P9-DEI-242

CRAZY

IS A

COMPLIMENT

CRAZY

IS A

COMPLIMENT

*The Power of Zigging
When Everyone Else Zags*

LINDA ROTTENBERG

COFOUNDER AND CEO, ENDEAVOR

PORTFOLIO/PENGUIN

PORTFOLIO / PENGUIN
Published by the Penguin Group
Penguin Group (USA) LLC
375 Hudson Street
New York, New York 10014

USA | Canada | UK | Ireland | Australia | New Zealand | India | South Africa | China
penguin.com
A Penguin Random House Company

First published by Portfolio / Penguin, a member of Penguin Group (USA) LLC, 2014

Copyright © 2014 by Linda Rottenberg
Penguin supports copyright. Copyright fuels creativity, encourages diverse voices, pro-
motes free speech, and creates a vibrant culture. Thank you for buying an authorized edition of this book and for complying with copyright laws by not reproducing, scanning, or
distributing any part of it in any form without permission. You are supporting writers and
allowing Penguin to continue to publish books for every reader.

Illustration credits
Page 44: Courtesy of Rodrigo Jordan
Page 112: Endeavor

LIBRARY OF CONGRESS CATALOGING-IN-PUBLICATION DATA
Rottenberg, Linda.
  Crazy is a compliment : the power of zigging when everyone else zags / Linda Rottenberg.
    pages cm
  Includes bibliographical references and index.
  ISBN 978-1-59184-664-2
  1. Entrepreneurship. 2. Career development. 3. Success in business. I. Title.
  HB615.R68 2014
  650.1—dc23
                              2014021105

Printed in the United States of America
10 9 8 7 6 5 4 3 2 1

Set in Warnock Pro
Designed by Jaime Putorti

For Bruce
Who believes in all my crazy dreams
and
For Tybee and Eden
Who inspire me to go home

OCT 2014

CONTENTS

Why Everybody Needs to Act Like an Entrepreneur

I want to tell you about Leila.

Leila Velez grew up in the slums of Rio de Janeiro. Her mother was a maid; her father, a janitor. In the early 1990s Leila was serving hamburgers at McDonald's. But she had a dream.

Leila was frustrated by how few hair products there were for the curly locks of Afro-Brazilian women like her. "Poor people deserve to feel beautiful, too," she told her sister-in-law Zica, a hairdresser. In 1993 the two amateurs turned Leila's basement into a mad scientist's lab. They tested their first product on their husbands . . . and the men's hair promptly fell out.

Going back to the sink, Leila and Zica perfected their formula and opened a salon. It was an unimpressive place, down a dark corridor, a mere three hundred square feet. "How can you be successful in such a pitiful space?" their friends said. But the sisters pushed on. Soon women in Rio were waiting four to six hours for an appointment, and customers were crediting their products with not only improving their hair texture but also boosting their self-esteem.

When I tell this story to friends, they often say, "That must be one of those charming stories we keep hearing about women in microfinance." But there's nothing micro about Leila's story. Within a few years her company, Beleza Natural, was selling an array of hair products in a handful of "hair clinics." By 2013 Beleza Natural was serving 100,000 customers a month, employing 2,300 people, and earning $80 million a year.

So how did Leila do it? How did she go from being an hourly worker at McDonald's to the leader of a multimillion-dollar franchise? And more to the point: What can the rest of us learn from her story to be more daring in our own lives?

We can learn a lot.

First, we can be reminded of the value of looking at the world through fresh eyes. The legendary retailer Sam Walton once said, "If everybody else is doing it one way, there's a good chance you can find your niche by going in exactly the opposite direction." Leila saw that everybody else was just selling hair products; she would sell confidence. She called her niche lipstick psychology.

Many of the best ideas fulfill a need no one else knows exists. Earle Dickson was a twenty-eight-year-old cotton buyer for Johnson & Johnson in 1920, whose wife, Josephine, kept cutting herself while cooking. To stanch the bleeding, Josephine used the standard remedy, a piece of rag attached with string. The contraptions quickly fell off. Her husband began tinkering and soon presented his wife, then his bosses with an alternative: a self-adhesive bandage with the cotton built in. Band-Aids, as they were called, failed to take off until the company gave away free samples to butchers and Boy Scouts. More than a hundred billion of Earle's inventions have since been sold.

Next, we can learn that psychology plays an enormous role in tackling risk. The biggest barriers to success are not structural or cultural; they are mental and emotional. At every turn, someone (or, more likely, *everyone*) will call you and your idea crazy. The job of the innovator is to push past naysayers and find a way to drive forward. Leila was soft-spoken and shy. She wasn't used to bold action, confrontation, or speaking out. Before she could foster confidence in others, she first had to discover it in herself.

Finally, we can learn that risk takers rarely go it alone. Those seeking to disrupt the status quo need support. And support doesn't just mean financial, though that always helps. More often it means advice on handling fear, navigating tricky growth decisions, and breaking an intimidating task into manageable chunks. When Steve Jobs was just starting out, he sought the counsel of Robert Noyce, the coinventor of the microchip and the unofficial mayor of Silicon Valley. As with everything he did, Jobs took this relationship to an extreme. He would drop by Noyce's house uninvited on his motorcycle or telephone around midnight. An exasperated Noyce finally told his wife, "If he calls one more time I'm just not going to pick up the phone!"

But of course Noyce always picked up. Entrepreneurs always find a way.

So where did Leila go to get the backing she needed?

That's where my story intersects with hers. In 1997 I cofounded an organization called Endeavor to support dreamers like Leila. In nearly two decades, Endeavor has screened forty thousand candidates and selected roughly one thousand individuals from more than six hundred fast-growing companies to be part of our network. We discovered these innovators in the least likely places: cyber cafés in South Africa, sandwich shops in Mexico, women-only gyms in Turkey; gamer hangouts in Indonesia; ceviche stores in the United States. We've worked with founders in such crazily diverse fields as biometric eye scanning, snail farming, pharmacy franchising, and wind turbine manufacturing. We've helped daring individuals operate in such challenging environments as Athens in the midst of a currency crisis, Cairo in the throes of a revolution, and Miami as it emerged out of recession.

We call these business leaders high-impact entrepreneurs, a term Endeavor coined in 2004. High-impact means individuals with the biggest ideas, the likeliest potential to build businesses that matter, and the greatest ability to inspire others. Once we invite these leaders into our network we do whatever we can to help them succeed, from forming advisory boards to accessing capital, from hiring talent to honing leadership. And we encourage them to nurture and mentor the next generation.

Today Endeavor has offices in forty-five cities around the world, employs 350 people, and has a pool of 5,000 volunteer mentors. While some of our ventures lose steam, the vast majority have grown at an impressive rate. In 2013 the entrepreneurs we support generated close to $7 billion in revenues and provided more than 400,000 jobs.

My experience has taught me that the capacity to dream big is not confined to any country, age, or gender. The desire to take initiative, be your own boss, advance your life, and improve the world is universal.

But the roadblocks are universal, too.

I've spent the last two decades working to identify the common mistakes and specific stumbling blocks that innovators face as they attempt to turn their ideas into reality. I've sought to isolate the mix of concrete steps, strategic support, and emotional encouragement they need to bring their ideas to the next level. And I've learned when change makers need a shoulder to cry on and when they need a kick in the pants.

When I met Leila, for example, she was eager to expand yet scrambling to keep pace with demand. She was overwhelmed. To help, we introduced her to mentors who could support her growth. We encouraged her to create a shareholder agreement with her in-laws. When she got divorced, Leila even found a new husband through our network. (She got what I call the full-service treatment!)

But most important, we showed her that instead of being alone, she's part of the biggest movement in the world today, the unstoppable, unwavering trend toward individuals who seek to improve their own lives and, in the process, improve the world around them.

She's an entrepreneur.

— *ENTREPRENEURSHIP ISN'T JUST FOR ENTREPRENEURS ANYMORE* —

I wrote this book because I believe that we all have a little Leila within us.

Every day I meet people with a dream. Those people are just like Leila—and just like you. Maybe you're serving coffee and fantasizing about launching a microbrewery; maybe you've skipped college and yearn to start your own design firm; maybe you're sitting in your cubicle and brainstorming a new idea that can improve your company; maybe you've got a plan to improve the environment; maybe you're a stay-at-home parent with an idea for a new mobile app; or maybe you're a retiree hoping to start a B&B.

You have a dream, but you don't know how to turn your dream into reality. Or you've already launched your dream, but you're unsure how to take it to the next level.

This book can show you the way.

I'm going to impart lessons I've learned from helping Leila and a thousand others like her. I'll disclose the results of intensive research conducted over several years by the Endeavor team and our partners at Bain & Company. I'll lay out the insights I've been taking to Fortune 500 companies the last few years because they, too, want to become more entrepreneurial. And I'll share my own up-and-down story of building (and occasionally rebuilding) a fast-growing organization that's a hybrid of nonprofit and for-profit.

Above all, I'm going to try to show you that no matter what you're doing right now, no matter what dream you're trying to get going or grow bigger, you need these lessons.

You need to think and act more like an entrepreneur.

When we started Endeavor in the late 1990s, the word "entrepreneur" was not very popular. It wasn't even used by most people who started companies. Adapted from the French word meaning "to undertake," entrepreneurship existed as an academic concept, but the expression—or any expression like it, for that matter—was barely used in most countries. Even most Americans viewed entrepreneurship as a rarefied notion that applied only to founders of the fastest-growing (or fastest-failing) enterprises. And at the risk of my pointing out the obvious, those leaders were mostly young, mostly in tech, and mostly male.

That stereotype no longer holds. Today entrepreneurship doesn't just mean starting a tech company. It means undertaking any bold venture—from improving your neighborhood to selling crafts out of your basement; from modernizing your family business to proposing a new initiative in your corporation. The techniques involved in sharpening your idea, facing down critics, recruiting boosters, and handling setbacks apply in almost every realm of work.

Entrepreneurship, defined as a nimble, creatively destructive, optimistic force, has become the go-to problem-solving technique of the twenty-first century. If some moments have been ripe for diplomats, financiers, soldiers, or politicians, today is ripe for entrepreneurs. Now, that may sound a little grand. But scroll through the Internet, flip through a corporate annual report, visit a college campus, listen to moms and dads at school drop-off: Everyone is talking about being a force of disruption, trying a fresh approach, becoming an agent of change. Alexis Ohanian, the founder of Reddit, put it well: "'I have a startup' is the new 'I'm in a band.'" Even the Boy Scouts now have an entrepreneurship merit badge and Mattel has Entrepreneur Barbie!

The reasons behind this shift are complex, but they come down to a simple reality: We live in a time of uncertainty. Our economies, our companies, our jobs are no longer stable and secure. Change is the only constant. To survive, we all need the skills required to continually reinvent ourselves. Everyone needs to take some risk or risk being left behind.

Here's the good news: Anybody can be a change agent today. There are no admission criteria. There is no wardrobe requirement. There is no secret vote.

Entrepreneurship is for everyone.

But here's the bad news: We don't really have a language to discuss this wide swath of workers who are becoming more entrepreneurial.

The word "entrepreneur," once underused, is now in jeopardy of being overused. As a result, lots of people (me included) began taking this clunky word and adding all sorts of qualifiers to it, making it even clunkier. Suddenly we had "social entrepreneur" to describe those building mission-driven organizations that focus on everything from human rights to the environment; "microentrepreneur" to describe individuals starting lifestyle businesses; "intrapreneur" to label change makers within large corporations; "copreneurs" to describe couples starting businesses; even "mompreneurs," "dadpreneurs," and "kidpreneurs." These terms became so unwieldy that on Twitter everyone just gave up and shortened "entrepreneurs" to #treps.

@*#&!

Trust me, as someone who's sat on a gazillion panels about the "future of entrepreneurship," I know we need a new lexicon.

In this book I want to try a different approach, one that I hope is clearer and certainly more fun. I've given each of these different groups a name. The names are simple, easy to understand, and reflective of the arenas in which people operate. They represent four different species, and they all need help in realizing their dreams. One of these species surely applies to you.

GAZELLES. This is the classic entrepreneur of myth and reality, someone who starts a new business venture and aims for it to explode into a white-hot phenomenon—Home Depot, Facebook, Jenny Craig, Under Armour, Instagram. High growth is the goal. The Endeavor entrepreneurs I work with fall into this category—or they aspire to, at least.

The term "gazelle" was coined by the economist David Birch in 1994. It describes high-growth businesses whose sales double every four years. Though only 2 to 4 percent of companies fit this model in the United States, this otherwise minuscule group accounts for nearly all private-sector job creation. When you hear politicians say, "Small businesses create most of the new jobs," they're really talking about the young and growing firms. They're talking about gazelles. Birch chose gazelles because they're fast moving and high jumping.

You would think gazelles already know how to be successful entrepreneurs, but in my experience, they don't. Sure, they know how to start something, but unfortunately they keep making the same mistakes over and over again: They expand too quickly; they lose focus; they tangle with their partners; they can't give up control. (And yup, I've made all those mistakes, too, which I'll discuss in detail.) After seeing these pitfalls repeatedly, I developed a list of the most common mistakes made by gazelles and a playbook for how to avoid them if you want your start-up to become a big enterprise.

SKUNKS. The term "intrapreneur," which first popped up in the 1970s and first appeared in the *American Heritage Dictionary* in 1992, is defined as a person within a large corporation who takes responsibility for "turning an idea into a profitable finished product through assertive risk-taking and innovation." While the word is no more pleasing today, the idea is a lot more popular: Encouraging people to be more independent and creative inside corporations has become an urgent cry.

In 2013 I was invited to speak at Dell World on a panel about disruption. The founder, Michael Dell, had just taken the company private after a long battle with shareholders. He declared his intention to restore the firm's entrepreneurial DNA, returning it to its roots in Room 2713 of the Dobie Center at the University of Texas. Michael opened the conference of six thousand people by saying, "Welcome to the world's largest start-up!"

But while encouraging employees to take more risks is simple, getting them to follow through is hard. "Some are afraid of change," Michael told me later. "This resistance is almost certainly a path of disaster in any fast-changing business." There are the quick, he said, or the dead.

Michael isn't the only corporate leader seeking to reclaim his company's entrepreneurial mojo. Most of the world's top CEOs realize they have to disrupt their own organizations before others beat them to it. Yet somehow this message is not getting through to many of their employees. If you work in a large corporation today, with a benefits package and retirement plan, you may think you're safe. You may think all this entrepreneurial undertaking is not for you. But you'd be wrong.

While starting something new involves peril, *not* starting something new today is just as perilous, if not more so. Pretending your job is safe and your company is stable leaves you dangerously exposed. If you think risk taking is risky, being risk averse is often riskier.

First of all, your company itself isn't safe. The topple rate of big companies, a metric that gauges how often they lose their leadership positions, more than doubled between 1965 and 2008. A new member of the S&P index in the 1920s could expect to remain on the list for sixty-five years. By 2012 that average had dropped to eighteen years. In the last five years alone, S&P 500 mainstays like Heinz, Sprint, Sara Lee, RadioShack, Kodak, Office Depot, and the New York Times Company all fell from the list.

Even if your company continues to thrive, your ability to survive in it depends on your capacity and willingness to innovate. Job security these days depends on the same qualities that make good entrepreneurs: agility, imagination, persistence, execution. To put it another way, adapt from within or you may be forced to adapt from without.

Become a skunk. I've adopted this term from the Lockheed Corporation, which during World War II set up a secret division to build fighter jets. It was called Skunk Works. Though rumor suggested the name came from the poor hygiene habits of the overworked employees, it actually came from the moonshine factory in the cartoon series *Li'l Abner*. (The moonshine was said to be created by grinding up dead skunks.) Either way, the message is clear: Entrepreneurs operating within large corporations go out of their way to stink up the joint.

DOLPHINS. For the last decade or so, there's been abundant lip service paid to the idea that the social sector must become more entrepreneurial. *Nonprofits need to employ more business techniques. Philanthropy needs to be more innovative and metrics driven.* I've been involved in this movement for twenty-five years and been lucky to have had the chance to work with two of its pioneers.

In 1989 I volunteered to help Wendy Kopp recruit college seniors to join her start-up, Teach For America. When she proposed creating a national teacher corps in her senior thesis at Princeton, her adviser responded, "My Dear Ms. Kopp, you are quite evidently deranged." But Wendy would not be deterred. Teach For America now receives more than fifty thousand applications each year and has an annual budget of $350 million.

I later went to work for Bill Drayton, the "godfather of social entrepreneurship." Bill was among the first to fund social entrepreneurs through his organization, Ashoka. Having supported more than three thousand nonprofit innovators across the globe, Bill champions the idea that anyone, anywhere can be a change maker. "Everyone gets to be a player," he said.

Despite these trendsetters, too many nonprofits, community groups, and social service organizations continue to lag behind the age of disruption. They lack leaders willing to deploy the full range of entrepreneurial skills needed to scale their ideas and maximize their impact. What they need are more dolphins.

Dolphins are my nickname for contrarians in the nonprofit or public sector who are willing to buck the conventions of their professions and agitate for real change. Why dolphins? Because they're smart and social (they live in cooperative groups, called pods) and are one of the few animals shown to be altruistic toward others. But they're not pushovers: Harm a dolphin's pod, and watch out! Today even causes for which there are no compelling private-sector solutions are ripe for entrepreneurial shake-up. It's dolphins making the waves.

BUTTERFLIES. There's a final collection of entrepreneurs who need these lessons, and they may be the fastest-growing group of all. These are small-scale or lifestyle entrepreneurs.

First among these are sole proprietors—plumbers, yoga instructors, freelance writers, organic farmers, artists. The U.S. Census Bureau estimates that a majority of U.S. businesses have no paid employees. Forty percent of American adults have now spent part of their careers working on their own, and 24 million more are expected to be self-employed by 2018. Globally the number of independent contractors will reach 1.3 billion by 2020. These fields are booming because they're open to anyone: moms, dads, grannies, twenty-somethings, even teens starting microventures in their basements, cars, or bathrooms. (Yes, bathtub brews are back!) As Jay-Z put it, "I'm not a businessman; I'm a business, man."

The second part of this group has just a handful of employees. There are seven million companies in America that employ workers; 90 percent of them have fewer than twenty. While some of these entrepreneurs aim to be fast-growing gazelles, most are content to stay small and local.

I'm dubbing this species butterflies because butterflies are varied (there are at least 17,500 different types of butterfly) and driven by freedom and individualism. In both Eastern and Western cultures, butterflies have long symbolized the soul, especially one reborn after a period of cocooning. Beyond personal transformation, butterflies are vital to their habitat and an indicator of its overall well-being. More butterflies equal a healthier ecosystem.

At first glance, this group would hardly seem a candidate for the skill set of groundbreaking entrepreneurs. Do you really need to be disruptive when you're selling homemade cheese at the farmers' market? The answer: You do, especially because your competitor probably has an in at Whole Foods, now accepts credit card payments with a Square reader, and has just launched a vibrant Web business. Etsy, the online arts, crafts, and food hub, now has more than a million "makers" selling goods directly to consumers. Even butterflies need to spread their wings.

Besides, butterflies are uniquely suited to this age of disruption. In chaos theory, "butterfly effect" is the term given to the idea that change can come from anywhere. The weather in Central Park can be affected by a butterfly's flapping its wings in South America.

I saw the sensitivity and fearlessness of butterflies firsthand on the eve of Superstorm Sandy, near my home in Brooklyn. I had stopped in to buy bread from my favorite local bakery, Bien Cuit. It was not long after the mayor announced evacuations. "I guess you'll be closing soon," I said to the man behind the counter.

"No way," he replied. "The neighborhood needs us. We're going to stay open all night."

Don't underestimate the tenacity of a butterfly.

Today, nearly two decades after I first started hunting down entrepreneurs, innovators of all types are popping up everywhere. They aren't waiting for changes to happen to them; they're making changes happen every day.

Whatever your passion, pick one of these species and start writing your story—or risk being an ostrich, with your head stuck in the sand.

— THE SECRET SAUCE OF ENTREPRENEURSHIP —

But once you've embraced the life of a change maker, how do you know what to do next?

Again, that's where I come into the picture.

I'd like to invite you into my bedroom for a second. You'll find several things of interest there. An African bedspread I brought back from my travels. A poem my husband wrote for me when he proposed. And on the nightstand next to my side of the bed, a stack of half-read books. They're all about entrepreneurship.

I love entrepreneurship. I don't love its literature. When I sat down to work on this book, I made a list of everything I didn't want it to be. It wouldn't be a how-to manual for writing a business plan, developing a marketing strategy, or reading a venture capital (VC) term sheet. It wouldn't be an academic primer on the history of entrepreneurship. It wouldn't be an inspirational graduation speech filled with feel-good bromides. And it wouldn't be the story of one person's journey to success. If that's what you're looking for, go read Howard Schultz's *Pour Your Heart Into It*, Richard Branson's *Losing My Virginity*, Tony Hsieh's *Delivering Happiness*, or Walter Isaacson's *Steve Jobs*, all books I read and enjoyed.

Here's what this book is: It's the story of the entrepreneurial journeys of many people—gazelles, skunks, dolphins, and butterflies—and what the rest of us can learn from them. It's my attempt to break down a process that often seems overwhelming into a series of achievable steps. It's my shot at answering this question: Since everybody has to take risks these days, how do you make sure you're taking smart risks?

To answer that, I've divided the book into three sections: "Get Going," "Go Big," and "Go Home."

In "Get Going," I'll lay out the road map for becoming an entrepreneur: from battling inner fear to fending off skeptics, to stalking supporters, to exploiting chaos. The theme in this section is attitude: how to get yourself the right one and brush off the wrong one.

In "Go Big," I'll talk about how to take your idea to scale. To do that, I'll help you figure out your entrepreneur personality, avoid rookie mistakes, find the right mentors, and learn how to lead. "Leadership 3.0" is my term for the new skills required to attract and retain today's hyperconnected, hyperskilled, hypersensitive talent.

Finally, in "Go Home," I'll discuss what it means to live like an entrepreneur. This includes how to cultivate meaning in your workplace and how to integrate your work with your family. If the first two sections are the craft of entrepreneurship, I consider this the art. This part is also the most personal to me. I believe deeply that part of the mantle of entrepreneurship is to inspire and help others to follow this path. Also, as a mom who runs a large organization I've fought hard to maintain a harmony between my professional life and my family life, and I encourage my team to do the same.

Altogether, these topics capture what I've learned in two decades of experiencing the ups and downs of the entrepreneurial life. They are why I wanted to write this book. But there's one more reason that explains why I wanted to write it now.

— YOU DON'T NEED A HOODIE TO BE AN ENTREPRENEUR —

In 2012 I visited Wilkes University, a vibrant campus tucked away in an old mining town in central Pennsylvania, to give a talk about entrepreneurship. Toward the end of the Q&A, a hand shot up in back. "I like your stories about entrepreneurs," he said, "but I'm wondering if they apply to me. I don't have an idea that's big enough. I don't have the right connections. And I don't live in Silicon Valley."

A little taken aback and somewhat distracted (I knew my seven-year-old daughters were waiting up for me at home), I said the first thing that came to mind: "Don't worry. You don't need a hoodie to be an entrepreneur. Anybody can be one." The answer worked fine enough, but all during my ride home, I was haunted by his question and increasingly disappointed by my glib response.

In the early years of Endeavor, whenever I bumped into anyone who didn't quite understand what we were doing (which is to say, most people I met), I would sum it up by saying, "We're taking the magic of Silicon Valley and sprinkling it in places with talent and big ideas, but no belief in the ability of individuals to turn those ideas into reality." I used to think that applied only to people like Leila.

Now everyone needs a bit of that magic.

We all need a little bit of Leila in our lives.

By the time I got home to Brooklyn that night, I had decided to write this book. I wanted to write it for those students in Pennsylvania. I wanted to write it for my twin daughters waiting up to say good night. I wanted to write it for all those who have a dream they don't know how to realize, who want to marry their passions with their everyday lives, who want to make an impact on their companies, their communities, or the larger world.

In her classic cookbook *Mastering the Art of French Cooking* Julia Child, herself a genre-making, ceiling-breaking entrepreneur, wrote, "Anyone can cook in the French manner anywhere, with the right instruction." This book takes a similar view toward dreaming big and making change.

I used to believe in the maxim that entrepreneurs are "born, not made." Now I believe that entrepreneurship, like great cooking, can be practiced and honed by anybody with a desire to learn. (Also, just like master chefs, even the most skilled entrepreneurs drop some pans and break a few eggs along the way.)

In the end, mastering the art of entrepreneurship is not simply about starting a business. It's about taking chances, overcoming doubts, managing risk, dealing with chaos, cultivating employees, coping with stumbles and successes, integrating work and family, and paying it forward to ensure that the next generation can dream big as well.

And it's realizing that all those people calling you crazy are giving you a huge compliment.

So let's get going.

PART I

Get Going

CHAPTER 1

Getting to Day One

*I*n the spring of 1998 I stepped into a small, unassuming office in a nondescript neighborhood of Buenos Aires. I went there to meet Wences Casares, a charismatic twentysomething with a crazy idea. When I walked out several hours later, I was carrying one of the more important lessons I ever learned about entrepreneurship: The most valuable backer you need to start any venture is not your mother, father, spouse, boss, banker, or friend. It's not anyone else at all. It's you.

And you're the hardest backer you'll ever have to win.

Before we talk about what it takes to get an initiative under way, we have to talk about what it means to get yourself in the proper frame of mind. You can't convince others until you first convince yourself. Few people I know have done this under more extreme circumstances than Wences.

Wences was born on a sheep farm in Patagonia—twenty miles from the nearest neighbor and one hundred miles from the closest town. His father was a rancher, but also a ham radio operator and DIYer. He gave each of his four children a computer in the bedroom and jerry-rigged a local network so they could communicate with one another.

"The biggest impact my father had on me was showing me how to be a doer," Wences said. "Living in the middle of nowhere, we constantly had to come up with creative ways of solving problems, like digging trenches or building bridges on the side of a mountain."

Being an entrepreneur is just a fancy way of saying you're a doer, he told me.

And did he ever do! In high school Wences started a T-shirt painting shop. He also downloaded a mismatched database of all the telephone numbers in Patagonia, corrected the mistakes, published a series of directories, and sold advertising. He earned $80,000. The first person in his family to attend college, Wences started yet another business while attending classes. It was the inaugural Internet service provider in Argentina. A year later he sold the firm in a deal he thought kept him as part of the team. After signing the contract, Wences showed up at his office and was locked out. He got virtually nothing.

In these early ventures, Wences was unbowed by fear, and no wonder, he had little at stake. But now the stakes were getting higher. While still enrolled at university, he set out to create a financial services portal for Latin America, a local E*Trade. But his studies were getting in the way, so he traveled one thousand miles back to Patagonia to inform his father he was dropping out of college. In what he described as the scariest moment of his life, Wences also told his dad he'd asked his two sisters to drop out of school, too, and join him.

His father considered the information for a few minutes, then said, "Do it right." His unspoken message: "Don't shame the family."

At this point things started to really get scary, and Wences, for the first time, began to question himself. He lived in a community where going it alone was not valued, family reputation was everything, and the ability of him or his sisters to build a career or find a spouse was now on the line. And worse, nobody liked his idea. Thirty-three investors turned him down. "We barely have a functioning stock market," he was told. "How can we possibly support an electronic trading platform?"

I listened to this story while sitting in Wences's grungy office in Buenos Aires, surrounded by a few broken-down computers and peeling wallpaper. "I want to keep going," he said. "But sometimes I look at my sisters sleeping in our tiny apartment, and I think, 'Am I crazy?'"

He turned to me. "Do you think I'm crazy?"

"Yes," I said. "But that's why you're going to succeed. Plus, I think I can help."

Wences's story shows that the first step to becoming an entrepreneur does not happen in a laboratory, a conference room, or even a pitch session. It happens in the mind. And not the part of the mind where the lightbulbs go off and the ahas are heard. It happens in the part where the darkness resides and the doubts cry out. It happens in that place where you start to get worried about your rent, your mortgage, your children, your debt building up on your credit card, your reputation in the cafeteria, your sisters sleeping on the couch.

It happens when you're exposed.

Jeff Bezos has a wonderful way of describing this heightened mind-set of being an entrepreneur. He calls the mix of anticipation, excitement, and uncertainty Day One. In Bezos's coinage, "Day One" is not a date on a calendar; it's a commitment to seeing every day as a fresh opportunity to create something new. Sixteen years after Amazon started, Bezos concluded a shareholder letter by saying his approach remains unchanged: "It's still Day One."

At Endeavor we adopted Bezos's concept and turned it into a rallying cry to help entrepreneurs acknowledge and overcome their moments of insecurity and fear. We even started a series of talks in which change makers described their Day One experiences. We tell speakers, "Don't focus on the idea; focus on the emotions, the challenges." When I gave one of these talks, my team rejected multiple drafts and pushed me to be more revealing.

In the next few chapters I'll talk about this process of overcoming emotional hurdles and getting an idea out of the shower, off the napkin, and into the world. While it may appear intimidating and others will surely call you nuts, there are actually a host of concrete ways to reduce your hazard and maximize your chances of success.

But first, I'm going to focus on what it means to give yourself permission to undertake such a challenge to begin with. To me this is the breakthrough step to thinking and acting like an entrepreneur. I'll even put it in a formula:

heart + mind - fear = entrepreneur

Or to put it another way, entrepreneurship begins with psyching yourself up instead of psyching yourself out.

— THE DISTANCE BETWEEN YOUR EARS —

In the early 2000s green products were gaining popularity in the United States, but one industry was stubbornly resistant: home cleaning products. Eco-friendly offerings brought in only 1 percent of the industry's $12 billion in sales. Clorox, the market leader, was particularly slow to adapt. It took two corporate skunks to crack the formula, but first they had to crack an even trickier code: how to be entrepreneurial in a conservative company while also finding time to be moms.

Mary Jo Cook was in a bind. She was a new mother eager to spend time with her young daughter, but she was also an ambitious executive at Clorox. So she did something virtually unheard of at the century-old company: She made her job part-time. "People were pretty shocked," she told me. "There was only one professional working less than full-time." Initially Mary Jo went to four days, then to three and a half when her second child was born.

Part of negotiating her own schedule meant designing a new role. "There weren't typical jobs you could just drop into," she said. The job she eventually created was heading a new division focused on innovation. When the job became too big, a colleague and fellow parent, Suzanne Sengelmann, proposed that the two share the role—another breakthrough. Their arrangement perfectly embodies the flexibility required of these entrepreneurial times. Beyond dividing responsibilities, Mary Jo and Suzanne merged themselves into one entity. Each worked three days a week, overlapping on Wednesdays. They shared a title (vice president), a voice mail, and an e-mail account. They even went by a joint name, Sam, a combination of Suzanne and MJ.

Initially, Suzanne and Mary Jo were apprehensive. "Our biggest fear was failing at the job," Suzanne told me. "Because we were so high profile in the company, we were fearful that if we blew it, we would rob other women of the opportunity—both at Clorox and perhaps even broader."

To their relief, not only did the new arrangement work, but it had added benefits. The act of thinking more creatively about their responsibilities encouraged them to think more creatively about their work. Also, the fact that they weren't stuck in the office all day meant they were hanging out with their customers at the playground. "Sam" kept hearing from fellow moms in the Bay Area that they were concerned about the impact of cleaning products on their children. And it wasn't just others. "You know what?" Suzanne said. "I have concerns. I clean. I grocery shop. Just having the opportunity to live the life of our core consumer was a huge advantage."

"Sam" had found a new calling: Clorox should create environmentally sensitive products targeted to moms.

But MJ and Suzanne had a problem, too. They knew their plan could face resistance from colleagues. Any "nontoxic" product threatened to make Clorox's other products look "toxic." This was their true test: Would they talk themselves out of their project before it got started or risk alienating those around them by challenging the core identity of the company?

Their answer: They gave themselves a quiet, under-the-radar mandate. In Mary Jo's phrase, they took "smart risks." That included giving themselves permission to spend a fifth of their time dabbling with their idea. "We told our boss it was ten percent," Suzanne told me, "but really it was closer to twenty." They called it their skunk project.

"The beauty of a skunk project," Suzanne said, "is you don't have to go through the same processes and approvals and questions and all that; you can just do it."

And they did. First, they went to their local supermarket and bought every green product. None impressed them. Next, they reached out to target consumers, whom they dubbed chemical-avoiding naturalists. Then they discovered another underground group at Clorox—this one comprised of chemists. (It, too, was headed by a working mom.) This group was also tinkering with biodegradable formulas and had adopted the nickname Project Kermit to celebrate its interest in all things green. The two teams merged forces. They kept their bosses informed but didn't ask for explicit sign-off; they paid expenses out of existing budgets.

Project Kermit's early efforts failed. "The first time there wasn't enough of a market interest," Mary Jo said. "The second time the technology wasn't good enough. The third time all the pieces came together." In late 2007 Clorox released Green Works. Through a novel endorsement deal, products were packaged with the seal of the Sierra Club. Within six months the new line had captured 40 percent of the natural market. Within five years Green Works was a $60 million annual business. It may not be easy being green, but with a little ingenuity, two skunks named "Sam" found a way to make it profitable.

What's striking about this story is the willingness of two part-time executives to resist their own temptation to hold themselves back as they pursued an unconventional project. Time after time I've seen people considering doing something bold get stuck at this stage. They keep waiting for someone else to give them permission, but here's what I've learned: That someone doesn't exist.

The only person who can give you permission to take risk is you.

When I asked Suzanne how people inside more traditional corporations can give themselves that green light, she said, "I believe that in every company, no matter how traditional, there are entrepreneurial idea people. But ideas are fragile. Ideas require conviction. They require knowing something is right in your gut because there's no physics or data that supports the idea."

Egyptian-born Amr Shady also had an idea in his gut, but before he could pursue his entrepreneurial dream, he first had to get over his fear of disappointing his father. Growing up in Cairo, Amr was a talented math and physics student. He went to university at fifteen and after graduation went to work at a safe managerial job in his father's electrical engineering company with offices across the Middle East. By twenty-one he was running the company's Egypt operations. Soon, though, he grew bored. He didn't want to take over his father's company, he realized; he wanted to start his own. But it took him years to muster up the courage to confront his dad.

"I didn't want to let him down," Amr told me. "I was supposed to be helping him, and now I wanted to go out on my own. Facing my father was the biggest burden I had."

Amr's father surprised him by giving his blessing. "I was happy he had the entrepreneurial spirit," he said. Amr started a telecom company that provided apps and other services for mobile phones. In 2010 he became an Endeavor entrepreneur.

What he took away from this experience was the importance of confronting your demons. "When I started out," Amr told me, "I thought the biggest business challenges had to do with things like raising money, the cost of complying with tax regulations, and issues with the legal and regulatory environment. But these turned out to be minor issues." Even the revolutions that have swept the region proved relatively minor compared with the biggest challenge Amr faced.

The real problem was self-censorship, he said. When I asked him to explain, he reminded me of the story of how the under-four-minute mile came to be. Before 1954 everyone thought the four-minute mile was the physical limit of the human body. When Roger Bannister broke the world record, he also broke a psychological barrier. By the end of 1957 sixteen runners had accomplished the feat. "Too many aspiring entrepreneurs make the pre-Bannister mistake," Amr said. "We censor ourselves. We discount our potential and therefore don't make it big. I'm still guilty of that myself."

Amr's chief lesson: Don't look to others to validate your desires; look to yourself. Or as the legendary Bob Jones said about golf, it's "a game played on a five-inch course—the distance between your ears."

— WHAT I'M SUPPOSED TO BE —

I relate to this idea of psychological tests because I faced one myself. I was raised in a traditional family in the suburbs of Boston. My parents were high school sweethearts in Rhode Island who met at a dance when they were fourteen and seventeen. My dad went on to become a lawyer; my mother, a homemaker. Throughout my childhood my parents were incredibly loving, intently focused on education, and almost genetically risk averse. Chance taking was for others; they valued steadiness and security above all else.

Some of this unease with risk rubbed off on me. I went to Harvard and then opted for the safe path and applied to law school. But once I got to Yale Law School, I quickly discovered that I didn't want to be a lawyer. This was hard for me to admit. I had spent my whole life playing it safe, trying to please others. Now I wanted to figure out who I was, and what I wanted to be.

I had a childhood pen pal in Uruguay and, on a whim, went to sleep on her couch. My parents said, "It's just a phase." (They also made sure I took the bar exam before I left.) Soon I moved to Buenos Aires and started dancing tango and cheering for local soccer teams. I paid my way by working at a local law school. But I was also looking over my shoulder and becoming enchanted with a new type of celebrity emerging back home: the start-up CEO.

This was the gilded age of Bill Gates, Michael Dell, and Howard Schultz. It was soon after the blockbuster initial public offerings (IPOs) of Netscape and Yahoo! sent Silicon Valley entrepreneurs scampering to start the "new new thing." It was when two computer science grad students named Sergey Brin and Larry Page were testing their idea to revolutionize Internet search; when Steven Spielberg, Jeffrey Katzenberg, and David Geffen were bucking the studio system to form DreamWorks; when Vera Wang left her mentor, Ralph Lauren, to revolutionize bridal wear; when Pierre Omidyar managed to auction a broken laser pointer on a new e-commerce site that would come to be called eBay; when Steve Jobs made his dramatic return to Apple; and when a Wall Street refugee named Jeff Bezos took a cross-country drive to Seattle during which he honed a plan to sell books online.

I became a convert to entrepreneurship. It seemed to fit the mood of rebellion and individualism I was experiencing. It seemed to offer the opportunity to remake the world in your image. It seemed daring.

Soon enough I tried out my newfound zeal in my newfound community. My friends were puzzled. "What do you mean start a business?" Once I told a group of students in Brazil the legendary story of Steve Jobs and Steve Wozniak's working on the first Apple computer in the Jobs family garage. "That's a nice story," one guy said, "but how does it relate to my life? No one will give me money to launch my idea . . . and I don't even have a garage!"

Then, one day, late for a meeting in Buenos Aires, I hopped in a taxi and struck up a conversation with the driver. He told me he had an engineering degree but couldn't find a job. The only employers hiring were government bureaucracies and old-school corporations, he said, neither of which had much use for someone with his skills.

"Forgive me," I said to the driver, "but wouldn't you rather be a—" I paused. I didn't know the Spanish equivalent for what I was trying to communicate. "An entrepreneur?" I asked, in English.

"A what?" he said.

"An entrepreneur," I repeated. "You know, someone who starts a business."

"Oh, you mean an *empresario*," he said dismissively, referring to the Spanish word for "big businessman," a term associated more with cronyism and greed than with innovation and growth.

"No, not *empresario*. What's the Spanish word for 'entrepreneur'?"

He shrugged. "I don't think there is a word like that here."

"Well, that explains it," I thought. No wonder I hadn't seen any high-flying, high-growth entrepreneurs in Latin America. Not only did these countries lack start-up capital, but they didn't even have a common word for such a person!

Suddenly I had a vision. What if there was an organization to help entrepreneurs around the world get started and go to scale? What if we harnessed the power of individual dreamers and high-growth businesses to transform local economies? What if we created a global movement around innovation?

I went back home to the United States and started talking up my idea. First, I went to my boss at my new job at Ashoka, the pioneering organization that works with social entrepreneurs. I suggested he branch out from nonprofit innovators (dolphins, in my lexicon) and start an arm to support for-profit entrepreneurs (gazelles). He told me he had his hands full. Next, I shared my idea with friends working in international development, on Wall Street, and even in Silicon Valley. Nothing.

I was beginning to learn an important lesson about starting anything new: Being misunderstood is part of the process. If contrarian thinking is the first step to becoming an entrepreneur, then you can't expect others—especially those following more traditional paths—to embrace your vision at the outset. Often your best hope is to find another outlier who's passionate about the same thing.

In my case that person was the twenty-seven-year-old American entrepreneur Peter Kellner. Peter's father is a Hungarian immigrant; his mother is from a suburb of Detroit. A JD-MBA student at the time, Peter had already started companies in Russia and Eastern Europe. When we met, he had just returned from China, where he, too, had the idea to support high-growth entrepreneurs. We quickly decided to team up.

In our first meeting we sat at my parents' kitchen table in Boston and, in cliché fashion, sketched out a plan to start an organization on the back of a napkin. Yes, an actual napkin. We chose our name from a quote Peter suggested by Henry David Thoreau: "I know of no more encouraging fact than the unquestionable ability of man to elevate his life by conscious endeavor." (I liked the word "endeavor" and ignored the whiff of sexism.)

My parents were listening from the other side of the room. They weren't pleased.

My mom interrupted. "Linda," she said, "you're not thinking of giving up your job for this, are you?" When I said yes, she glanced at my father with a look that said, "Alan, *you* talk her out of this!"

My dad calmly said, "You know we didn't send you to college and graduate school just to have you take early retirement." He reminded me I didn't have a trust fund and needed to be financially independent. He mentioned the promise I'd made after law school: I would take some "time off the treadmill" but would ultimately get a traditional job. If I wasn't interested in practicing law, then how about a consulting firm?

Sensing my father's approach wasn't working, my mom tried a different tack. "You know your eggs aren't getting any younger," she said. I was twenty-eight, and by that age my mom already had given birth to me and my brother and was about to become pregnant with my sister. Her message: I needed to think more about my ticking clock and less about my expanding dreams. She continued. "And you definitely need to stop getting on planes all the time if you ever want to get married."

So here I was, caught between what my parents wanted for me and what I wanted for myself. It's the same moment that Amr Shady experienced with his father, that Mary Jo and Suzanne faced when they first heard from moms on the playground, that Wences sensed when he looked at his sisters sleeping on the other side of the room, that almost every entrepreneur I've ever met confronted at one time or another. It's that juncture between doing what's safe and expected and doing what's uncertain and unknown. It's the crux between fear and hope.

I chose hope. "I can't turn back," I told my mother, tearing up. "I've been thinking about this too long. This is what I need to do. This is who I'm supposed to be."

My mother looked stunned; my dad was speechless. Peter immediately jumped in to support me. "Debbie," he said, "I understand Linda needs to have some stability. We've agreed that she'll move to New York, set up our operations, and try to raise money." Then he turned to my dad. "And I've decided to take a semester off from grad school and move to Latin America. I'll be sharing the risk." My parents nodded silently. To this day I assume they thought our dream would fizzle, and I would be back applying for a "real" job.

In the years that followed, I've thought often of that scene at my parents' kitchen table. In many ways, my passion to help entrepreneurs is fueled by my desire to help them push through similar inflection points in their lives: when few others believe; when they feel anxious and alone; when they're on the verge of figuring out who they want to be.

As it happens, the figure that best captures that moment is Kermit the Frog. In the opening of *The Muppet Movie* (1979), Kermit sings a hymn to becoming something more than what you are. "Why are there so many songs about rainbows?" he asks. Rainbows are about visions, illusions, and dreams. Rainbows are about hearing voices and people calling your name. The "rainbow connection" is what you feel when you finally discover what you're supposed to be.

To me, getting to Day One is finally embracing what you're supposed to be.

— FAN THE FOOLISH FIRE —

Thomas Edison was being stubborn. Though he would later be known as the Wizard of Menlo Park, Edison in the late 1870s was considered the fool of New Jersey. Having already invented the telegraph, he had moved on to one of the more elusive goals of modern science, the incandescent lightbulb. One critic called the pursuit "sheer nonsense"; another predicted "final, necessary, and ignominious failure."

A chief problem Edison and other inventors faced was that electricity was considered extremely dangerous—*ignis fatuus*, "foolish fire." Health experts warned that too much exposure to light would cause eye ailments, nervous breakdowns, and—horrors—freckles! Even defenders admitted it made the interiors of houses look wan, gave food an unappetizing paleness, and exposed the wrinkles on the faces of ladies.

In 1879 Edison threw open the doors of his Menlo Park workshop to introduce the prototype of his incandescent light— the "little globe of sunshine" that promised a softer glow. Skeptics were unmoved. They called Edison a con man and taunted him to prove his bulb could light up a larger stage.

That soon happened, but not by him. On a cold December night in 1880, an inventor named Charles Brush strung twenty-three arc lamps on fifty-foot poles along a short stretch of Broadway from Union Square to Madison Square in New York City. Endeavor's headquarters are on this stretch today. The daughter of the city's treasurer was supposed to flip the switch, but she feared electrocution and backed out. When the lights finally came on, they filled the air with intense brightness and stark shadows. A *New York Times* reporter captured the scene: "The great white outlines of the marble stores, the mess of wires overhead, the throng of moving vehicles, were all brought out with an accuracy and exactness that left little to be desired." (This account earned Broadway its enduring nickname, the Great White Way.)

The arrival of electric light into public places was greeted with all the warmth of the plague. Pedestrians used umbrellas to shield themselves; people complained they looked like ghosts.

Despite the naysayers, Edison pushed on. Brush pushed on, too, though unlike Edison, a gazelle who employed hundreds of engineers and dreamed of building a big business, Brush was a butterfly, preferring solitary nights of tinkering away in his one-man lab. Edison would be the one to assuage critics and make the lightbulb a household item. More important, he owned the key patent and formed the Edison Electric Light Company, with backing from J. P. Morgan and the Vanderbilts.

What Edison and Brush both demonstrate is the importance of sticking with your vision, knowing what you want out of your entrepreneurial venture, and being strong enough to accept criticism for your choices.

In my experience, almost all entrepreneurs at one point or another have been accused of being out of their minds. You can't rock the boat without being told you're off your rocker. Consider just a few examples:

Gazelles

- When Sam Walton had the idea to create a discount store at age forty-four, his brother dismissed it as "just another of Sam Walton's crazy ideas." Walton himself said everybody he met "really did think I'd completely lost my mind."

Skunks

- In 1999 four Microsoft employees met over a bowl of jelly beans to concoct a game console that could take on the Sony PlayStation. They called it Xbox; their skeptical colleagues dubbed it coffin box. Even their partners at Intel scoffed. "We laughed at the idea they would blow a few billion dollars," one executive said. But the jelly bean club kept scheming and recruiting allies, until they wooed the biggest ally of all, Bill Gates. Xbox went on to become Microsoft's largest "internal start-up."

Dolphins

- When Raymond Damadian, a little-known professor in New York, first had the idea that he could detect cancerous tumors in the body using nuclear magnetic resonance, his academic colleagues called him a crackpot, a charlatan, and a screaming lunatic. Worse, they denied him tenure. "It's a totally harebrained theory," one colleague said. Undeterred, Damadian filed for patents and raised just enough money to build a device. In 1977 he conducted the first full-body MRI.

Butterflies

• Twenty-two-year-old Jeffrey Braverman was earning six figures on Wall Street when he left in 2002 to join the struggling family business started by his grandfather. The Newark Nut Company, which had once employed thirty people, was now down to two. "My dad and my uncle both thought I was crazy," Jeffrey said. He took the business online and relaunched it as Nuts.com. In under a decade the company employed eighty people and generated more than $20 million in annual revenues.

Why is it that so many entrepreneurs, in so many divergent fields, are all called, well, nuts?

The short answer is that seeing things in an unconventional way is threatening: It's threatening to those who benefit from the status quo, and it's equally threatening to those outside the establishment who might have had that idea or taken those steps, if only . . . Niccolò Machiavelli made that point in *The Prince*: "There is nothing more difficult to carry out, nor more doubtful of success, nor more dangerous to handle, than to initiate a new order of things." Machiavelli's explanation: The reformer has fierce enemies in all those who profit from the old order and only fair-weather supporters among those who would profit from the new one.

So given that you're going to be criticized for your crazy idea, how should you respond?

Own it.

I learned this in one of the defining moments of my career. A few months after the showdown with my parents, I got a call from Peter, who was living in South America searching for entrepreneurs, while I was in New York searching for funders (and, yes, Mom, a husband, too).

"Linda, pack your bags," Peter said. "I've gotten you a meeting with a real estate tycoon here in Argentina. His name is Eduardo Elsztain." In a legendary story, Eduardo, a college dropout, had talked his way into George Soros's office in 1990 and pitched his unlikely vision that Argentina was emerging from decades of debt crisis and was ripe with opportunity. Eduardo walked out of the meeting with a $10 million check, which he proceeded to turn into the nation's largest real estate empire.

Eduardo had given me ten minutes. Five minutes into our meeting he looked at his watch and explained he would do his best to secure an appointment for me with Soros. "Thank you very much," I said. "But I'm not looking for a meeting with George Soros." Puzzled, he motioned for me to continue. "Look, Eduardo, you're an entrepreneur. I'm an entrepreneur. Endeavor is all about supporting entrepreneurs. Here's what I do want: your time, your passion, and two hundred thousand dollars."

Our meeting had been in English, but after my direct request, Eduardo turned to his right-hand man, Oscar, and started speaking in Spanish. "*Esta chica está loca!*" he said. He went on, telling Oscar that meeting with me was like being in a bad horror movie in which the protagonist at first appears charming, but then you find yourself in the shower, and she's coming at you with a knife.

This bad-movie character, however, understands Spanish. When he finished, I smiled and said, "Eduardo, *estoy muy decepcionada*. ["I'm very disappointed".] I didn't expect to hear this from the man who walked into a billionaire's office and walked out with a $10 million check. You're lucky I asked you for only two hundred thousand!"

Eduardo gaped at me, looked back at Oscar, and took out his check-book. He handed me $200,000 on the spot and, along with his dona-tion, agreed to become the founding chairman of Endeavor Argentina.

That experience led to one of my guiding principles of entrepre-neurship: Crazy is a compliment!

I also propose this corollary: If you're *not* called crazy when you launch something new, it means you're *not thinking big enough*.

The point is: Given that you're going to be called bonkers when-ever you threaten the status quo, you might as well accept the term as a source of pride. I did this myself. For years, many in Latin America referred to me as *la chica loca*, and the nickname later spread to the Middle East. Instead of taking offense, I wore it as a badge of honor.

If you're going to agitate for change, you're going to generate push-back. Don't be surprised; don't be hurt; don't give up. Press on.

Fan the foolish fire.

— *STOP PLANNING, START DOING* —

In 2013 I appeared on the *Today* show in a segment about helping peo-ple start their own businesses. My fellow guest was an MBA-trained Internet entrepreneur who explained that she had written a seventy-five-page business plan before starting her business. She recom-mended that viewers do the same. I almost fell off my stool. "On that we can agree to disagree," I said.

Wait! Everybody knows that the one thing you need to execute an idea is a step-by-step plan. Everybody agrees that once you have your crazy idea, you should put it on the page to make it seem more real. You should add numbers, buzzwords, projections, graphs. You should create a PowerPoint to impress your bosses, your friends, your lover. You should draft a business plan.

Well, let me tell you: "Everybody" is wrong. There's another way to approach this phase of entrepreneurship. Stop planning. Start doing.

Vinny Lingham grew up in the Eastern Cape Province of South

Africa during apartheid and was raised in a segregated area designated for Indians. He remembers watching the movie *Wall Street* as a boy and thinking, "I want to be something more." Vinny developed a passion for starting enterprises, from selling stickers in grade school to managing rock bands in college. In 2003 he left his first corporate job, sold his house, and convinced his fiancée and two friends to join him in launching an online marketing company. He was finally living the self-made life he'd dreamed of.

But Vinny wasn't satisfied. He'd identified a new problem: Many small businesses lacked the capital or know-how to create Web sites. So he left his own start-up and launched another one. Soon Google chose his new firm, Yola, for a major initiative, and HP offered to pre-install its product on its computers. In 2009 *Businessweek* declared Yola one of "Fifty Startups You Should Know." Several years later Vinny launched yet another new company, Gyft—a mobile gift card wallet—that was nurtured by Google Ventures.

Vinny is a serial gazelle, and he soon became a mainstay of Silicon Valley. Along the way he developed strong opinions about most entrepreneurs he met: They overthink, they overplan, they overanalyze. I once moderated a panel involving Vinny, Leila, and other entrepreneurs before a roomful of finance types. "You guys think too much," Vinny told the audience. "You spend all your time talking about ideas, learning theory, and writing business plans, and not enough time trying stuff out." He added this kicker: "By the time you've perfected your plan on paper, guys like me will have signed up loads of real-life customers for our businesses."

Vinny is not alone. Research we did of the nearly one thousand Endeavor entrepreneurs found that two-thirds did not write formal business plans when starting their ventures, more than 80 percent launched their first product within six months, and nearly half changed their business model at least once. Wences didn't have a business plan when he started his company, and neither did Leila.

Our gazelles are in good company. A 2002 survey of the founders of Inc. 500 companies revealed that only 12 percent conducted formal market research before launch and only 40 percent wrote formal business plans. Of those who wrote plans, two-thirds admitted they ditched them later. The founders of Microsoft, Pixar, and Starbucks didn't follow business plans; Intel's business plan was a mere 161 words, with a number of those words, including "and," being misspelled.

Corporate skunks, too, can use this stop-planning, start-doing approach. When I asked Mary Jo Cook, of Clorox, what advice she would give to those in big companies who were thinking of becoming more entrepreneurial, she said, "Instead of analyzing and analyzing and analyzing and trying to predict the perfect case in an imperfect, messy, constantly changing world, just try something." The key to entrepreneurship, she said, is to "learn by doing." What's valuable about this approach within corporations is that instead of trying to impress your boss with a PowerPoint, you can make your case with proof points.

Consider what happened at Pfizer, one of the world's largest pharmaceutical companies, with more than ninety thousand employees. In 2005 Jordan Cohen, a mid-level human resources officer, noticed that a new father on his team was staying late to create spreadsheets and do research online. Cohen didn't think this was a valuable use of time and wondered if individual employees could outsource grunt work to India.

Instead of crafting an elaborate proposal, Cohen tested the idea using a handful of workers and his own limited budget. He dubbed his initiative Office of the Future and kept it secret from his superiors for an entire year to gain evidence, traction, and allies. The first test failed miserably. Assignments came back filled with typos; data were riddled with errors. Cohen discovered his colleagues weren't being specific enough with their outsourced assistants about what they needed, so he spent months breaking down projects into four usable tasks: creating documents, manipulating spreadsheets, scheduling meetings, and conducting research.

At this point he recruited a senior manager from a different department, who offered to pilot the program and pay for it out of his budget, giving Cohen both resources and cover. Pfizer's top brass was still kept in the dark. Word of the program began to spread, and two hundred employees eventually joined the initiative. Armed with a trove of data showing thousands of employee hours saved, Cohen and his adviser finally pitched top execs, who green-lighted a company-wide program. Today the renamed pfizerWorks serves ten thousand managers, including the chairman and CEO. In internal surveys, employees rated it the company's most popular service, even though they have to pay for it out of their own department budgets.

Butterfly entrepreneurs often dive into their enterprises without a plan. They see something that needs fixing, and they go about fixing it. In their case, it's often not a choice because many don't even realize they're starting something when they do. That was the case of Margaret Rudkin.

The oldest of five children in an Irish American family, Rudkin (née Fogarty) was born in 1897 in New York. With the reputation of being a fiery redhead, she was her high school valedictorian and went to work at a Wall Street brokerage firm, where she met her husband. The two had three sons and moved to a lovely piece of property in Fairfield, Connecticut. The year was 1929. When the stock market crashed, the family suffered, selling apples and pigs to pay their bills. But Rudkin's bigger challenge was the severe allergies and asthma of her youngest son, Mark, who was unable to eat processed foods.

When a doctor ordered Mark to go on a diet of natural foods, Rudkin decided to try baking him some stone-ground whole wheat bread. "My first loaf should have been sent to the Smithsonian Institution as a sample of Stone Age bread," Rudkin said. "It was hard as a rock and about one inch high." After a few tries she finally had an edible loaf. Mark loved it, and so did his doctor, who started "prescribing" it to his patients. Rudkin promptly marched to her local grocer and asked if he was interested in selling her bread. "No way," the grocer said. Rudkin had no experience in the baking business; besides, she wanted twenty-five cents a loaf instead of the going rate of ten cents.

So she cut him a slice. The grocer tasted it and bought every loaf on the spot; then he called her later and ordered some more. Rudkin named her bread after her beloved home in Connecticut, Pepperidge Farm, which itself was named for an old pepperidge, or tupelo, tree. "Although I knew nothing of manufacturing, of marketing, of pricing, or of making bread in quantities," she said, "with that phone call, Pepperidge Farm bread was born."

Margaret Rudkin had become an accidental entrepreneur. All she had was a motive, a kitchen, and a recipe, as well as a husband who was willing to tote her loaves to Grand Central Station to sell. Within a few years she had moved her operation to her garage. After *Reader's Digest* touted her bread in 1939, demand exploded. As one reporter noted, "In response to this growing demand, Margaret Rudkin pushed her vivid red hair back from a perspiring brow and said she had always known the people of the United States wanted homemade bread—but did they have to have it all at once?"

Lots of butterfly entrepreneurs begin like this, often after someone loses a job or when their kids no longer need them full-time. They don't write business plans because they don't have the knowledge or resources—and wouldn't know what to do with such a plan if they had it.

Still uneasy about forgoing that plan? Bill Sahlman, the guru of entrepreneurial finance at Harvard Business School, wrote a piece for *Harvard Business Review* titled "How to Write a Great Business Plan." His surprising conclusion: "In my experience with hundreds of entrepreneurial startups, business plans rank no higher than 2—on a scale of 1 to 10—as a predictor of a new venture's success." Sometimes, he continued, "the more elaborately crafted the document, the more likely the venture is to, well, flop."

Bill's explanation was that most business plans spend too much time on padded numbers and inflated language that fail to acknowledge that smart businesses adapt and change. Early ventures bear little resemblance to what they ultimately become. Bill even included a handy key explaining what business plan–speak really means.

What They Say . . .	What They Really Mean . . .
We conservatively project . . .	We read a book that said we had to be a $50 million company in five years, and we reverse-engineered the numbers.
The project is 98 percent complete.	To complete the remaining 2 percent will take twice as long as it took to create the initial 98 percent and cost twice as much.
Customers are clamoring for our product.	We have not yet asked them to pay for it.

To be clear, I'm not saying that business plans themselves are bad. Nor is Bill Sahlman saying that. Vinny, for example, eventually did write a plan for his various ventures when the time came to raise money from VCs. (Actually, he hired an MBA to do it for him.) Jordan Cohen ultimately did write a proposal to expand his outsourcing initiative across Pfizer. It's when you make your plan that's important. Do it too early, and it's likely to stifle your momentum and bury your enthusiasm under a deluge of doubt and made-up numbers.

Instead, the lesson of this early stage of becoming an entrepreneur is that the most important things you can do relate to mind-set: (1) First, give yourself permission to be a contrarian, to flout convention, to follow the unsafe path, to zig when everyone else zags; then (2) take some action to get going. Allow yourself to try; then try. As Wences would say, be a doer.

Keep moving toward Day One.

Be warned, you will be called crazy for having a big dream, for taking a career-threatening chance, for plunging in without knowing exactly where you're going. That is an undeniable side effect of being an entrepreneur. There is no reward without some risk.

But if I could stress one thing, the smartest entrepreneurs don't take blind risks; they take smart risks. They don't risk it all; they risk just enough to get going, then hedge those risks at every step along the way.

It's how to pull off that delicate balance that I want to turn to next.

CHAPTER 2

Derisking Risk

Sara Blakely felt like a failure. She tried to become a stand-up comedian but fell short. She planned to go to law school but bombed the LSAT. She became a cast member at Disney World but quit after three months. Finally she found work selling fax machines.

One day, suffering in the heat and humidity of Florida, Sara needed panty hose to wear with white pants and sandals, so she cut the feet off a regular pair. They rode up her leg, annoyingly. "I needed an undergarment that didn't exist," she said. She started researching fabrics at night and eventually designed a product she liked. She even taught herself patent law to save money. Her total investment: $5,000. She called her product Spanks.

"I knew that Kodak and Coca-Cola were the two most recognized names," Sara said, "and they both have 'K' sounds in them." As a comedian she also knew that *K* sounds make people laugh. At the last minute she changed the *KS* to an *X* after learning that made-up words make better brands and are easier to trademark. "Spanx is edgy, fun, extremely catchy, and for a moment it makes your mind wander (admit it)," she said. Her slogan: "Don't worry, we've got your butt covered."

I love this story for a lot reasons: It's fun, impressive, inspiring. In 2012, at age forty-one, Sara became the youngest self-made woman to make the *Forbes* billionaire list. (And well, I like the product, too. I'm happy Sara has my butt covered!) But I especially like that it encompasses a number of key lessons I've learned about becoming an entrepreneur—namely, how to take big, unmanageable dreams and slice them into small, manageable tasks.

It's what Sara did after committing to her dream that's so illustrative. Although she knew nothing about the hosiery business, Sara didn't bog down in some meta-analysis. Instead, she hopped into her car and drove door to door in North Carolina, trying to talk mill owners into manufacturing her product. They always asked the same three questions: "And you are?" "And you are representing?" "And you are backed by?"

"When I answered 'Sara Blakely' to all three," she said, "most of them sent me away."

But faced with multiple rejections, she didn't cave. She pushed on. Finally one mill owner who had sent her away called back. "I've decided to help make your crazy idea," he said. Why? she asked. "I have two daughters," he replied.

Sara's experience embodies the second key step of becoming an entrepreneur: deciding how much to put on the line, developing a prototype, finding users, and (my favorite) stalking supporters. If the first step to becoming an entrepreneur is about managing mind-set, this one's about managing risk. Specifically, it's about derisking risk.

When Sara first had the idea for butt-flattering panty hose, for example, she didn't quit her day job selling fax machines. For *two years*, Sara hawked office products nine to five on weekdays and sold panty hose on nights and weekends. She didn't resign until she was fairly confident her entrepreneurial venture would take off. What gave her that confidence? Oprah had picked Spanx as one of her "favorite things."

While the popular impression of entrepreneurs is that they're reckless cowboys, the reality is quite different. Dig below the surface and what smart entrepreneurs actually know is how to get an idea going with minimal expense, nominal exposure, and limited liability.

So how do you do that? How do you differentiate smart risks from foolish ones? The four strategies in this chapter can help. Contrary to what those inspirational posters say, the first step is not always the hardest.

This one is.

— DON'T BET THE FARM —

One of the trickiest questions entrepreneurs face early on is: Once you have your idea and are convinced it will fly, how far should you go? The popular myth goes something like this: Go all in. Sell the baseball card collection. Mortgage the house. Max out your credit cards. Dip into your IRA.

Bet the farm.

The legendary CEO of McDonald's, Ray Kroc, captured this sentiment well: "If you're not a risk taker, you should get the hell out of business." Like a lot of the lore around entrepreneurship—and business in general—this myth appeals to a kind of macho bravado. In fact, the phrase "bet the farm" comes from poker tables in the Wild West, where betting the farm in a game of five-card draw proved you had cojones.

Well, boys will be boys, but entrepreneurs will be savvy. Talk to actual entrepreneurs, and the story around risk is often quite different.

Richard Branson is certainly no wimp. Yet as he wrote in *Losing My Virginity*, "If you are a risk-taker, the art is to protect the downside." When we honored him at one of our annual Endeavor galas, he told the story of his ill-fated foray into soft drinks, Virgin Cola. "I thought we could take on Coca-Cola," he said. In Branson's telling, Virgin Cola was a disaster, but it was a "contained disaster." It was the result of a calculated entrepreneurial risk that didn't threaten the

Virgin brand. His lesson to our entrepreneurs: "Make sure a single failure won't ruin everything."

Many entrepreneurs I've worked with echo this idea. Rodrigo Jordan is one of the biggest adventure junkies I know. The Chilean-born CEO loves extreme sports, including rock and ice climbing. In 1992 he became the first South American to scale Everest, a feat he has repeated many times. (In 2012 he texted me a fun photo of the Endeavor flag staked on the summit.)

Rodrigo leveraged his mountaineering techniques to form a corporate leadership training company, so I was surprised when he told me this: "The common wisdom is all wrong: Entrepreneurs don't like to take risks. I hate risks. I'm always trying to avoid and minimize risks. An entrepreneur should never be a daredevil who puts it all on the line."

Endeavor's research backs this up. When we asked our entrepreneurs to rate their attitude toward risk, the overwhelming majority veered toward the middle, not the extreme. Ninety-five percent said they did not risk their ability to provide food and shelter for their families when starting their businesses. More than 80 percent had enough savings or other resources set aside to cover basic expenses for at least one year. This doesn't mean they were rich—most lived on very tight budgets at the outset—but it does speak to their attitude toward limiting liability and continuing to provide for their families while they pursued their crazy dreams.

Still, some risk is necessary. So how much? If you're not supposed to bet the farm, what amount should you bet?

Just enough to get you into the game. Sixty-one percent of the 2013 Inc. 500 entrepreneurs originally wagered less than $10,000 on their businesses. For most start-ups, the number is significantly less. In *The Lean Startup*, Eric Ries advocates investing just enough for a starter product—nothing too fancy, nothing too expensive. The goal is to create what he calls a minimum viable product. "This is a hard truth for many entrepreneurs to accept," Ries wrote. You may be wishing for a mind-blowing prototype that will change the world or one that will impress that snarky cousin at Thanksgiving.

The smarter approach is to take incremental steps, get feedback, and adjust. Ries labels this the "build-measure-learn" feedback loop. It's the same reason you shouldn't fuss over a business plan: You'll quickly outgrow your prototype. As Reid Hoffman, cofounder of LinkedIn and an Endeavor board member, says, "If you're not embarrassed by your first product, you've waited too long."

One advantage of not betting the farm is that you're not laying out a lot of cash. In 1999 a former ticket seller for the San Diego Padres, Nick Swinmurn, had the provocative idea that people might be willing to buy footwear from a grand online emporium. It's fairly easy to see the appeal: infinite selection, year-round. Also, $2 billion of shoes were annually purchased at that time through a catalog. But it's also easy to see the downside: I, for one, have problematic feet and have to try on multiple pairs before I find one that fits.

Swinmurn could have spent years studying the market, analyzing consumers' buying habits. Or he could've invested in a warehouse and stuffed it with shoeboxes from floor to ceiling. He might have racked up debt only to discover that people were no more likely to buy shoes online than martinis. Instead, Swinmurn tried an experiment. He walked into a shoe store in Sunnyvale, California, one day and asked if he could take pictures of its products and put them online. If people bought the shoes, he would return to the store and buy them at full price.

This obviously was not a viable business model, but here's the thing: Swinmurn's experiment wasn't designed to *be* a business; it was designed to *test the idea* for a business. And it worked: He quickly proved that people would be willing to buy shoes online. Even more important, he garnered key information about his customers: who they were, what products they liked, how many samples they wanted to try on before making a purchase, etc. In June 1999 Swinmurn opened ShoeSite.com, which he soon rechristened Zappos.com.

Using low-risk tactics to launch high-risk ventures is especially valuable in larger corporations, where failures can potentially derail your career. Two skunks at MTV understood this. In the mid-1990s the Internet was just catching on, and two mid-level employees at MTV Europe wanted to find a way to incorporate e-mails and user-generated content into a show. But instead of marching into the CEO's office to get a sign-off, Henrik Werdelin and Eric Kearley began stealthily developing a pilot. Werdelin borrowed equipment from technicians he hung out with after work; Kearley paid for a camera out of his own pocket. They built a prototype studio inside an unused tiny room near Kearley's office. They even managed to recruit a well-known MTV anchor, using only a bottle of scotch.

Still, a prototype was not enough. The two skunks needed to air their show live to prove the technology would work. But how could they convince their superiors to cede valuable airtime to their cobbled-together idea? The answer: They didn't. They persuaded some technicians in the control room to air their pilot in the middle of the night, when the network normally ran taped programs. The risk was minimal, they argued. If the show went horribly wrong, the technicians could simply switch back to the canned programs.

That didn't happen. The show was a hit. "When I approached our CEO," Kearley said, "I was able to tell him that we had a new idea, that we had made it work technically, that we had already broadcast it successfully." The concept became the award-winning *Top Selection*, and the technology they pioneered went on to form the backbone of *Total Request Live*, MTV's groundbreaking show hosted by Carson Daly, that propelled the careers of Britney Spears, Christina Aguilera, and Justin Timberlake.

This incremental approach to developing an idea is also valuable for butterfly entrepreneurs, who often don't have the cash to build expensive prototypes or the freedom to quit their jobs and ignore the kids. Cleveland-born Warren Brown had an undergraduate degree from Brown University and a JD and master's degree in public health from George Washington University. He was working as a litigator for the Department of Health and Human Services when he hit a wall of frustration. A lifelong tinkerer in the kitchen, Brown made a New Year's resolution in 1999 to learn to bake. He worked during the day, baked cakes every night, and stopped in on bakeries during business trips.

Before visiting relatives in New York one weekend, he prepared a simple chocolate cake, put it on a white plate, and carried it on the plane. "Walking through the airport and onto the plane, security guards, flight attendants, passengers, and other travelers came up to me. *Did you make that cake? Is it your birthday? Are you a baker?*" It was like a focus group, he said: cake = love. "Waiting by the curb that night for my aunt Yvette, I realized I was staring at my future."

In the mythic version of this story Brown quits his job, borrows money from friends and family, and opens a bakery. But in the actual version of this story he worries, is afraid to tell his friends and family, and works himself into a state of agitation. Six months after that flight, in a whirl of working, baking, and running errands for his sideline business, Brown collapsed at his home, unable to move or breathe. "I was confused, tired, and desperate," he said. "I wanted to bake, but I didn't know how I could pull it off. How do I tell my parents, who sent me to law school?" A friend drove him to a hospital, where doctors instructed him to slow down.

Brown went to his boss and asked for a three-month unpaid leave of absence. He didn't quit outright, but he did think he could write a business plan (sigh), raise some money, and open a store. He rented a kitchen, baked fifteen showcase cakes, and invited seventy-five friends to a tasting. And yes, he also invited his parents. His mother said, in a small voice, "Well, if that's what you really want to do . . ." His father said his passion had better come with a real salary.

Three months later he hadn't written a word of the business plan and hadn't raised a nickel. He got some orders—birthday parties, weddings, a few restaurants—and decided to extend his leave. The *Washington Post* caught wind and wrote an article—not about his store but about his decision whether or not to open one. The headline: WILL WARREN BROWN GIVE UP A PROMISING LEGAL CAREER TO MAKE CAKES? The *Today* show called. *People* magazine labeled this handsome thirty-year-old African American one of "50 Most Eligible Bachelors in America."

But still no store! "The process is long and tough," he said. "Starting a business is not easy." Another year passed. Finally he got a small business loan, and in 2002, almost four years after his resolution, Brown opened CakeLove in Washington, D.C. The next year he started a café; a cookbook followed, as did six other stores and a Food Network series. But as Brown said, his fast growth would not have been possible without his slow start.

"You listen to entrepreneurs talk about their experience," he said, "and you often don't hear all the difficult things that happened along the way." Brown added, "You have to be a little unhinged" to do what he did, but you also have to push forward without throwing everything you've built out the door.

In my experience, most entrepreneurs are not risk maximizers; they are *risk minimizers*. They don't focus on optimal returns; they focus on acceptable loss.

Leave the high-ante games for the poker table. When it comes to your ideas, don't bet the actual farm. Wager a few chickens at a time.

— FRIENDS DON'T LET FRIENDS TEST-DRIVE THEIR IDEAS —

But how do you know if betting even a few chickens is a good idea? Your inclination may be to go to the people you trust the most: your friends, your family, your jogging partner, the neighbor across the street, the smart guy in the cubicle around the corner. So you build up the confidence, you practice your pitch, you slide on the Spanx (yes, they have them for men, too), and you ask: "So tell me, is my crazy idea brilliant or is it just crazy?"

Please ignore whatever they say.

As the old saying goes, love is blind, and what you need at the moment is to see your idea more clearly. Sara Blakely, when she started dabbling with nylons, didn't tell her friends and family. The only people who knew, apart from patent lawyers she consulted, were her roommate and her boyfriend. "My family knew that 'Sara's working on some idea,'" she said, "but I never told them what it was." Her reason: "Ideas are fragile in their infancy, and I sensed that if I talked about it with friends, I might be discouraged."

Your loved ones are likely to greet your idea in one of two ways, neither of which is all that helpful to you. For some, it will be mindless flattery: "OMG, that's the greatest idea I've ever heard! You're a genius. You'll make millions!" It's the equivalent of taking a bridesmaid to the final fitting of your wedding dress and expecting anything other than "You look perfect!" These responses may boost your mood, but they don't help you test the quality of your idea.

For others, it will always be negative: "You're thinking of quitting your job to do WHAT?" "Somebody else is bound to do it first—and better." "How will you ever send your kids to college?" This is what Warren Brown's parents effectively said to him.

In both cases, the people you're talking to are usually responding out of emotion—either trying to make you feel good or trying to make themselves feel good (or at least justify their own risk aversion). Neither does you much good at all.

Consider these two cautionary tales, both involving butterflies, but with very different endings.

Mel and Patricia Ziegler were weary of their high-stress, low-wage jobs. He worked as a reporter; she, a courtroom sketch artist. They were young, newly in love, and unbeknownst to each other, both quit their jobs on the same day in hopes of building a life of freedom and travel. First they downsized; then they read a book on how to start a business; then, out of nowhere, Mel got a freelance writing gig in Australia. Looking for cheap clothing in Sydney one day, Mel happened on a secondhand British Burma jacket. "Made of thick but soft khaki cotton twill, it looked like a safari jacket," he recalled. "It had the tailored feeling of a fine garment." He topped it off with an olive green Australian bush hat.

Patricia almost didn't recognize her clothes-averse boyfriend when he walked through customs two weeks later. "Something was different," she said. "Had he acquired this new worldliness, this rather heroic nonchalance from his adventures Down Under, or was it the jacket?" Impressed with its "perfect color" and "slightly worn collar and cuffs," she set about doctoring the jacket, adding suede elbow patches, leather trim, and wooden buttons. Mel wore it almost every day, and everywhere he went, people stopped him. "Where did you get that fabulous jacket?"

"The jacket had a message for me," he said, "and it didn't take me long to get it: here was the business we'd been looking for." Patricia got the same message, too.

They invested $750 into a line of used, short-armed Spanish paratrooper shirts (the British Burma jackets were impossible to find and, even used, too pricey). Mel and Patricia described the move as their stop-planning, start-doing moment: "Therein lay the full and complete business plan of a writer and artist who had quit their jobs to make it on their own."

After a few hot afternoons hawking their wares at a flea market, the couple decided to spend their remaining cash on a homemade catalog filled with Patricia's hand-drawn illustrations and Mel's quirky, conversational dialogue. (Mel dubbed himself minister of propaganda.) The pair eagerly took their pride and joy, fresh off the printer, to two friends. After flipping through the pages, one friend said, "You don't expect this to sell anything, do you?" The other added, "You sure you want to mail this?" Shaken, Patricia turned to Mel after they left and asked if they should quit. "We can't turn back now," he said.

Patricia and Mel's quirky idea, Banana Republic, has grown to more than six hundred stores across the globe. Five years after Mel first bought that used jacket, the couple sold their company to the Gap and left to pursue their dreams of freedom and artistry. A key reason Gap took an interest in Banana Republic: Its eccentric, chatty, hand-illustrated catalogs had taken off. Had the Zieglers listened to their friends, they never would have taken it off the drawing board.

One problem with listening to those closest to you is that they might rain on your safari. But the opposite problem is equally bad: Your friends might butter you up. And if your dream is to make jam, that butter might be awfully tempting.

Alison Roman and Eva Scofield were coworkers at Brooklyn's trendy Momofuku Milk Bar who longed to join the artisanal food movement sweeping through their neighborhood. Offered the chance to sell something at Brooklyn Flea, the trendy market at the pinnacle of the farm-to-table trend, they jumped. They started testing recipes in off-hours; each put in a couple of hundred dollars for ingredients.

Finally they came up with a winner: fresh organic fruit jams with unusual flavors—vanilla-lemon, grapefruit-hibiscus. One particular jar caught Roman's eye: It was well-made, gorgeous, but, at $1.85 a pop, costly. Things went smoothly at first. The jams tasted great. Friends cheered them on, even pushing them to raise their prices, from the already expensive $7 to downright outrageous $9 per jar. "Handmade in Brooklyn with local fruit" drew a crowd. People raved about the jars. Maiden Preserves appeared to be another dishrags-to-riches success story.

But the reality was more bitter. The company never broke even. "Friends would say, 'You guys are doing so well,'" Roman said. "I'd say, 'No, we're not.' There's this fantasy, but it's not as simple as putting fruit in a jar and selling it." Soon the partners were bickering over strategy. Roman wanted to go more nichey, selling to baby and bridal showers and cute boutiques. Scofield wanted to spin off a line with cheaper jars. "It was becoming clear we didn't have the same vision," Roman said. Soon they stopped making jam together.

For most entrepreneurs, the surprising truth is that the people you trust most are usually the least trustworthy when it comes to your ideas. A team of researchers from Babson College and IPADE Business School surveyed 120 founders in Hong Kong, Kenya, Mexico, Nigeria, the United Kingdom, and the United States, asking for the biggest mistakes they had made. One conclusion: selling early to family and friends.

This problem was particularly pronounced in the clothing, food, and financial services industries, the researchers found. (The founders of Banana Republic and Maiden Preserves were not alone.) "You never know why relatives are buying from you," the researchers said. "Often their motivation is love, pity, or a sense of obligation, not compelling product quality." Founders, in retrospect, wished they had ignored what family had to say and instead pursued "arm's-length transactions with customers who would have given them candid feedback."

The appeal of turning to loved ones for early input is obvious: They're close; they're cheap; they often share your tastes. But the downsides are equally great. Smart entrepreneurs move as quickly as possible from finding their true passions to finding their true customers, and they often skip the troublesome step of asking what those around them think.

Next time you consider phoning a friend and sharing your crazy concept before it's ready for prime time, remember: Friends don't let friends test-drive their ideas.

— FOLLOW THE CROWD —

So once you have a minimum viable product in hand, how do you test its appeal? Specifically, how do you test it in a cost-effective way that doesn't imperil your idea, your life savings, or your ability to pay the electric bill?

Like so many other areas of contemporary life, the Internet has opened previously unimaginable paths. Crazy dreamers now have a new way to stop planning and start doing, avoid betting the farm, and sidestep letting their friends test-drive their ideas. This way was not available to Edison or Branson or to the founders of Banana Republic or even Spanx.

That new way is the crowd.

In 2002 Perry Chen was an electronic musician and busboy living in New Orleans, experimenting with what he calls dropping out of society. He tried to bring a pair of Austrian DJs to town for JazzFest. The duo asked for $15,000 plus five business-class tickets, an insurmountable sum for the barely employed Chen, who would be left to foot the bill if no one bought tickets for the show. But he "had a feeling that this was a problem that should be solvable," he said. What if he could ask those who might enjoy the show to precommit to buying tickets?

Though it took him seven years to flesh out his idea, in 2009 Chen and two cofounders launched Kickstarter. A missionary dolphin at heart, Chen insisted he was building an ecosystem to help creative people, not a business. Three weeks in, a twenty-two-year-old singer-songwriter from Athens, Georgia, tried to raise funds to release an album titled *Allison Weiss Was Right All Along*. She reached her goal in ten hours. "That's when we knew a movement had been launched," Chen said.

It took Kickstarter four months to fund one hundred projects and a year to reach a thousand. By year two it was funding a thousand projects a month; five years in, Kickstarter had enabled fifty thousand projects to raise $850 million from over five million contributors. Today more than five hundred crowdfunding sites have joined the revolution, and the field continues to double every year.

Crowdfunding has proven especially powerful for butterflies because the medium thrives on helping underdogs. Movie directors can bypass Hollywood studios; musicians can avoid record companies; authors can sidestep publishers. The same is happening with comic books, video games, and theater productions. In 2013 alone Kickstarter helped *Moby-Dick* get translated into Emojis and the documentary *Inocente* win an Oscar.

Yet it's not just butterflies. Dolphins, too, are taking advantage of the crowd. A number of Kickstarter-like platforms have popped up to help cause-driven organizations. Do Good Bus, the brainchild of a team of Los Angeles musicians, embarked on a bus tour of twenty-two cities promising "altruistic adventurism." They played music and promoted programs for at-risk youth. Their appeal attracted 680 backers and $101,000.

Crowdfunding is not foolproof, and it's not easy street. Only 44 percent of Kickstarter projects ever get funded. Also, while persistent creators find ways to build word of mouth, many projects start off with a built-in base of friends, family, and fans. As one aspiring creator said, "You have to bring your own crowd." (And to be clear, just because you don't ask friends for their opinion before you get going, once you're under way, there's no reason not to ask them to help spread the word and rustle up customers.)

Still, crowdfunding has already altered the start-up landscape. First, it's democratized access to capital, especially for people in out-of-the-way places. Second, it provides valuable market feedback.

Instead of spending precious time and money on prototypes or store-fronts, entrepreneurs can ask potential customers to give input, vote on features, and place preorders. Imagine if Warren Brown had launched a Kickstarter campaign after he appeared on the *Today* show and in *People*. He might not have had to wait an entire year to get a loan for his first CakeLove store.

Third, crowdfunding sites offer publicity in case you're one of the millions of entrepreneurs who aren't Sara Blakely or Warren Brown and don't find yourself on national television. A leading scholar of crowdfunding, Anindya Ghose of New York University, said the exposure is often more valuable than the money. "Crowdfunding helps to create a lot of buzz, word-of-mouth, and awareness of a project." Finally, crowdfunding has made looking scruffy desirable. While start-ups long wanted to appear polished and professional, now they often want to appear scrappy and grassroots.

Even corporations want some of that scrappiness. IBM launched an internal crowdfunding platform where skunks pitch projects to one another (instead of their bosses) for $2,000 in seed money. Coca-Cola announced it was "crowdsourcing happiness" through a "smile-back" video campaign; Sam Adams produced the first "collaborative ale." And in 2013 GE formed a partnership with Quirky, a platform on which "citizen inventors" submit ideas that the crowd can vote on, improve, and bring to market.

Using customers to help design products is another way the crowd is helping entrepreneurs cut down on risk. Two entrepreneurs in our network did just that. Jo Bedu is a Jordanian apparel company that selects designs for its edgy products through crowdsourcing. Michael Makdah and Tamer Al-Masri were high school friends who reunited in their twenties and discovered a way to merge their passions in art and marketing. They withdrew $4,200 from savings and created six hundred T-shirts from Tamer's witty designs. They stored inventory at Tamer's house and sold the shirts at Souk Jara, a local street market. The products were well received; they hired their first employee. But sales soon stalled.

Then the two had an idea. Why not outsource designs to the eventual buyers? They launched a Facebook campaign inviting their followers to submit design ideas. Jo Bedu then bought the best designs and printed them. The resulting T-shirts sold forty thousand units. With proof in hand, the company opened its first store; within two years it was selling Jo Bedu clothing and accessories at the Virgin megastore in Amman. Today the company still solicits customer designs and receives two thousand submissions for every request.

These days the best way to stand out from the crowd is to follow it.

— *THE LOST ART OF STALKING* —

All these techniques are legitimate ways of testing your idea and getting it going without assuming unnecessary risk. But there's one more strategy I want to mention. It's part of what we might call the dark arts of entrepreneurship, the kind of thing that's not taught in business school but that every entrepreneur I know uses at one time or another.

Several years after my meeting with Eduardo Elsztain, where I earned my *la chica loca* moniker, I was invited to address the first-year class at Harvard Business School. On that day the school was unveiling a new case study about Endeavor. It had been commissioned by Bill Sahlman, the same guru of entrepreneurship who mocked business plan doublespeak. Bill introduced me by explaining how I had built Endeavor by using a nonconventional technique to recruit boosters: I trapped them in confined spaces from which they had little chance to escape. I loitered outside airplane bathrooms; I lurked in fancy restaurants; I hovered around gym treadmills.

"Linda was a stalker," Bill announced to his class.

I chuckled. "And from what I've seen, stalking is an underrated start-up strategy!"

Bill himself had been among my victims. Six months into the life of Endeavor I began to realize we needed some "cred." By then Peter and I had recruited two friends, Gary Mueller and Jason Green, to join our board. Gary was a successful Internet entrepreneur; Jason, an up-and-coming venture capitalist. Still, everywhere I went, people kept asking who our backers were. They would say something to the effect of "We've never heard of you. This is an outlandish idea. Prove to us you can attract big names."

So when I heard that Peter Brooke, the legendary pioneer of international VC and private equity, was slated to speak on a panel at Harvard Business School, I pounced. Literally. I attended the event, eyed the sixty-eight-year-old Brooke walking offstage and into the men's bathroom, and waited.

When he emerged, I stepped in front of him. "Hi, my name is Linda, and I've started an organization to support entrepreneurs around the world. I'd love to come by your office for a few minutes to tell you more about it." Brooke did not miss a beat. I clearly was not the first person to accost him like this.

"Who else is backing you?" he said.

"Um, well, Bill Sahlman is a supporter," I said, improvising.

"Really? Sahlman is backing this? In that case, here's my card. Give me a call."

Minutes later I marched up to Bill's office and said, "Guess what? I'm pretty sure Peter Brooke is going to cochair our global advisory board. And he's asked for you to be the other cochair."

Not until three years later, at the third annual gathering of Endeavor's global advisory board, did the two cochairs realize that neither had ever officially agreed to play any role in our organization.

A crazy lady coming at you with a knife, indeed. Only it's a butter knife. The better way to butter you up.

There's a common misperception in the world of entrepreneurship that in order to be successful, you must start with personal wealth, a fancy degree, a golden Rolodex, or some combination of the three. The reality is often the opposite. Most of the entrepreneurs I encounter on a daily basis lack connections to elite networks and don't have trust funds as a safety net. What they do possess is chutzpah.

Still, learning to deploy that audacity is tricky. There are a number of ways you can perfect the art.

Stalk the competition. You can never learn too much about the field you're trying to disrupt. If a major consulting group is working on a case for a cruise line, it pays its junior employees to dress as tourists, go on rivals' cruises, and take lots of pictures. When Sam Walton was getting started, he loved to sneak around rival stores on family trips. His wife would wait in the car with the kids, who always complained, "Oh, no, Daddy, not another store." Once Walton was slinking around a Price Club in San Diego, making notes on a tape recorder, when an employee caught him. Forced to hand over the incriminating evidence, Walton wrote a note to Robert Price, the owner's son. "Robert, your guy is just too good. Here's the tape. If you want to listen to it, you certainly have that privilege, but I have some other material on here I would very much like back." Four days later the tape recorder was returned, with all of Walton's notes still on it.

The Internet has made this kind of sleuthing a lot easier. You can set a Google alert for your competition or track its personnel moves on LinkedIn. A LinkedIn career adviser told *Forbes* that not stalking competitors was one of the biggest mistakes novices make. "If you're a game developing startup," she said, "you should absolutely be following Electronic Arts," which allows you to know who's left the company. "Maybe you want to hire them, maybe they've got some dirt they can share, but either way, keeping track of the industry players can give you a competitive advantage."

Stalk customers. Sometimes, if you're new to a field, you have to try unconventional ways to attract customers. If that field is protection from cybercriminals, well . . .

Marcelo Romcy and João Mendes were teenage hackers from rural Brazil. After meeting in college, they decided to go straight and set up a cybersecurity business, Proteus. When I met them, Marcelo and João had achieved regional penetration and were eager to expand overseas. But there was a problem: They had built their business using a hazardous technique. They would pick a bank or financial firm they wanted as a client, breach its firewall, and temporarily "borrow" $10,000. Then they would knock on the CEO's door with the money in hand, explain how they'd got it, and pitch themselves to fix the problem. Their strategy paid off: Proteus soon became one of South America's leading IT auditing firms.

My first suggestion was that they not try this strategy in the United States, where this technique would likely get them a visit from the SEC! Instead, I encouraged them to fly to Jordan, where I was hosting an event. There they zeroed in on one of the region's top CEOs, with six thousand employees and lots of contacts around the world. After Marcelo made his pitch, the CEO turned cocky. "We have the best IT security in the region," he said. "Why do we need you?"

Marcelo offered to hack into his system to show how much he needed Proteus.

"Go ahead," the CEO said. "You won't find a hole."

Three days later Marcelo called the CEO. "Would you like for me to tell you the password to your e-mail?" he asked. "I'm looking through your messages right now." The company became a client and soon recommended Proteus to others.

Stalk allies. If you're a skunk trying to drum up an entrepreneurial idea in a large corporation, stalking often means finding subtle ways to beat your own drum. Instead of badgering higher-ups, you're often better off subtly pestering your colleagues, reminding them that you're working on a new idea, gently leaving the door open if they want to walk through it. One of the most ubiquitous products in American cubicles came from this approach.

In 1968 a chemist at 3M named Spencer Silver invented the first superadhesive that could be peeled off surfaces without ruining them. It seemed like a blockbuster product, but the company couldn't figure out what to do with it. Silver became known as Mr. Persistent because he wouldn't give up, always knocking on people's doors, forever slipping his product into presentations. Silver kept at it for five years; still, the invention sat unused.

Then in 1974, another 3M scientist, Art Fry, who had heard one of

Silver's countless talks, was fiddling with his hymnal at church one day when he had a revelation. During Wednesday night choir practice, Fry would bookmark his hymnal with pieces of paper, but by Sunday morning they would have fallen out. "What I need is a bookmark that would stick to the paper without falling off and not damage the sheets," Fry thought. The next day, recalling Mr. Persistent, Fry requested a sample of Silver's adhesive. It took several more years to hone the product, and Fry's supervisors initially balked, fearing the product would seem "wasteful." But 3M executives began noticing more and more employees using the new sticky notes to remind them of their to-do lists. The executives got on board. Today 3M sells 50 billion Post-it notes a year.

Stalk gatekeepers. There's an undercurrent that runs through many stalking stories. Entrepreneurs are often outsiders. They're usually not from the best families, the best schools, or the best neighborhoods. That's a key reason you find guerrilla tactics in so many stories of women entrepreneurs. We're not part of the old boys club; we don't tend to hang out in smoke-filled rooms; we're not likely to be sitting at the poker table.

When Sara Blakely was struggling to get Spanx into stores, she cold-called the buyer from Neiman Marcus, who offered her "five minutes" if she flew to Dallas. The two met in a conference room, but after a few minutes Sara realized she wasn't connecting. So she took the woman to the ladies' room, pulled a sample out of her "lucky red backpack," and performed a live demonstration. Three weeks later the product was on Neiman Marcus shelves. "I became notorious for lifting up my pant leg to every woman walking by," Sara said.

One of the most iconic female business leaders of the twentieth century used a similar technique. Josephine Esther "Estelle" Mentzer was the embodiment of an outsider. Born to Hungarian Jewish immigrants in an Italian neighborhood of Queens, Estelle lived over her father's modest hardware store, where she longed for a life of affluence and glamour. When she asked a woman at the beauty salon where she had bought her lovely blouse, the woman coolly replied, "What differ-ence could it possibly make? You could never afford it."

Estelle walked away, heart pounding, face burning. She vowed she would someday have whatever she wanted—"jewels, exquisite art, gra-cious homes, everything."

Estelle's uncle was a struggling chemist with a line of skin creams he couldn't sell. Estelle tried a new approach: stalking. She stopped women on trains, in elevators, at the market, on the way to a Salvation Army meeting. She whipped out her jar of Super-Rich All-Purpose Cream, pointed out wrinkles on her unsuspecting victims, and in-sisted she could make them glow. When the ladies demurred, saying they really had somewhere to be, Estelle cut them off mid-sentence. "Just give me five minutes," she implored.

She stalked retailers, too. Because luxury was what Estelle wanted, luxury was what she presented. She changed her first name to Estée and, coupled with her married surname, sold her creams under the brand Estée Lauder—but only in salons and boutiques, never in drug-stores. She also kept her sights focused on the grand prize, Saks Fifth Avenue. She hounded the store's cosmetics buyer, Robert Fiske, who made it clear that Saks was not interested in an unproven product by an unknown brand.

So Estée waited for an opening. At a charity luncheon in 1948 at the Waldorf Astoria, she gave away lipstick in metallic sheaths, a sig-nificant step up from the more commonly used plastic. When women asked where they could buy the product, Estée smiled and told them to go across the street to Saks.

As Fiske recalled, "There formed a line of people across Park Ave-nue and across 50th Street into Saks asking for these lipsticks, one af-ter another." The next day Fiske placed an order for $800.

Altogether, the techniques of stalking, following the crowd, build-ing prototypes, and betting just a few chickens at a time highlight a broader theme of getting started as an entrepreneur: What seems like a daunting process from the outside can actually be broken down into less daunting steps. You don't need to risk everything to be an entre-preneur, but you do need to take smart risks. And the key word here is "take." None of these strategies will work if you don't muster the cour-age to try them.

A few years ago the fashion designer Tory Burch invited me to an event hosted by her foundation. It was a speed dating session between mentors and butterflies. Mentors were stationed at long tables; men-tees sat down for ten minutes and at the sound of a bell moved to the next person. I met a woman who ran a catering company and another who sold flower arrangements. Then a young clothing designer sat across from me.

"I'm so happy to be here!" she began. "I know this is cheesy, but To-ry's like my role model. She has had an amazing career, and her de-signs—"

At this point I stopped listening and started looking around the room. Spotting Tory, who was leaning against a wall, I turned back to the young designer and said, "You should say all of that to her. She's right there."

"But—what?" the young designer stammered. "Am I supposed to, like, go up to Tory Burch?"

"Yes!" I said.

"Oh, no, I couldn't do that," she said, shaking her head.

"Look, Tory *invited* you here," I said. "She's an entrepreneur. Go talk to her."

At that point the bell rang, and the woman moved on to the next table. But as the evening was drawing to a close, I saw the young de-signer chatting with Tory, proudly handing her business card to her role model.

Entrepreneurs know how to hedge their bets, but they also know when to play their cards.

CHAPTER 3

Chaos Is Your Friend

W alt Disney was on top of the world. At twenty-six the fiercely determined, relentlessly optimistic movie director, who still looked so young he wore a mustache and carried a pipe to appear sophisticated, had come to New York to celebrate his new movie series featuring the character Oswald the Lucky Rabbit. He even brought along his wife, Lillian.

Walt was finally ready to cash in on the success he had been seeking his entire life, but unbeknownst to him, he was about to receive the biggest blow of his career. The way he responded led to a defining moment in American popular culture and created a signature lesson for entrepreneurs: How you handle defeat is even more important than how you handle success. What you do in the face of fear will ultimately determine whether you surmount that fear. Succumb, you'll always stay small. Overcome, you give yourself the chance to go big.

Walter Elias Disney was a classic entrepreneur. His father, an itinerant carpenter and cabinetmaker, was a teetotaling disciplinarian. He staunchly disapproved when his fourth child showed an interest in drawing. "Walter, you're going to make a career of that, are you?" he said. Walter certainly tried. After a stint in France during World War I,

Walt was repeatedly rebuffed as a newspaper illustrator and went to work at an ad company, where he met a fellow illustrator, Ub Iwerks. The neophytes quickly left to form their own art studio. It failed in a month. They turned to animation, making cartoons in a backyard shed. That company went broke in a year.

During those years Walt learned resilience, what it meant "to take advantage of opportunity." When his brother Roy moved to Los Angeles, Walt followed. He had just forty dollars in his pocket. He sent a proposal to Margaret Winkler, a film distributor in New York, to make a series of short films about Alice in Wonderland and a new creation, Oswald the Lucky Rabbit. Winkler gave him funding, and Walt naively gave her control of the rights. Walt, his brother, and Iwerks hired a team of animators.

When "Ozzie" scored with audiences, Walt traveled to New York to meet Winkler's new husband, Charles Mintz. Walt intended to ask for higher profits; instead he got a nasty surprise. Mintz had secretly hired away Disney's team of animators. Mintz offered Walt a pay cut and demanded full ownership of Oswald. This was Walt's equivalent of Wences's sisters-on-the-couch moment. Lillian was terrified; Roy urged him to settle. But Walt marched into Mintz's office, shoved the new contract in his face, and said, "Here. You can have the little bastard!"

On the long train ride home, Walt brooded. "He was like a raging lion on that train," Lillian said. He had no contract, no income, no employees. Worse, he had no cartoon character. With cats, dogs, bears, rabbits, and every other lovable animal taken, there was nothing left. "About the only thing that hadn't been featured," he thought, "was the mouse."

So he began sketching on train stationery, and by the time they reached Kansas City, he had created a mouse with red velvet pants and two pearly buttons. Walt reportedly wanted to call it Mortimer, but Lillian hated the name. "Too sissy," she said. What did she think of Mickey, an Irish name, an outsider's name? "It's better than Mortimer," she said.

One of the most epic creations in the history of popular culture grew out of a combination of fear and desperation. Mickey Mouse was conceived in a moment of chaos. As Walt summed up his own personality, "I function better when things are going badly than when they're smooth as whipped cream."

Which is why he was such a great entrepreneur.

Setbacks. All dreamers face them. No matter what kind of risk taker you are, eventually you . . . will . . . hit . . . a . . . wall. And if you don't slam into the wall yourself, some external force will send you hurtling toward it.

How you respond represents the third big challenge of getting going: handling moments of instability. One thing I learned working in unstable economies over the years is that stability is the friend of the status quo; chaos is the friend of the entrepreneur. When Endeavor surveyed two hundred entrepreneurs to identify their strengths and weaknesses, the most commonly selected strength was "I see opportunities where others see obstacles."

So how should you react to disorder? Instead of fearing it, embrace it.

Make chaos your friend.

To help you remember, I've organized this chapter into an acronym: CHAOS.

— _C_HAMPAGNE FOR YOUR ENEMIES —

The first thing to know about chaos is that it happens to everybody. Turbulence is the official climate of entrepreneurship. Sometimes the source of unrest is external: a natural disaster, a revolution, a war, or, as happened to me, a high-risk pregnancy. Whatever the situation, the key is not to flee from the situation but to run into it.

Like many, I had little choice but to confront my chaotic test. After six years in Latin America, we began to explore taking Endeavor to new continents. Edgar Bronfman, Jr., the CEO of Warner Music, became chairman during this time and vowed, "I don't want us to be charming; I want us to be important." Our first target was South Africa, and I began traveling back and forth to meet potential board members. Over the course of a year I made nine trips.

And then, I got pregnant. With twins. Fulfilling the promise I had made to my parents at their kitchen table, I had managed to find a husband, the author and *New York Times* columnist Bruce Feiler, who was also a dreamer, with just enough "crazy" in him. (He had once been a circus clown.) Suddenly, though, our lives were upside down.

During the most pivotal moment in Endeavor's existence, I was put on bed rest for three months, gave birth to two beautiful daughters, and learned to breastfeed using the "double football" technique, a baby tucked Heisman Trophy–like in each arm. Once, one of my girls slipped off the armrest and tumbled to the ground. My sister-in-law comforted me with a quote from Dr. Spock: "If you haven't dropped your child before age two, you're an overprotective parent."

It was chaos, indeed.

But that disruption forced me to change as an entrepreneur. When I returned from maternity leave, I had no choice but to restructure our organization so it was less reliant on me, a common mistake I had seen other entrepreneurs make yet still repeated myself. I recruited some senior management. I built an international expansion team. I enlarged our board.

By acknowledging the challenging situation, we were forced to become creative, and in the process became stronger. Over the next three years, Endeavor launched offices in five countries in Africa and the Middle East, some that I didn't even visit until they were open. And I never dropped a football again.

The act of turning hardship into change is especially true for dolphin entrepreneurs in the nonprofit sector. Some of the highest-profile social entrepreneurs have turned personal tragedy into groundbreaking initiatives that transformed debates, changed public policy, and saved lives.

• In 1980 thirteen-year-old Cari Lightner of Fair Oaks, California, was walking along a quiet road on her way to a church carnival when a driver swerved out of control and killed her. When Cari's mother, Candace, learned the driver had a record of arrests for intoxication (including a hit-and-run and drunk-driving charge booked only a few days earlier), she decided to fight back. She founded Mothers Against Drunk Driving, which became one of the country's leading organizations pushing for stricter alcohol policy.

• In 1990 Michael J. Fox, already a three-time Emmy Award–winning actor at age thirty, woke up one morning to find a tremble in his left pinky. It was the first sign of Fox's early on-set Parkinson's. He kept the disease secret for eight years. When he finally went public, he vowed to turn his plight into medical breakthroughs. In 2000 he quit his role on *Spin City* and launched the Michael J. Fox Foundation for Parkinson's Research, which has raised more than $400 million.

• The supermodel Petra Nemcova and her fiancé, the photographer Simon Atlee, were vacationing in a beachfront bungalow in Thailand in December 2004, when the Indian Ocean tsunami ripped through their resort and swept them away. Nemcova's pelvis was shattered, and her arm crushed; Atlee was killed. When Nemcova returned the following year, she discovered that emergency relief efforts had stalled and many children had no schools. She founded the Happy Hearts Fund, which has built more than seventy schools in countries affected by natural disasters.

These individuals stumbled into awful situations for which there were no existing solutions. The only solution was to take the initiative themselves to help others prevent, or handle, similar misfortunes.

External chaos often affects for-profit entrepreneurs differently.

You're a gazelle; you're going along quite nicely when you suddenly find yourself in the middle of a turmoil you did nothing to create. That's when your entrepreneurial IQ gets tested. In my experience, the flat-footed grow conservative; the nimble-footed get imaginative.

Cairo today has 20 million people and 14 million vehicles, making it one of the world's most crowded and clogged metropolitan areas. Getting stuck in traffic is inevitable. People schedule workdays, weddings, even walks outside around traffic patterns. A recent World Bank study found that Cairo congestion costs the economy $8 billion a year. A presidential debate in 2012, hailed as a sign of burgeoning democracy, was delayed when one of the candidates got stuck in traffic. A CNN reporter tweeted: "No matter who is running [for president], #cairotraffic always wins."

Five cousins set out to create a mobile solution. In 2010 they created an app to crowdsource traffic reports in real time. They named it Bey2ollak (yes, that's a 2, but the name is pronounced bay-oh-lek), Arabic for "it is being said." The name evokes an expression used by frustrated drivers when they roll down their windows and shout traffic warnings to others. Hoping to inject fun into an annoying situation, Bey2ollak invites users to report road conditions using cheeky options like "sweet" (no traffic) and "no hope" (avoid this road at all costs).

While the Israeli crowdsourced traffic app Waze was soaring at the time, the Bey2ollak founders set their sights low. "We didn't really expect that much success," one cousin said. "At the beginning we just wanted to create it because we all got stuck in traffic." But the Egyptian app gained instant traction, amassing five thousand users in its first day. One week after launch Vodafone reached out for an exclusive sponsorship.

Then came the Egyptian revolution. Weeks of instability became months, became years. The stock market plummeted; investment dried up. Did the founders give up and go home? Nope. They adapted. They found a new niche, adding options they never would have imagined, one that gave protesters a list of emergency numbers; a second that marked areas too dangerous because of vandalism. When fuel shortages caused a panic, the Bey2ollak team added a feature displaying the location of gas stations. By 2013 Bey2ollak, which became an Endeavor company, had enlisted more than six hundred thousand subscribers and had expanded into Europe.

The lesson from this story is that events that kick up dust and topple regimes favor the quick and nimble. Because disruption is the essence of entrepreneurship, the more disruptive the world becomes, the more you should look for openings—and keep looking. This strategy can be especially effective for skunks. In the face of sudden change, sometimes even the most plodding companies can drop their normal tendency to drag their feet.

In August 2005 Hurricane Katrina stormed ashore on the Gulf Coast. Marian Croak, a researcher at AT&T's Bell Laboratories, watched the weak relief efforts with dismay. "If people needed clothes, if they needed money, it wasn't clear how to get it to them quickly," she said. Croak had spent her career studying breakthroughs in data communications; she was the first woman in the history of AT&T to receive one hundred patents. She recalled that AT&T had set up a text message voting system for *American Idol* in 2003. If viewers could use their mobile phones to cast votes for Carrie Underwood and Jennifer Hudson, why not have them do the same to donate money to those in need? The contribution would be charged to the customer's cell phone bill, and AT&T would pass the funds quickly to organizations like the Red Cross.

Croak had the idea in late August; she filed for a patent that September. Now that's a skunk who can sprint! When a magnitude 7 earthquake hit Haiti in 2010, relief organizations collected more than $30 million through Croak's text-to-donate invention.

These stories have one thing in common: flashes of entrepreneurship emerging from flashes of instability. My favorite story of this kind occurred two hundred years earlier in an entirely different sort of upheaval.

In 1813, during the Napoleonic Wars, Russia had just invaded France. When Russian troops occupied Reims, in the Champagne region, soldiers were given free rein to loot and pillage local vineyards, including one run by Barbe-Nicole Ponsardin, the young widow of François Clicquot.

But Veuve Clicquot, as she was widely known (*veuve* is French for "widow"), was a cunning adversary, who also happened to have a sharp business mind. Born to prominent parents, Barbe-Nicole Ponsardin had married the heir to the House of Clicquot. He died six years later, leaving the twenty-seven-year-old novice in charge of the family businesses, including banking, wool, and sparkling wine. At the time champagne was a small-time enterprise. Veuve Clicquot revolutionized the industry by storing the bottles upside down in special racks, turning them, then freezing off the excess yeast. The new technique resulted in a sharper taste, less sweet, with smaller bubbles. Her 1811 vintage is said to have been the first truly modern champagne.

Yet no sooner had she perfected it than swarms of Russian soldiers were at her cellar door. Her more experienced rivals chose to go underground. They shuttered their businesses and protected their vineyards against marauding soldiers. At first, Widow Clicquot considered this approach. "Everything is going badly," she wrote a friend. "I have been occupied for many days with walling up my cellars, but I know full well that this will not prevent them from being robbed and pillaged. If so, I am ruined."

Then Clicquot did what all good entrepreneurs do. She pivoted to seize a marketing opportunity. She resolved to get the Russian Army wasted. Her bet was that when the soldiers returned to Russia, they would have an insatiable taste for her champagne. "Today they drink," she said. "Tomorrow they will pay!" She drowned them in wine but smartly held back the vintage of 1811. When French soldiers arrived a few months later to push out the Russians, she repeated her stunt. She gave Napoleon's officers free champagne and glasses, but because they couldn't hold the flutes while riding on their horses, they took their military sabres and lopped off the necks of the bottles. The ceremonial custom of *sabrage* was born.

Veuve Clicquot's biggest gambit came in 1814. When it became clear that the war would soon end, she took several thousand bottles of that 1811 vintage and decided to risk them all, running the blockade, shipping them to Russia, beating her competitors to a lucrative market. The plan worked. Russians had already been clamoring for the Widow by name. The moment a cease-fire was announced, her bottles arrived in Moscow and St. Petersburg, a drinking frenzy ensued, and Czar Alexander soon declared he would drink nothing else. Veuve Clicquot became a leading international luxury brand and the Grande Dame of Champagne is often credited with becoming the first woman to lead a multinational business.

There is a kicker to this story. In recognition of the Widow's achievement, Veuve Clicquot today gives annual awards to female business leaders. In 2008 I won one of these awards. The prize was having a grapevine in Reims named after me. The Rottenberg grape may be coming to a vintage near you someday soon!

In case after case, entrepreneurs who succeed in times of turmoil manage to contain their fear or anxiety. They don't succumb to the agitation around them; they stay calm, recognize the opportunities that the disruption around them creates, then seek to exploit them. They respond to chaos not with panic but with strategic precision. If anything, they use the disruption to outflank their competitors.

So next time adversity approaches or you face down a foe, don't rush for shelter. Instead, channel the Widow, pop some bubbly, and clink with the enemy.

— HUG THE BEAR —

Bubbles don't only burst in war, of course. Sometimes the chaos that hits an entrepreneur is economic: recession, downturn, credit crunch, market collapse. Through no fault of your own, suddenly expenses mount, business dries up, donations wither. Then what?

Whet your appetite.

Warren Buffett says his approach to investing is: "Be fearful when others are greedy and be greedy when others are fearful." Entrepreneurs can learn a lot from that attitude. When markets collapse, the temptation is to retrench, harbor assets, wait out the storm. To be sure, sometimes you do need to step back and conserve resources to prepare for growth later, but whenever possible, resist that temptation.

Downturns are often the best time to strike big. The history of entrepreneurship shows that moments of distress—the ones that are most miserable for entrenched players—are precisely the ones that are most favorable for outsiders. A study by the Kauffman Foundation found that over half of today's Fortune 500 companies were started during recessions or bear markets. The list includes IBM, General Motors, and Microsoft. Some of the country's most storied brands were launched in troubled times: Hyatt, Revlon, IHOP, Burger King, *Sports Illustrated*, CNN, and MTV. FedEx was started during the oil crisis of 1973, HP during the Great Depression, and Procter & Gamble as far back as the Panic of 1837.

The same dynamic occurred in the Great Recession of 2008. Kauffman has tracked the number of new firms started in the United States ever since 1996. Before the recession the number stood at 470,000 a month; afterward it reached 565,000 a month. The rate of start-ups surged 15 percent between 2007 and 2009.

How can instability be good for business? Two ways.

First, it's a good time to hire. Jim Collins, the author of the management classics *Good to Great* and *Great by Choice*, said, "In rapid-growth times it's hard to get the right people—you're more likely to compromise on who you get." In periods of uncertainty, that logjam opens. Many talented people get laid off, leaving them more willing to consider nontraditional careers, even take pay cuts. Many workers who still have jobs meanwhile start to realize their positions are not safe, opening them up to new opportunities with more flexibility and freedom.

This freeing up of talent clearly benefits dolphins. At first blush, nonprofit entrepreneurs would seem to be in for rough times when the economy gets tough. And it's true that government grants and philanthropic dollars often shrivel up during recessions. But hiring gets easier. When making money gets more challenging for people, having more meaning becomes more important. A report from Johns Hopkins University chronicling employment for the first decade of the twenty-first century, a period that included two recessions, found that nonprofit employment grew at an average annual rate of 2.1 percent while for-profit employment declined 0.6 percent.

I saw this firsthand at Endeavor. Starting in 2009 we were able to bring on a suite of senior managers—executives with twenty years of experience in top-flight companies like Dell and Bloomberg. We became a magnet for college and business school grads seeking jobs with impact and meaning. And we weren't alone. Applications at Teach For America grew by a third; at AmeriCorps, they tripled. Diana Aviv, head of a nonprofit trade group, said it became common to hear of more than one hundred applications for a single position. "Some of these people haven't been employed for a while and are happy to have something," she said. "But once they're there, they've recalibrated and reoriented themselves toward public service."

Second, periods of instability provide a good opportunity for taking chances.

A great case study is Greece in the wake of its 2009 economic meltdown. Entrepreneurship boomed. Forty-one thousand new businesses were formed in 2012. Ninety percent of these newcomers were small-scale enterprises—restaurants, cafés, clothing stores. But the biggest gains came from the minority of high-growth businesses. A 2013 study by Endeavor Greece found that this group, which included energy, technology, and food-processing companies, grew by 40 percent a year for three consecutive years. Most of these founders were not people who were forced into starting businesses. They were young people between twenty-five and forty-five, with high education and at least three years' experience in the private sector. They had options. Still, the destabilized economy had turned them into entrepreneurs— gazelles—by choice.

Nikos Kakavoulis and Phaedra Chrousos are good examples. They met at Columbia Business School in 2006 and bonded over their love of Athens. Nikos returned to Greece to launch digital editions of *Vogue, Glamour,* and *Men's Health.* Phaedra worked as a consultant. When the economy spiraled downward, the two grew frustrated by all the negative press. Nikos began sending friends daily e-mails listing one unique local discovery in Athens, a "best-kept secret," from a hidden bakery to a hush-hush event.

The e-mails went viral. From a few dozen friends, Daily Secret grew to more than thirty thousand members in just three months. The curated notices attracted users with their upbeat tone and stunning visuals. "It wasn't too long before we realized that cities all over the world were starving for a daily dose of positive energy," Nikos said. Daily Secret soon launched in Istanbul and has rolled out a new city nearly every month since. By early 2014 the company was covering thirty cities worldwide and had grown to over a million and a half subscribers.

I met Nikos and Phaedra in 2012, just as Endeavor publicly launched in Athens. They were among our first entrepreneurs in Greece. That September I appeared on CNBC's *Squawk Box* to announce our first country operation in Europe. The host, Andrew Ross Sorkin, was skeptical. "If you were going to start doing business in Europe," he said, "why in God's name would you choose Greece?"

"Because when economies turn down, entrepreneurs look up!" I said.

Now I'm not Pollyanna. I know that entrepreneurship is hard and that recession can make it harder. Most firms will not survive. But working with gazelles in places where the environment is brutal even in the best of times has convinced me that periods of decline are when entrepreneurs show their grit. If anything, entrepreneurs feel more at home during these times because it reminds them of their earliest days, when their families wouldn't support them, banks wouldn't lend to them, and industry bigwigs wouldn't respond to them. They had no choice but to be scrappy.

Even people who've never done anything entrepreneurial but then suddenly lose their jobs have reason to feel optimistic about their new-found willingness to take risk: They're in good company. Bernie Marcus (forty-nine years old) and Arthur Blank (thirty-six) started Home Depot after being booted from Handy Dan. Michael Bloomberg (thirty-nine) used his severance check from Salomon Brothers to launch his firm. Maybe the most famous of these inadvertent entrepreneurs is the twenty-six-year-old woman who was sacked from her secretary job in London.

In the late 1980s Joanne Rowling was working at Amnesty International, supposedly researching human rights violations but secretly writing stories on her work computer. She was fired. Next, she took a secretarial job at the Manchester Chamber of Commerce but was, in her own words, "the worst secretary ever." Again she spent her days inventing characters. Again her employers got fed up and gave her the boot. Not long after, Rowling was on a long train ride from Manchester to London when a thought popped into her head: What if a little boy embarked on a train that enabled him to escape the boring adult world and enter a place where he was literally and metaphorically powerful? She had outlined several books of the young wizard's adventures by the time her train pulled into the station.

Rowling's butterfly path was hardly direct. She had briefly married, had a child, divorced, and was forced to live on the dole with her young daughter before she finished her manuscript. It was rejected by a dozen publishers. The chairman of Bloomsbury, however, brought it home for his eight-year-old daughter to read. The little girl loved it. Rowling received an advance of £1,500 for *Harry Potter and the Philosopher's*

Stone. Fearing that boys would not want to read a book by a woman, the publisher insisted she adopt a gender-neutral pen name. With no middle name, Rowling added the *K* in honor of her grandmother Kathleen. (The comedian in Sara Blakely would approve.)

Part of acting like an entrepreneur is learning to turn around bleak situations. I'm not suggesting it's easy. It's not *supposed* to be easy. But if you want to overturn the old order, what you need is a little disorder. Embrace it. If you can't run with the bulls, you might as well hug the bear.

— ADMIT YOU SCREWED UP —

Sometimes the chaos you face as an entrepreneur is not outside your control. It's a crisis of your own doing: You picked the wrong strategy; you made the wrong bet; you executed poorly; you lost your way. In short, you screwed up. Your instinct may be to pretend it didn't happen and hope the problem goes away. You're not alone. Lots of entrepreneurs have chosen this path, but it's the wrong one. The truth is, there's only one way out.

Own it.

Leon Leonwood Bean was managing his brother Ervin's dry goods store in Freeport, Maine, in 1911, when he decided to address a pressing problem: his constantly rain-soaked feet. He hit upon the idea of sewing lightweight leather uppers to the rubber soles of galoshes and convinced a local cobbler to make him a pair. Eureka! Bean became so convinced these boots were his ticket to financial success that he had one hundred pairs made and set out to sell them through the mail. He obtained the addresses of out-of-state Maine hunting license holders and sent each a flyer, in which he proclaimed: "You cannot expect success hunting deer or moose if your feet are not properly dressed. The Maine Hunting Shoe is designed by a hunter who has tramped the Maine woods for the last 18 years. We guarantee them to give perfect satisfaction in every way."

His marketing worked: All one hundred pairs of shoes were sold. Ninety were promptly returned. The stitching that held the leather tops in place had come undone as soon as the shoes were out of the box. Bean lived up to his word: He refunded everyone's money. But he also went a step further. He borrowed money and convinced the U.S. Rubber Company to mold a heavier bottom that would support the stitching. Then he sent every unsatisfied customer a new pair of shoes, free of charge. Word of mouth about his honesty and quality service spread; more orders poured in; Maine had its first retailing superstar, L. L. Bean.

Bean's near-fatal mistake formed the bedrock of his business philosophy. He would field-test every new product the company sold, sneaking out of the office for afternoons of camping, hunting, and fishing. Reminiscent of the Banana Republic founders, Bean also wrote his own advertising copy and personally responded to customer letters. As one observer wrote, "It's as if Bean were family, some sort of mildly eccentric but amiable uncle who lives up in Maine and sends us packages." And it wasn't just hype. Customers could return any L. L. Bean product for a replacement or full refund, and he never even charged for shipping. Bean's brand became known for its 100 percent satisfaction guarantee.

A century later the founders of another clothing company learned a similar lesson, though in their case it was more than a pair of boots that needed repairing. Bonobos is an online men's clothing retailer founded in 2007, but a mistake in 2011 almost brought down the company. It happened on Cyber Monday. Bonobos was offering discounts as large as 60 percent, and executives knew that traffic would be hefty. CEO Andy Dunn had hired a new head of technology, and the two had spent weeks bracing for orders. Still, they were unprepared for the volume. Internet sales exploded that year, and Bonobos was swamped. The site crashed.

Dunn took ownership of the problem. He took the site down and announced he was leaving it dark for as long as it took to fix the glitches. More important, he fessed up. In place of the cleanly designed Bonobos home page, he put a "fail whale" page that showed a guy with his pants at his ankles and the line "Caught us with our pants down." He told *Inc.* magazine later, "We were saying, 'We screwed up.'" Using the hashtag #SaveBonobos, the company also took to Twitter with witty self-deprecating remarks. On Quora, a question-and-answer Web site, Bonobos's design team began a dialogue with customers.

The Web site remained off-line for another two days. When it went back live, customers who had missed out on the sale were offered discounted prices. The company had an awful month, "because we deserved it," Dunn said. "It felt insurmountable, but it brought people together. I remember seeing everybody jamming on a Saturday and seeing the good energy and thinking, 'We'll be OK.'" Customers agreed. On social media, shoppers praised the company's honesty. One Facebook user wrote: "You guys have always topped my Best Customer Service list and have handled this outage beautifully. Keep up the great service and great communication! Signed, Customer for life."

One of the more dramatic business turnaround stories of recent years hinged not on one apology but two. In July 2011 Reed Hastings, the CEO of Netflix and *Fortune*'s "Businessperson of the Year," announced he was splitting his company into two services, one to ship discs, the other to stream video. Eight hundred thousand customers immediately bolted. Hastings issued an apology on the company's blog. "I messed up," he wrote. "It is clear from the feedback that many members felt we lacked respect and humility in the way we announced the separation." He went on: "In hindsight, I slid into arrogance based upon past success." He even issued a video confession. But he continued to move forward with the unpopular strategy, and the stock continued to plunge.

Media critics swarmed. Even *Saturday Night Live* mocked Hastings and his Hawaiian shirts. Three weeks later Hastings posted another entry on his blog. The company would stay as one. "It is clear that for many of our members two websites would make things more difficult, so we are going to keep Netflix as one place to go for stream-ing and DVDs." The stock kept falling, from a high $298 to $53.

At that point Hastings stopped talking and went back to work. He rebuilt his business; he invested $100 million in *House of Cards*; he even changed how he dressed (less beachwear, more business attire). The turnabout worked. The company added millions of streaming subscribers; *House of Cards* was a critical and commercial hit. Netflix ended 2013 as the single best-performing stock in the S&P 500, rising 298 percent. By early 2014 the stock was trading near $400.

So what did Hastings learn from the debacle and recovery? "I real-ized, if our business is about making people happy, which it is, then I had made a mistake," he told the columnist James Stewart. "The hard-est part was my own sense of guilt. I love the company. I worked really hard to make it successful, and I screwed up. The public shame didn't bother me. It was the private shame of having made a big mistake." Hastings said he didn't expect the apology alone to turn things around. "I wasn't naïve enough to think most customers care if the C.E.O. apologizes, but I thought it was honest and appropriate." His new fo-cus: "pleasing and growing our membership."

Apologies need to be real and meaningful to make a difference. Dov Seidman, the founder of LRN, a firm that advises companies on their cultures, dismissed most CEO mea culpas as "apology theater." In 2014 Seidman, along with the *New York Times* journalist Andrew Ross Sorkin, established an "apology watch" to call out fakers. The one CEO Seidman cited whose genuine apology and subsequent actions succeeded: Netflix's Reed Hastings.

Entrepreneurs face enough setbacks that you can't control. If you're the source of your problems, be honest, be forthright, be con-trite. Then get back to work.

— _ONCE UPON A TIME_ —

The easiest thing to do when your company hits rocky waters is to abandon your core principles and do anything to survive. That's understandable. It's also misguided.

One consistent theme of entrepreneurs who deftly navigate chaos is they don't just look forward; they also look back. They don't just seize opportunities, own their mistakes, and move on. In the midst of whatever mess they're in, they also return to their core values. They reconnect with their origin stories. As the great business historian Alfred Chandler, Jr., liked to put it, "How can you know where you're going if you don't know where you've been?"

One stunning example of this strategy is Howard Schultz. In January 2008 Schultz, the chairman and retired CEO of Starbucks, called an emergency meeting of the board. With the stock down 50 percent, Schultz announced that he had fired his handpicked successor and was returning to run the company. Executives had "watered down" the Starbucks experience, he said, crowding counters with stuffed animals, eliminating aromas by pregrinding coffee, and, worst of all, installing automated espresso machines that removed the "romance and theater" of the barista's work. "It is not going to be good enough to 'go back to the future,'" he said. "There is a piece of the past that we need; we have to find and bring the soul of our company back."

Those are just words, of course, but Schultz took unheard-of actions. First he closed all 7,100 stores in the United States for three and a half hours on a Tuesday afternoon to retrain the baristas in the "art of espresso." Wall Street was furious. Analysts were more upset when he spent $30 million taking ten thousand store managers to New Orleans for a retreat. Schultz said he wanted to be "vulnerable and transparent with them about what is really at stake here, how desperate the situation is." He also batted away personal pleas from big investors to cut back on health care costs and dial back on quality, a potential savings of hundreds of millions of dollars.

From its all-time low a few months after Schultz retook control, Starbucks stock rose nearly tenfold in the next five years. Asked why, Schultz credited the company's return to its bedrock: "The equity of the brand is defined by the quality of the coffee, but most importantly, the relationship that the barista has with the customer."

Founders aren't the only ones who can return to their entrepreneurial origins in times of turmoil. Consider Angela Ahrendts, whom I think of as the skunk in a trench coat. In 2006 Ahrendts, who grew up in New Palestine, Indiana (population 2,053), was not a likely candidate to take over the iconic British fashion brand Burberry. One of six siblings growing up in a modest house, Ahrendts had slept in a coat closet underneath a stairwell and sewn her own clothing. The London press mocked her midwestern style and unglamorous roots.

But the six-foot-three-inch-tall Ahrendts, who went on to work at Donna Karan and Henri Bendel, had a formidable business sense. She loved strong, consistent brands that hewed to their traditions. Burberry was far from that. The 150-year-old company was faltering. At a time of rapid expansion in luxury brands, Burberry was flat. The company had twenty-three licensees around the world, each selling something different, from dog leashes to kilts. "In luxury, ubiquity will kill you," Ahrendts said. "It means you're not really luxury anymore."

The turning point came in her first strategic planning meeting. Her top sixty managers had flown to London from around the world. The weather was quintessentially British—chilly, gray, and damp. But not one of the managers was wearing a Burberry trench coat. Ahrendts thought, "If our top people weren't buying our products, despite the great discount they could get, how could we expect customers to pay full price for them?"

Ahrendts turned to a young designer from her Donna Karan years, Christopher Bailey, to help her return Burberry to its roots. The process was messy. She dubbed Bailey the brand czar and declared all designs would go through his office, no exceptions. She then fired the entire Hong Kong–based design team and brought designers from around the world to the U.K. to be retrained by Bailey. At one point, Ahrendts was called to testify before Parliament about her controversial decision to shutter a Welsh factory. But she never deviated. Burberry must return to its heritage: rainwear.

In the 1880s young Thomas Burberry, a former draper's apprentice, had invented gabardine, a waterproof fabric that he used to make raincoats. He was asked to design a durable coat to be worn by British soldiers in the trenches of World War I. After the war the Burberry "trench coat" became synonymous with British culture, eventually earning a royal warrant that entitled the company to supply the royal family. The explorer Ernest Shackleton wore his Burberry across Antarctica; George Mallory wore his on his failed attempt to scale Everest. Hollywood stars, from Humphrey Bogart to Greta Garbo, donned them in movie stills.

Ahrendts wanted to return the company to that glittering past. "I always remind employees that we didn't found the company, Thomas Burberry did—at the age of 21. He was young. He was innovative. We say that his spirit lives on, and that it's this generation's job to keep his legacy going."

Being nonconventional skunks, she and Bailey weren't content with the familiar beige and plaid. They added metallic purple and alligator epaulets. While her brand czar pushed the designs, Ahrendts focused on expansion. In six years she opened 132 stores, all focused on selling outerwear. She reeducated the staff to sell the Burberry craftsmanship and reoriented the marketing around a new generation of customers: millennials.

In 2011 Burberry was named the fastest-growing luxury brand on the Interbrand index and the fourth fastest-growing brand overall, behind Apple, Google, and Amazon. The next year the company reached $3 billion in revenues, double the amount of five years earlier. In 2013 Ahrendts announced she was leaving Burberry to join Apple—not as CEO but as the skunk in charge of retail. Score one for trench coat warfare!

Score another for one of the key lessons for entrepreneurs in chaos: If you're feeling lost in the woods, go back to "once upon a time."

— SHIFT HAPPENS —

A year after my children were born, I took one of my trips abroad, to São Paulo. While there, I went to see Jorge Paulo Lemann and Beto Sicupira, who now run 3G Capital, one of the most influential global investment firms in the world, owners of Anheuser-Busch and large chunks of Burger King and Heinz. Both men were founding board members of Endeavor Brazil. I was still tender from all the turmoil Endeavor had been going through and expressed my frustration and fear.

I wanted to understand from Beto and Jorge Paulo what I was doing wrong. Weren't things supposed to get easier? Beto, who is the scrappier, more tactical of the two, gave me a brisk pep talk. "You're a pioneer. It's supposed to be hard. If it were easy, someone else would have done your idea before you." He patted me on the shoulder and walked out of the room.

Then Jorge Paulo said something that has stuck with me ever since. A graduate of Harvard and onetime tennis prodigy who played in Wimbledon, Jorge Paulo has a smooth, avuncular manner that masks a steely will. He told me to imagine the hard times he and his partners had faced: currency devaluations, triple-digit inflation, stock market crashes, coups, general strikes. "Every day in our world is another existential threat," he said.

But that's what made them strong, he continued. "Our main advantage is that we've been tested in an environment of great economic turmoil and major transformations. The ups and downs of the economy prepared us to deal with adverse situations."

His point was clear: Entrepreneurs have to be masters of chaos.

Research backs him up. A major study of business leaders in emerging markets, conducted by professors at the University of Pennsylvania and the University of Oviedo in Spain, found that because they came of age in turbulent environments, they're less crippled by fear than their U.S.-bred counterparts and better positioned to exploit opportunities. The study concluded: "All companies need to be able to function in chaotic, unpredictable business environments."

I heard the same point as well from two Endeavor entrepreneurs I met on that trip to Brazil. Mario Chady and Eduardo Ourivio were running several quick-dining restaurants when the country's monetary system collapsed. Inflation spiked 70 percent a month. "We changed the menu pricing once a week," Mario said. "Life was crazy. I raced back and forth among my restaurants on my motorcycle." Unable to withstand the pressure, the entrepreneurs declared bankruptcy.

Then they set out to rebuild. Mario went to work full-time at his worst-performing store. Each corner of the restaurant had a different food station, and Mario and Eduardo soon noticed that the most popular was the pasta station, where the chef prepared meals in front of the customers. Seizing on that insight, they created the concept of Spoleto, where the customer can choose the ingredients of a meal— the pasta, the sauce, the toppings—then watch it being prepared.

Next, Mario and Eduardo turned to culture. With so much turmoil, employees felt anxious about their future. While few emerging market firms offer profit sharing or stock options, Spoleto offered both. "We wanted everyone, from the CEO down to the dishwashers, to share our dream," Mario said. Even fewer companies go public, meaning that the stock options were not likely to amount to much. So Mario and Eduardo infused every aspect of Spoleto with their own natural enthusiasm and fun. They hired a former actor to train the waitstaff on presentation and a circus performer to teach chefs how to juggle. Allowing the team to make meal preparation more theatrical empowered the staff to feel like ambassadors for the company.

The bet paid off. In an industry racked with high turnover, Spoleto's turnover is a third of the national average. In 2013 Spoleto generated annual revenues of $340 million, employed 7,000 people, and managed 470 restaurants. They were also preparing to open the first Spoleto outlet in the United States.

Reflecting on his journey, Mario told me, "Even when it's hard, even on those days when you want to crawl back into bed, you have to keep remembering the big dream. Don't let outside chaos, like the economy, deter you. Use it to your advantage."

Eduardo added, "In businesses like ours, *shift* happens!"

When I first started out, I believed that rough patches were just that, rough patches. Now I know better. I tell our entrepreneurs not to make the same naïve mistake I did. After the hard spells things don't "go back to normal." Hard *is* normal. Status quo is Sturm und Drang.

Or as Eduardo put it, shift happens.

So be prepared. When chaos is the everyday, you'd better make chaos your friend. If not, while you're busy complaining about your misfortune, somebody else will board a train somewhere and conjure up Harry Potter, Mickey Mouse, or some other crazy invention.

And you'll be stuck holding Oswald the rabbit.

PART II

Go Big

CHAPTER 4

Your Entrepreneur Personality

Katherine Briggs didn't dislike the man her daughter, Isabel, brought home for Christmas in 1915. But she did think their personalities were incompatible. Isabel was spontaneous, imaginative, and whimsical. Her boyfriend, Clarence "Chief" Myers, was logical, deliberate, and meticulous. Yet the two appeared happy. How could that be?

Inspired by her daughter's unusual taste in men, Katherine began scouring biographies and identified four personality types: meditative, spontaneous, sociable, and executive. When she hit upon Carl Jung's book *Psychological Types*, she told Isabel, "This is it!" and integrated his research into her typology. Both mother and daughter, now married to Chief, continued observing people and labeling their "types" for the next two decades. (Actually, Isabel continued for sixty-one years, the length of her marriage to her "incompatible" boyfriend.)

After the start of World War II Isabel read an article in *Reader's Digest* about how women flooding into the workplace were having trouble finding the right job. She realized her mother's research might be able to help women secure work that fitted their personalities. Isabel began testing everyone she could find—friends, students, office workers. The test she created, the Myers-Briggs Type Indicator, be-came the most popular workplace diagnostic ever, taken by over 50 million people.

I'm a big fan of Myers-Briggs and other tests like it. (I'm an ENTP in Myers-Briggs, an ID in DISC, and a Type 7 in Enneagram.) I know from experience they help me understand myself better. And as some-one who's occasionally accused of being impatient, I also know they've helped me at work to realize that not everybody is motivated in the same way. Perhaps that's why, a few years into running Endeavor, after realizing that almost every entrepreneur I met kept tripping on famil-iar hurdles in his or her quest to go big, I decided to do something similar. I set out to create a personality test that could help entrepre-neurs identify their best and worst traits.

The process took several years. First, my team and I analyzed the thousands of entrepreneurs we screened over the years and the fifty international selection panel events, during which we debated the merits of candidates at their inflection points. Then we brought in from Bain & Company a top team that sent a detailed questionnaire to two hundred of our entrepreneurs. Bain followed up with in-depth in-terviews; we crunched the data; we debated. In the end we settled on four entrepreneur personality types:

Diamond: *Visionary dreamers leading disruptive ventures*

Star: *Charismatic individuals building personality brands*

Transformer: *Change makers reenergizing traditional industries*

Rocketship: *Analytical thinkers making strategic improvements*

These types are different from the species I've been talking about so far—gazelle, skunk, dolphin, and butterfly—which have to do with the field you work in. The profile types are more focused on your per-sonality: your strengths and pitfalls as a leader; your good tendencies as a change maker and your bad ones. The more you know about your instincts as an entrepreneur, the more effective you'll be.

That's especially true at the stage I want to turn to in this section: going big.

Many books about entrepreneurship play the same trick, and it's the same one they pull in romantic comedies in Hollywood. They show the meet-cute moment between the founders, the amusing hurdles they face on the way to the altar, and the drive they make into the sunset, after they have their first big win. From there on it's happily ever after.

If only.

"Starting a company is like getting married," said Georges Doriot, the father of venture capital. "Most of the problems are discovered after the honeymoon is over."

In this section I'm going to help you tackle those post-honeymoon problems. Over the next few chapters, I'll focus on the raucous day-to-day challenges of managing a fast-moving enterprise, especially honing your leadership skills, finding and keeping talent, and getting the most out of your mentors.

But I want to begin with what I believe is the first critical step to going big: knowing who you are. Just as all the new workers flooding into the workplace in the 1940s needed to understand who they were, so all the entrepreneurs flooding into the workplace today need to know who they are. Every entrepreneur has a personality type. What type are you?

— DIAMONDS —

Steve Jobs. Mark Zuckerberg. Sergey Brin and Larry Page. Ted Turner. George Lucas. Elon Musk. Diamond entrepreneurs are brilliant dreamers who start bold, disruptive organizations. They are charismatic evangelists who capture the imagination of everyone they meet as they talk about revolutionizing people's lives. Diamonds envision a more exciting world, then inspire others to help them achieve it. But diamonds often lack a clear road map for growth; they tend to have highly unstable and unpredictable futures. When diamonds succeed, they can be game changers. But when they fail, it's often quick and messy.

Endeavor entrepreneur Brahms Chouity grew up in Lebanon and Saudi Arabia, studied hospitality in Switzerland, and started a number of companies in the Middle East that ranged from interior design to finance. He even opened the Saudi office for a line of British sports cars. He moved fast, acted quickly, and took ninety trips a year. Then, in 2010, when his wife announced she was pregnant, Brahms declared he was taking a sabbatical. His wife was thrilled. Yet when he stationed himself on the couple's couch in Beirut and proceeded to indulge himself in his favorite pastime, playing video games, her patience ebbed. Three days into Brahms's sabbatical, she gave him an ultimatum: "Find some way of making money or no more consoles in the house."

He needed a new scheme, quick. Late one night, after a daylong binge of gaming, he watched *The Social Network*, about the early days of Facebook. This was his level-up moment: There was no social network to connect gamers across different platforms—Xbox, PlayStation, PC. "If Mark Zuckerberg can do it, why can't I?" he said. "That little kid is younger than me." So he did. With the help of a designer, Brahms created At7addak (pronounced at-ha-dak), Arabic for "I challenge you." Gamers flocked to the site, EA and Activision offered sponsorship, but revenues were modest. So Brahms pivoted to a more user-generated model. He invited contributors to submit reviews and videos, offering to split the advertising with them. Within two years he had 600,000 active users and 8 million monthly page views.

Brahms's strengths as an entrepreneur are apparent to anyone who meets him. He's driven; he's confident; he's an idea machine. But his weaknesses are also clear. He's impulsive. One minute he's studying hotel management, the next he's selling sports cars, soon he's building a social network. Can he stick to anything? Does he have the patience to build a sustainable business, or will he jump at the new, new thing the second he has the chance?

Brahms, in my classification, is a diamond. Entrepreneurs like him either go big or fail fast.

With each profile type, we've identified key questions the entrepreneurs should be asking, along with their backers, team members, mentors, even friends and family. With diamonds, these questions are:

- Is there a big enough idea, product, or service that gives the enterprise an edge?

- Is the entrepreneur likely to stick with this venture or will s/he cut and run the minute a shiny, new opportunity presents itself?

- Is the entrepreneur open to feedback and criticism?

- Does the entrepreneur share credit?

These last points are particularly critical for diamonds. Consider Elon Musk, the South African entrepreneur behind PayPal and the groundbreaking mind who created SpaceX and Tesla. Musk is frequently described as a genius, a tech wunderkind. When Musk started Tesla Motors, the electric car company, in 2003, he declared, "We're going to be the next GM," and vowed to put 100,000 cars on the road by 2009. Though he missed his initial goal by 99,400 cars, eventually Musk's relentless vision won out: *Consumer Reports* named the Tesla Model S its overall top pick for 2014 and that year the electric car maker reached a valuation of $30 billion, or just over half of GM.

But this gazelle-diamond is equally often described as autocratic and stubborn. His first CEO sued him, saying Musk had slandered him and taken undue credit for founding the company. When the *New York Times* criticized the Model S, Musk called the story a "fake" and an "ethics violation" and launched a month-long personal attack on the reporter.

Diamonds are brilliant, but it's often all about them.

The ultimate diamond was Steve Jobs. On the upside, at every stage of his storied career, Jobs succeeded in bending reality to fit his vision. A member of his Macintosh design team likened Jobs's mixture of stubbornness and creativity to the reality distortion field in *Star Trek.* "In his presence, reality is malleable," the designer said. But that conviction meant he tuned out others (including customers) and was unwilling to share the spotlight. Apple's design guru Jony Ive described what it was like to bring Jobs fresh ideas. "He will go through a process of looking at my ideas and say, 'That's no good. That's not very good. I like that one.'" Later Ive said, "I will be sitting in the audience and he will be talking about it as if it was his idea. I pay maniacal attention to where an idea comes from, and I even keep notebooks filled with my ideas. So it hurts when he takes credit for one of my designs."

A diamond is not always an employee's best friend.

Not all diamonds are fast-growing, profit-seeking gazelles. Some, like me, are dolphins. When Peter and I founded Endeavor, we believed we had a revolutionary idea. We vowed to build something unique on the basis of a future only we could see. That confidence was our positive. Our negatives were that we both are stubborn, I'm easily distracted and was slow to prove I could work with others, and Peter generates lots of ideas and left the daily operations of Endeavor after a year to pursue another one. That left me to prove I could focus, hire the right people, and give them the freedom to succeed.

Each entrepreneur type has risks. Knowing your potentially fatal flaws—or what I call "red flags"—can help you avoid disaster. For diamonds, this is my advice:

Listen to learn. *Diamonds often say they want to be their own bosses, but no one can do it alone. You need a robust team of* *mentors, partners, and employees. If you're too stubborn to take criticism, you'll be too slow to uncover problems.*

Share your success. *Hiring a team is not enough; you need to reward your team. And remember, everyone is not like you. Some people like praise; others like perks; others prefer a challenge they can master or time off. Find out what motivates and inspires your team members and give it to them. Remind yourself to share the credit and spread the spoils.*

The customer is sometimes right. *Your personal drive and vision may be your greatest assets, but sorry, you're not Steve Jobs. Don't dismiss your customers. Your organization might be offering something totally groundbreaking, but that doesn't mean users will unconditionally like it. Design the right feedback system and act on what you hear.*

— STARS —

Oprah Winfrey. Martha Stewart. Richard Branson. Estée Lauder. Giorgio Armani. Jay-Z. Star entrepreneurs are dynamic trendsetters with big personalities who inspire deep loyalty among diverse audiences. Stars instinctively know what's coming in the culture; they're two steps ahead of everyone else. Stars become a source of pride for their communities, their cultures, and their countries. When they become big, they can go global. But they're often one-person shows, change their minds frequently, and can be undisciplined with time and money.

The Endeavor entrepreneur Anton Wirjono wanted to be more than just the best DJ in Jakarta. While studying business in California, the Indonesia native had spun records to earn extra cash. Returning home, he put aside his accounting books and pursued his passion for dance music. He quickly became the godfather of Indonesia's hip-hop scene. MTV Indonesia named him one of "10 People with a Midas Touch."

Inspired by Jakarta's overnight markets, Anton and four partners organized a series of four-day pop-up fashion markets. They attracted seventy-five thousand people. The group opened a department store called The Goods Dept that sold carefully curated products. A Goods Café followed, along with two more stores and an e-commerce site. With Indonesia's creative class booming, the Goods Group was becoming the go-to destination of a new class of urban sophisticates. Anton was its icon or, as he billed himself, the "universal provider of everything cool."

When I met Anton, his strengths as an entrepreneur were clear: He's charismatic; he's hip; he has an eye for trends. Also, he attracts loyal followers and gives them a satisfying experience. He's a tastemaker. But Anton's weaknesses were equally clear. Would his artistic sensibilities take precedence over his business instincts? Knowing the latest trends is great, but sooner or later you're going to need those accounting books under the bed. Was he willing to sully himself with day-to-day management? If not, maybe he'd be better as the chief curation officer instead of chief executive officer. Finally, would he lose his touch for taste making?

Anton, in my classification, is a star. Some stars continue to burn bright, while others ignite quickly then fade.

Stars face steep challenges to going big:

- Can the idea grow beyond the entrepreneur's charisma? Is it a cult of personality, a one man/woman show?

- Because many stars charge premiums, is the reputation of the entrepreneur's brand strong enough that consumers will pay extra for the product or experience?

- Is the entrepreneur comfortable using data and analysis and not just marketing, creativity, and artistic vision?

- Does the entrepreneur have what it takes to build a great organization in addition to a great brand?

The trouble with many stars is they are constantly told how charismatic and appealing they are. They're "rock stars." But in order to grow, they need collaborators. When this type of entrepreneur asks my advice on how to go big, I say, "Be a rock band, not a rock star."

Consider one of the biggest rock stars in the food world. Wolfgang Puck was raised by a coal miner father and pastry chef mother in Austria. He started working in restaurants when he was fourteen and came to America at twenty-four. After serving as chef at Ma Maison in Los Angeles in the mid-seventies, Puck decided it was time to open his own restaurant. In his vision, it would have red-checkered tablecloths and a poster of Mount Vesuvius on the wall. But in the mind of his soon-to-be wife, Barbara, Spago had spacious windows, white tablecloths, and the first-ever open kitchen where patrons could watch Puck prepare California cuisine. Barbara's vision prevailed, and Spago was an instant hit. Soon Puck became a fixture on talk shows, red carpets, bookshelves, and supermarket shelves. He was America's first celebrity chef with a food empire worth $400 million.

Puck was always honest about knowing little about business. He had no financial skills, fell asleep at the accountant's, and dealt with money pressures by putting on weight. "A good chef has to be a manager, a businessman, and a great cook," he said. "To marry all three together is sometimes difficult." To get around this problem, he hired a Harvard MBA to help run his businesses, but the MBA ran up too much overhead, and Puck fired him. Barbara was a good businesswoman, so for a time she managed the restaurants and negotiated the endorsement deals. But when the two divorced, Puck was on his own. Today Puck focuses on being the public face of the brand and partners with firms like Campbell Soup to run the businesses with his name. His lesson for star entrepreneurs: "The brand has to be bigger than the person."

Collaborate or be content to remain small.

Stars also face another minefield. When an initiative is based largely on the personality of the founder, what happens if that personality is tarnished? When Donald Trump goes in and out of the gossip pages (or the political arena), it jeopardizes his brand as a luxury icon. When Tiger Woods gets caught in a sex scandal, it causes headaches with his corporate sponsors. When Martha Stewart gets sent to prison, it flatlines her billion-dollar lifestyle empire.

Nonprofits built around stars are especially vulnerable. The Lance Armstrong Foundation was one of the most recognizable brands in the nonprofit world. The ubiquitous yellow wristbands representing strength in the face of cancer were a case study of the power of entrepreneurial ingenuity. But when doping allegations against the star became too big to ignore, donations plummeted— down 45 percent in three years. After Armstrong admitted the allegations were true, the foundation's board asked him to resign from the organization and took his name off the door. The Lance Armstrong Foundation became Livestrong. The head of external affairs said, "When you have a famous face as the head of your organization, the urgency to explain what you do isn't that great—but now the urgency is really great."

Live by the star, die by the star.

To avoid that plight, heed these red flags:

Follow the full recipe. *Cooking a complete meal requires more than one ingredient. The same goes for creating an enduring brand. Your organization has to deliver on the promise of your personality. Make sure someone is keeping an eye on all aspects, from operations to customer service.*

Build up promoters inside and out. *Strong personalities need other strong personalities around them. When building your team, don't be tempted by flattery. Rather than people who* *compliment the boss, you need people whose skills comple-ment your own.*

Find a "left brain." *Stars are often right-brained individuals, meaning you think more intuitively, imaginatively, and cre-atively. Terrific, but your venture also needs someone who's more left-brained—analytical, rigorous, and happy to wade knee-deep into the data.*

— TRANSFORMERS —

Howard Schultz. Ray Kroc. Ingvar Kamprad, the founder of Ikea. Anita Roddick, the founder of The Body Shop. Blake Mycoskie, the founder of Toms Shoes. Transformer entrepreneurs are catalysts for change. They typically operate in old-line industries yet aspire to transform their firms or causes through innovation and moderniza-tion. Ray Kroc brought franchising to the ho-hum hamburger drive-through; Ingvar Kamprad replaced the staid furniture showrooms with sleek Swedish designs in trendy warehouse settings. Change can be good, but can it be enough to restore growth to a sector that's lost its luster?

Consider the case of the Endeavor entrepreneur René Freuden-berg. In 2006 he took over his father's industrial grease company in Guadalajara, Mexico. On the surface, what can be less glamorous than grease! Yet this lowly niche, which includes everything from machine oils to rust preventatives, brings in $8 billion a year worldwide. René's father had started the first grease producer in Latin America, but his son wanted to shake things up. "I shared my dad's philosophy, but at a certain point I no longer admired him because he kept repeating the same things," he said. When René took over, he shifted focus to the high-end market and green technology. Interlub became an industry leader in eco-friendly, custom-made products that increased efficiency but cost more. He set an ambitious goal of 20 percent annual growth.

To achieve that, René rebranded the company. He tried to make lubrication, well, sexy. He began referring to Interlub as a "world leader in the field of tribology," a fancy word for "friction." He put jazzy music on the company's Web site and changed the tagline to "X-treme lubrication." The moves worked. Interlub captured half of the Mexican market and sold its products in thirty countries. In 2013 Interlub's annual revenues reached $27 million; its profits doubled.

René clearly showed entrepreneurial prowess. He took a decades-old business that made a boring product and turned it into a cutting-edge producer of a hot commodity that people paid top dollar for. He even added an environmental twist, biodegradability. But he and his company also had shortcomings. For all the company's sizzle, Interlub was still making grease for factories, a decidedly nineteenth-century product. Also, would bigger and better-financed competitors eventually steal back the market share Interlub had poached? Finally, René wasn't the best manager. He was "not cold enough," he told us. He "cared too much about protecting people" and "needed to make decisions faster." Could he sustain major growth?

René, in my classification, is a transformer. Like him, many transformers are socially oriented with a strong desire to improve the world. Think of Toms Shoes' giving away a pair of shoes to the poor with every pair sold to a customer or The Body Shop's denouncing animal testing. Transformers take the old and make it seem new again, often by adding a cause.

They also face questions:

- Is the "transformation" they're focused on truly meaningful or just window dressing?

- Is the "change-the-world" mission backed up by a solid business model?

- Will the entrepreneur be able to overcome the traditional obstacles that have hamstrung its industry?

- Will the mission have to be scuttled in order to take the initiative big? Will selling more require selling out?

A good example of the dramatic impact—and potential downsides—of transformers can be seen in one of the more colorful entrepreneurs of the last generation. The Texas lawyer Herb Kelleher and a partner created the concept for Southwest Airlines in 1967 on, yup, the back of a cocktail napkin. They battled lawsuits for four years before flying their first plane. Nearly everything about their business model threatened the traditional carriers. While other airlines flew many types of planes, Southwest flew only one, the Boeing 737, minimizing maintenance costs. While other airlines touted their inflight services, Southwest touted their absence—better to keep prices down. While most airlines operated in a hub-and-spoke model, Southwest flew point to point, often landing in secondary airports. The company made a profit every year beginning in 1973.

Central to the company's image was that of its founder. Kelleher was a Stetson-wearing, bourbon-drinking, chain-smoking renegade. He told the truth about the crappy service of most airlines and in doing so advanced the message that Southwest would be different. The company ran an ad that taunted other carriers: "We'd like to match their new fares, but we'd have to raise ours." When other carriers started raising service fees, Southwest placed inserts in newspapers that read, "Don't #$*!% Me Over," accompanied by "Southwest is the only airline that accepts this coupon." It elaborated: no checked bag fees, no change fees, no fuel surcharges, no snack fees, no phone reservation fees.

Money magazine named Kelleher one of the top ten entrepreneurs of his generation.

Inevitably, when Kelleher stepped down in 2008, he took his reputation as a transformer with him. The new CEO, Gary Kelly, was a numbers guy. Soon enough, he stopped touting the company's low frills and ran ads declaring Southwest "America's largest domestic airline." Instead of tweaking the big guys, Southwest had become a big guy. Plus, Southwest's prices were no longer the cheapest in most markets, and Kelly even hinted the airline would drop its long-standing policy of free bags. Transformers can be forward-thinking iconoclasts, but in the end, the organizations they build often revert to the means of their industries.

A vivid example of this paradox is the quixotic story of one butterfly transformer, an original farm-to-sink entrepreneur. In 1984 Roxanne Quimby was a thirty-three-year-old, down-on-her-luck, single mom having difficulty finding a job. One day, while hitchhiking to a post office in Dexter, Maine, she was picked up by Burt Shavitz, a beekeeper in his late forties who lived in a turkey coop and made $3,000 a year selling jarred honey out of the back of his pickup truck. Locals called him the bee guy. The two became lovers.

One day, looking at all the unused beeswax he had accumulated, Shavitz recommended that Quimby make some candles and sell them at the local crafts fair. She started tinkering—first with candles, then with furniture polish, eventually with lip balm. "It was clear, very early, that people bought lip balm ten times faster than they bought beeswax furniture polish," Quimby said. "Next was a moisturizing cream. It sold better than the polish too." A onetime graphic designer, Quimby crafted a logo featuring a man drawn in Shavitz's likeness with a well-worn face, beaming eyes, a faint smile, and a hefty beard. She labeled the products "Burt's Bees." Her timing was impeccable. The interest in eco-friendly products was just taking off, and Burt's Bees's homespun packaging and all-natural ingredients were a perfect fit. By 1993 the company was earning $3 million a year; by 2000 the amount was $23 million.

Quimby and Shavitz were the ultimate transformers. They had taken a staid industry, with low-margin products like lip balm and skin salve, and revitalized it with a cutting-edge, organic brand that made people feel good about paying more for items that would rattle around in their pockets for a few weeks, then get lost before they got finished. Their story was a landmark success. But then trouble.

First, their relationship failed. After the couple moved to North Carolina to save on taxes, the two split. Shavitz moved back to Maine, and Quimby bought out his one-third share of the company by purchasing him a house for $130,000. A few years later she sold 80 percent of the company to private investors for $175 million; Shavitz's share would have been worth $59 million. (He complained, and Quimby gave him $4 million in a settlement.) A few years after that, Clorox bought Burt's Bees for $913 million, netting Quimby an additional $183 million.

That's when the real problems for the brand began. Like many transformers, Quimby had built her company's reputation as being socially conscious, natural, and homespun. Those were not exactly ideas associated with Clorox. (The sale took place a few months before the company released its Green Works line.) Executives at Clorox said they hoped to learn about natural practices from their new acquisition, but consumers were skeptical. They accused Quimby of selling out. Loyalists even created a petition on Change.org accusing Clorox of tampering with the recipe for Burt's Bees products.

Burt's is not alone, of course. Tom's of Maine, the makers of natural toothpaste, sold a majority stake to Colgate-Palmolive for $100 million. The Body Shop sold to L'Oréal for more than $1 billion. Ben & Jerry's sold to Unilever for $326 million. Four years later Ben & Jerry's own audit of its social practices said, "We are beginning to look like the rest of corporate America."

And that's the point: Transformers can be transformational, but their success is often built around temporary advantages or the founders' direct touch. When those go away, the changes often recede.

With that in mind, transformers should watch out for these red flags:

Make sure your business model is as compelling as your mission.
Transformers want to prove that those in traditional fields can still innovate. But innovation isn't enough. You also need a strong strategy to sustain your change over time.

Get real. *Sometimes transformers propose changes, but they're more cosmetic than real. Be prepared to defend your innovations as worth the costs and risks involved, and align your team to push back against critics.*

Don't shy away from data. *Entrepreneurs who focus on social goals often downplay finances and dismiss pesky data. While your sense of purpose is important, try to balance it with objective analysis. It's hard to change the world if your numbers don't add up.*

— ROCKETSHIPS —

Jeff Bezos. Bill Gates. Fred Smith. Michael Dell. Mike Bloomberg. Rocketship entrepreneurs are penetrating thinkers who apply a laser focus on metrics to accelerate growth and change. They are tinkerers and fixers, with a relentless drive toward efficiency, who aim to improve every element of their endeavors, making them cheaper, faster, better. Rocketships often have a background in mathematics, science, systems, or management and use their analytical minds to set clear goals and formulas for success. They are the rocket scientists of the entrepreneurial world. In an increasingly data-driven universe, they are uniquely poised to soar. But their obsession with numbers comes with clear risks.

The Endeavor entrepreneurs Nicolás Loaiza and Gigliola Aycardi like to crunch numbers. As MBA students in Bogotá, Colombia, the sports-loving friends complained about the lack of high-quality gyms in their country. They undertook a market analysis of Colombia's personal fitness industry and determined that a private gym offering individual exercise regimens would have huge potential. They started a company, Bodytech, which positioned itself as a medical sports center instead of a gym. Bodytech's highly qualified medical experts offered personalized health services, educating members about how to avoid chronic illnesses and how to identify personal exercise goals. They set a target of one thousand new members in six months; in the first thirty days they signed up eighteen hundred. In surveys, half the members said they had not exercised regularly before joining Bodytech.

Buoyed by their success, Nicolás and Gigliola expanded Bodytech rapidly. Over the next decade they opened twenty-six branches in six Colombian cities and signed up fifty thousand members. They merged with another chain and increased their membership by 34 percent. They did an exhaustive analysis of neighboring countries and concluded that the penetration rate of gyms in Latin America was a fraction of that in North America. Then Nicolás and Gigliola went out to raise enough capital to realize their aggressive expansion targets. By 2012 Bodytech had become the largest chain of gyms in South America.

When I met the founders, I was impressed with their strengths. They're analytical, data oriented, and laser focused on growth. They're doers—superefficient and effective. They set milestones, achieve them, then calculate new ones. They embody drive and success. But they showed some weaknesses, too. They came across as somewhat cocky. They're quick talkers, who have an answer for everything and bombard naysayers with a blizzard of statistics. We weren't sure they would listen. Also, they move so fast they might overlook the needs of their employees. Were they all in their head? we wondered. Where's the heart?

Gigliola and Nicolás, in my classification, are rocketships. They reflect the current vogue in business toward metrics, but they raise issues about the tendency to value numbers above all else. Rocketships should mind these flags:

- Confidence is one thing, but overconfidence is another. Will the entrepreneur be open to critical feedback?

- Tinkering around the edges is fine, but is there real differentiation here from what's currently available?

- In the entrepreneur's relentless push for efficiency, is there sufficient room for creativity, passion, and occasionally a new idea based on intuition, not spreadsheets?

- Does an uncompromising focus on customer satisfaction come at the cost of employee satisfaction? Can these entrepreneurs rally their own troops?

Jeff Bezos is the quintessential rocketship. In 1994 he was a senior vice president at a New York financial firm studying the Internet. He realized he wanted to be part of that movement. But instead of leaping into his passion, Bezos followed a methodology. First, he systematically analyzed business activities that could be enhanced by the Web. He concluded he should be a middleman between manufacturers and customers, selling nearly everything all over the world. Since starting with everything was impractical, he next made a list of twenty possible categories. He chose books. Then he approached his boss. "You know, I'm going to do this crazy thing," he said. "I'm going to start this company selling books online." The boss's response: "This actually sounds like a really good idea to me, but it sounds like it would be a better idea for somebody who didn't already have a good job."

This gave Bezos pause. So he did the most rocketship-like thing imaginable: He created a "regret minimization framework" to reduce the chances that he would regret his decision. Here's how he explained it: "I wanted to project myself forward to age 80 and say, 'Okay, now I'm looking back on my life. I want to have minimized the number of regrets I have.'" He wouldn't regret participating in the Internet, he concluded, and he wouldn't regret failing. "But I knew the one thing I might regret is not ever having tried."

Once under way, Bezos continued his focus on data, analysis, and efficiency. He sweated the small stuff. He crossed out every word on press releases that distracted from the company's core message: Amazon is the cheapest, friendliest place to buy books. (Later "books" changed to "everything.") He insisted that every Tuesday every department hold metrics meetings, in which employees were asked to justify every decision based on numbers. And he openly distributed his e-mail address, so customers could send complaints directly to him. He then forwarded those complaints to relevant employees with just one addition, a question mark. Nothing was said to elicit more fear than one of Bezos's voiceless queries: "?" When one worker asked at a company retreat why entire teams were required to drop everything on a dime to respond to a "question mark escalation," his savvier colleagues explained: They were jeff@amazon.com's way of making sure the customer's voice trumped all.

So what's the downside? Well, while Amazon's efficiency was a boon to consumers, sometimes it chafed employees. Bezos thrives on conflict. He prefers an adversarial work atmosphere to one based on cohesion. Also, one of his leadership principles is frugality: He refuses to spend money on anything not directly related to customer happiness. Even at the height of the Internet boom in the late 1990s, Amazon employees never had perks like other tech firms: no free massages, no free food, not even free parking. The only thing workers received free was aspirin. But when the tech boom went bust, Bezos had to convince investors he was cutting costs. Out went the aspirin.

Rocketships have formidable minds, but sometimes they give those around them headaches.

The same applies to rocketships in the nonprofit sector. Bill Gates is the rare entrepreneur who has been a pioneer in both the for-profit and nonprofit worlds. And in both arenas his entrepreneurial profile—data driven, efficiency focused, metrics obsessed—has been key to his successes and shortcomings.

Gates is often credited with spearheading the personal computer revolution, but he was less of an inventor and more of a curator. Others created the first operating system. Gates's brilliance was creating a business that bundled that operating system with a suite of services (spreadsheets, word processing, e-mail, etc.), then requiring hardware makers to preinstall it. Also, Gates was a tireless competitor. One of his early backers said, "This guy knows more about his competitors'

products than his competitors do." Finally, Gates was relentlessly focused on the bottom line. An e-mail once warned employees, "If you
find yourself relaxed and with your mind wandering, you are probably
having a detrimental effect on the stock price."

Over time these attributes proved costly. Gates dismissed the Internet, which soon passed him by, and he missed what Steve Jobs understood: that creativity and passion also drive people's attachments
to their technology. Sure enough, Apple's products were described as
art; Microsoft's, as artless. It's hard to build brand loyalty on that.

But what's even more telling is that when Gates stopped running Microsoft and turned his attention to his philanthropy, he brought the same
single-minded commitment to metrics and results. In the often squishy
and subjective world of nonprofits, the impact has been profound. Every
grant of the more than $3 billion the Gates Foundation gives out each
year comes with a framework to measure performance quantitatively. As
the foundation explains, these evaluations "can help depersonalize decision making and provide objective data that can inform action."

I know of few stories that better capture the ability of these profile
types to transcend fields of activity than how Bill Gates, the gazelle-
rocketship who had been running Microsoft, became Bill Gates, the
dolphin-rocketship who took over the Bill and Melinda Gates Foundation. The arena was different, but the man was the same. And so was
his entrepreneurial personality.

I tell rocketships to keep these issues in mind:

Look beyond the numbers. *Rocketships love analytics, but you
won't always have the data you need to feel 100 percent confident. Learn to be comfortable with ambiguity and taking edu-
cated risks. Anecdotal feedback from users may feel "soft" and
unreliable, but it can reveal insights that the data may miss.*

Let your creative juices flow. *Rocketships approach change differently from other entrepreneur types. They look to bridge a*

market gap or solve a customer need rather than embrace innovation for its own sake. Many rocketships prefer tinkering with already proven models rather than discovering untested ones. While this can cut down risk, it can hold you back. Mix in some novelty.

Heart matters. *Emotions might not be quantifiable, but they matter. Some of the most successful brands get that way because they appeal to the hearts and minds of both customers and employees. If you aren't comfortable getting outside your head every now and then, surround yourself with some people who are.*

— *YOUR ENTREPRENEURSHIP PERSONALITY* —

The idea of identifying different personality types goes back to antiquity. The ancient Greeks analyzed body fluids (blood, bile, and phlegm) and linked them to moods. Two hundred years ago scientists measured bumps on people's heads to ascertain certain personality characteristics. The idea of actually *asking people about themselves* didn't take hold until a century ago, first in the military. Personality tests have been a fact of life ever since—and a pretty good business, too, half a billion dollars a year in the United States alone.

It's time we bring that rigor to the fastest growing groups of workers today, entrepreneurs.

The main lesson of these four profile types is this: Just as there is no singular path to being an entrepreneur today, so there is also no set entrepreneur personality. There are multiple paths and multiple personalities. Each has its strengths and weaknesses.

So instead of peering outward, picking a hero to emulate, then struggling to model yourself on that ideal, look inward. Figure out what you're good at—and what you're not—then play up your strengths. The first step to going big is to know thyself.

CHAPTER 5

The Whiteboard

*B*y the time Henry Ford had his do-or-die moment as an entrepreneur, he was already something of a success. Yet he was still unprepared for the magnitude of the pressure. Moments like these happen to all entrepreneurs. They occur at unexpected times, when you're about to release a transformational product, land a massive client, move into a fresh space, or secure the long-awaited OK to take your idea to the world. You're about to go big when suddenly you're caught short. Now what do you do?

For years I've been studying these moments and how entrepreneurs react to them. I've tried to identify patterns to help people get through them more easily. My nickname for them comes from the man who was called Crazy Henry.

Ford faced his test in 1908, when he was forty-four years old. The Michigan native had built his first automobile in a backyard shed in 1896 at age thirty-three. Soon after, he quit his job at the Edison electric plant to start the Detroit Automobile Company. It failed without producing a car. Next he turned to building race cars. When one of his creations won a race, he secured funding to start the Ford Motor Company. Within two years the company was producing 1,700 cars a year in three different models.

Still, something nagged at Ford. A stop-planning, start-doing entrepreneur, he despised business plans and ran his company on instinct. The smart business move was to sell expensive cars to the elite, but Ford wanted to build a car for the masses. "It will be so low in price that no man making a good salary will be unable to own one," Ford declared. He would create a four-cylinder five-passenger touring car that would retail for the shockingly low price of $825.

He picked a room on the third floor of his factory at 461 Piquette Avenue in Detroit and staffed it with his smartest designers. He called it his experimental department. The tiny space was filled with a blackboard, milling machines, and drill presses. Ford sat in the middle in his "lucky" rocking chair that once belonged to his mother. He was a gazelle who was skunking himself.

But his plan enraged his backers. Investors were furious that his new car would undermine profits. Banks were concerned about the costs and refused to loan him money. Suppliers pushed back on his exacting timelines. The only people enthusiastic were his competitors. "How soon will Ford blow up?" they asked.

Finally, in early 1908, forty members of his secret team and many of his harshest critics gathered for the ceremonial assembling of the first prototype. Workers wrapped the engine in fifty feet of rope, hoisted it into the air, and began lowering it into the chassis. But as the future of the company slowly descended, the engine started spinning faster and faster and eventually broke free of the ropes, crashed to the ground, and smashed into pieces.

This was Ford's test: Go big or go home?

He quietly stepped forward and announced he would personally build a replacement. Six months later the Model T went on sale. Ford's populist dream, derided as foolhardy and dismissed as socialist, went on to sell 15 million cars over the next twenty years, making it the most successful invention of the automotive age and what many consider the most influential consumer product ever created.

To me, the image of that first Model T engine lying in pieces on the

concrete floor perfectly captures a turning point that all risk takers encounter. All entrepreneurs I know have confronted at least one of these
engine-on-the-floor moments, a crucial juncture where everything
they've worked for up until that point is at stake, and they have to make
what seems like *the one decision* that will determine whether their ideas
go huge or fall flat. I've seen the fear in entrepreneurs' eyes in these moments. I've watched them break down in tears. And I've learned what
they need most in that instant is the reassurance that they're not alone.

Well, you're not alone. Even better, solutions do exist. When I first
started noticing similarities in these moments, I kept a running tally
in my head. Later I started scribbling notes in the middle of the night.
Eventually I decided to do something with this list other than leave it
by the side of my bed (and bug my husband with it in the morning). So
I bought a whiteboard.

I leaned it behind my desk, and when entrepreneurs came in and
shared their problems, I would grab the board, point to an entry, and we'd
start brainstorming solutions. Entrepreneurs liked it because it gave them
relief that there was a path forward. I liked it because it gave me a way to
help someone who was feeling desperate. Here's what it looks like today:

1. Close Doors
2. Fire Your Mother-in-Law
3. Minnovate
4. Drop the Pens
5. Dream Big but Execute Small
6. Eat the Elephant One Bite at a Time

This list is by no means exhaustive. Some of these items might apply to you; others might not. We've done research at Endeavor to back up most of them. In effect, this list is the product of my own experimental department. It's my attempt to put into one place solutions to the make-or-break problems entrepreneurs confront in their attempt to go big.

The next time you drop an engine on the floor, perhaps one of these lessons might help you pick it up and move on.

— 1. CLOSE DOORS —

Two Endeavor entrepreneurs from Jordan came to my office one afternoon. Ramzi Halaby and Zafer Younis were at a breaking point. Their company, The Online Project, helped businesses manage their social media strategies. The firm had secured a number of top clients and employed over seventy people. But most clients wanted to deal directly with one of the founders, not their highly trained staff. Ramzi and Zafer outlined the situation, we discussed possible solutions, but they still seemed tense. Feeling more like their mom than their adviser at this point, I asked if anything else might be contributing to their stress.

"Well, we still own the radio station back in Amman," Ramzi said. "That takes about twenty percent of our time. We have an offer to sell it, but we're not sure we're ready to let go."

I grabbed my whiteboard. "You guys need to close doors," I said.

In the early stages of being an entrepreneur a little foot-dragging is understandable. Sara Blakely kept selling fax machines until she got booked on *Oprah*; Henry Ford kept working at the power plant while he was building his first car. In the year that it took to get Endeavor off the napkin, I wrote grant applications for other organizations on the side to earn extra money.

But at some point the hedging has to stop. This issue comes up at Endeavor selection panels. The executives and VCs we bring in to screen gazelles at their scale-up moments say it's a deal breaker if a founder isn't willing to give up outside projects and go all in.

The same applies to mission-driven dolphins aiming to go big. Bill Drayton, my former employer at Ashoka, insists that social entrepreneurs' willingness to leave everything else behind is a precondition for support. "It usually takes about three years," he said. "They have to test and refine their idea. They have to build an organization and start a movement." Only after the founders agree to quit their day jobs does Ashoka give them funding.

Often the reluctance to cut the cord is financial. You need the money. This is understandable at the outset. I'm all for not betting the farm on Day One. But once you're up and running, and there's some money coming in, your unwillingness to commit full-time becomes a hindrance. You can't expect to go big without accepting some added risk.

Bette Graham is a good example of how it can take years to reach that point. In 1951 Graham was a divorced single mom living in North Dallas. She wanted to be an artist but took a job as a bank secretary. Unfortunately, she was an awful typist, and the only way to fix her many mistakes was to retype the entire page, a Sisyphean torture. One day she watched some painters make a slipup on the bank's Christmas windows and cover over their blunder with white paint. "Why can't I do that with my bad typing?" she thought.

She mixed up some tempera at home, brought it into work, and used a watercolor brush to neaten up her errors. She called her concoction Mistake Out. For five years she kept her elixir secret from everyone, including her boss. Eventually her colleagues caught on and wanted some for themselves. She sold her first bottle in 1956.

Unable to afford employees, Graham recruited a high school chemistry teacher to make the product dry faster and roped in her son to fill bottles in their garage. (That son, by the way, went on to become a founding band member of The Monkees.) By 1957 Graham was selling around one hundred bottles a month and renamed her product

Liquid Paper. But she kept her secretarial job—until she used her own letterhead in lieu of the bank's one day and was fired.

This was her first close doors decision: Would she find new employment or attempt the life of a solo entrepreneur? Graham chose the freedom of a butterfly. She would brew her concoction without a safety net. Three years later she faced another juncture: Should she stay a mom-and-son operation or aim bigger? Again she chose the more daring path. She hired her first employee, moved into a shed in her backyard, and later bought a factory. By 1969 Graham's Liquid Paper Company was selling a million bottles a year; a decade later she sold it to Gillette for $47.5 million plus royalties.

The calendar here is instructive. For five years Graham kept her avocation a secret; for the next two she sold her product but kept doors open by keeping her job; finally she closed that door but stayed small for another three years. Not until a decade after her initial inspiration did she finally take maximum risk and try to go as big as she could.

An even better example of this measured pace—and the one I told Ramzi and Zafer that morning—is all the more startling because it involves somebody who's often thought of as a go-for-broke entrepreneur.

Phil Knight was a teenage runner in his home state of Oregon who hated clunky American athletic shoes, which were mostly made by tire companies. After a stint in the army, Knight attended Stanford's business school, where he wrote a paper on the high quality and low cost of Japanese sports shoes. In 1962 the newly minted MBA traveled to Japan, where he struck a deal to distribute Onitsuka Tiger shoes in the United States. Along with his former track coach, Knight sold Tiger shoes out of the back of his green Plymouth Valiant. But he was still under the influence of his father, who insisted he get a "real job" as an accountant. So Knight had someone else sell the shoes while he did other people's books.

Not until 1971, when a colleague conjured up the name Nike and Knight paid $35 for the "swoosh" ("I don't love it," he said, "but I think it will grow on me"), did Knight finally hang up his wingtips. The next year he sold $3.2 million worth of shoes. The "just do it!" moment for Phil Knight came nearly a decade after he'd first had the idea.

To be sure, not everyone wants to go big. Some entrepreneurs aspire to have lifestyle enterprises. Remember those Brooklyn jam makers: one wanted to stay local; the other wanted to scale. Both paths can be meaningful.

But as I told Ramzi and Zafer, many entrepreneurs cling to their conventional work out of fear rather than necessity. They continue typing other people's letters or doing other people's taxes even after their ventures produce sufficient income. My advice: Cut the umbilical cord.

When we're young, we're often told to keep as many doors open as possible. But for an entrepreneur seeking to scale, the better path forward is to close doors.

— 2. FIRE YOUR MOTHER-IN-LAW —

Gabriel and Guillermo Oropeza had a vision. The two brothers from Mexico City would reinvent the traditional document storage companies of Latin America. They started by taking over their father's firm and introducing a more sophisticated information platform. When they showed up at an Endeavor selection panel, the two boasted impressive technology, traction in their home market, and stellar résumés. Guillermo had studied at MIT and worked at the Boston Consulting Group; Gabriel had an MBA and experience at Coca-Cola and Johnson & Johnson.

But they faced a potential calamity. It may be the biggest single problem I've seen in all my years working with entrepreneurs. Yet like most who face it, the Oropezas weren't even aware of it.

They were precariously mixing their personal and professional lives.

Gabriel and Guillermo, both in their early thirties, held the titles of commercial director and director of planning; each owned 16.67 percent equity in the company, called Doc Solutions. The father, meanwhile, still held the title of CEO and controlled 50 percent of the equity. Although Guillermo senior was largely disengaged from the day-to-day business and had little understanding of the new IT platform, he still controlled the company.

We turned the Oropeza brothers down. One panelist said: "Tell your father to become nonexecutive chairman and then come back." To my surprise, a year later the pair showed up at another panel—with dad in tow. "Hola, Linda," Guillermo senior said, shaking my hand. "I'm here now as chairman." He promised to sit in the back and say nothing to prove his sons were in control. He did, and the brothers became Endeavor entrepreneurs. Since then Doc Solutions has grown to $12 million in revenues and nearly one thousand employees.

A few years ago I asked our in-house research group at Endeavor to examine the best- and worst-performing entrepreneurs in our network. The goal was to see if we could detect any commonalities linking those in the top quartile and those in the bottom.

Here's what we found: Three-quarters had launched their business with a partner, and 70 percent of these partners were people close to them—a best friend, a family member, a spouse, an in-law. Things start off swimmingly. "We know each other so well!" the cofounders effuse when we meet them. "Our skills are complementary!" "We practically finish each other's sentences!"

Then trouble brews. Cash problems arise, and cuts need to be made. Or business booms, and one partner wants to expand while the other prefers to stay small. Or it becomes clear that one partner lacks the skills to take the venture to the next level.

Yet the founders have no mechanism in place to handle these routine disputes. Familiarity breeds informality.

Half the entrepreneurs in the bottom quartile of our network shared one thing in common: They lacked a shareholder agreement among partners.

In many firms we work with, it's a founder's sibling who's in charge of business development, an in-law who controls the finances, or the father who claims to be "letting go" while still retaining power and majority ownership. Wences used that approach; he hired his sisters. So did I; my sister, Rebecca, was head of marketing at Endeavor for a few years. While that familial structure may work early on, it often presents challenges as the company matures. Suddenly the interests of different family members start to diverge. In Rebecca's case, she left to pursue an independent career. But in many cases family members hang on past a healthy point.

That's why the second item on my whiteboard is: Fire your mother-in-law. That may sound harsh, but there are ways to do this gracefully.

Endeavor entrepreneurs aren't alone in this struggle. More than 80 percent of American business is family owned; outside the United States the number is 90 percent. Also, look around. Gossip pages are filled with tales of business family feuds gone bad. From the sons of the IKEA founder Ingvar Kamprad to the wives of Rupert Murdoch, from Beyoncé's dad to Usher's mom ("I never fired my mother," Usher told Oprah. "I relieved her of her duties"), families that work together often stop playing together. The celebrity chef and reality TV star Gordon Ramsay had to split with his father-in-law, business partner, and best friend, Chris Hutcheson, after discovering that Hutcheson had been funneling money to a mistress and their secret family for thirty years. Talk about a kitchen nightmare!

The way to keep these issues out of the boardroom is to create what I call a start-up prenup, a document that puts the rights and responsibilities of each partner on paper. Just as it can seem inconceivable for a young couple in love to plan in case of divorce, so it can seem awkward and insulting to draft a formal contract between a parent and a child or two best friends from childhood. But too often I've seen the dreadful alternative. Even Leila had to tiptoe through the minefield of divorcing her partner-husband (who left the company) and renegotiating with her other partner, now her ex-sister-in-law Zica (Leila officially became CEO while Zica remained the face of the Beleza Natural brand).

These agreements work. John Davis, a family business expert at Harvard, told me that his research confirms what I've seen on the ground. "One of the basic rules of families is that structure is your friend," Davis said. The best way to avoid problems is to write down in advance what happens if someone wants to leave, cash out, or spend more time at the beach. "If you have a plan in place," John said, "then you still can show up at family occasions together."

A vivid illustration of how shareholder agreements work, whenever they're created, is Lucille Ball and Desi Arnaz. The redheaded comedian and the hotheaded Cuban met in 1940 on a movie set. Though she was six years his senior, the two soon eloped. A decade into their tempestuous marriage, they decided to make a sitcom. When the network balked at the awkward pairing, the two formed Desilu Productions, the first independent television production company, and spent $5,000 of their own money on the pilot of *I Love Lucy*.

Lucy and Desi were savvy pioneers. They insisted their shows be shot on film, which allowed the first-ever reruns; they cut their salaries in order to own the shows; and they sold syndication rights for $5 million, then plowed the money back into their studio, acquiring thirty-three sound stages—more than MGM or Twentieth Century Fox. *The Dick Van Dyke Show*, *The Andy Griffith Show*, and *My Three Sons* were all shot on their lot.

Yet the king and queen of television never improved their relationship. They divorced in 1960 but continued to work together. When that partnership finally soured, they took a coolly rational approach. "Instead of divorce lawyers profiting from our mistakes, we thought we'd profit from them," Lucy said. In what we might call a start-up postnup, the pair drafted an agreement: Lucy bought Desi's shares for $2.5 million and became the first female CEO of a major production company. Five years later Lucy sold the company to Paramount for $17 million. Her final act was green-lighting *Star Trek* and *Mission: Impossible*.

Whether you're a comedian, technologist, or hair colorist, avoid the single most common mistake we see in entrepreneurs: absence of a shareholder agreement. Put the terms of your partnership on paper. It's okay to love Lucy, but make sure you know what to do if the love goes away.

— *3. MINNOVATE* —

As entrepreneurship has gotten sexier in recent years, a few flashy stories have dominated the discussion: Apple, Facebook, Twitter. These businesses have one thing in common: They were based on big, breakthrough ideas that created new markets where none existed.

As influential as those stories have been in encouraging others, they've also had the opposite effect: They've discouraged even more people from chasing their dreams or taking their initiative to the next level. Why? Because they leave a false impression. They lead people to believe that the *only way to be a successful entrepreneur is to have a big, breakthrough idea.* In fact, the opposite is true. Most entrepreneurs don't have a big idea at all; they have lots of small ones.

The Babson College professor Dan Isenberg nailed the term for this phenomenon. Successful entrepreneurs don't innovate; they minnovate. They don't create Google; they create a more targeted search engine that serves a market or location that was overlooked. Two-thirds of Endeavor entrepreneurs started out by minnovating. The technique has multiple benefits: It mitigates risk by starting with a proven business model; it saves costs by making small adaptations instead of massive ones; it works.

In 1999 two Argentinean Stanford graduates, Marcos Galperin and Hernán Kazah, launched MercadoLibre ("free market" in Spanish), an online auction company modeled on eBay. Some said they were creating a copycat. Actually they minnovated. When the company started, only 2 to 3 percent of Latin Americans had Internet access. Also, neither buyers nor sellers trusted the notoriously inept and corrupt local postal system. So MercadoLibre tweaked the model. First, it focused on selling new goods, not used, so buyers could trust the quality. Second, when consumers balked at online auctions, the company moved to fixed prices. Finally, it encouraged buyers and sellers to meet in cafés and other public places to exchange goods instead of putting them in the mail.

The founders became Endeavor entrepreneurs, and the site became Latin America's number one e-commerce platform, serving 100 million users in twelve countries. In 2007 MercadoLibre went public on NASDAQ at a valuation of $400 million. Six years later it was worth $6 billion.

While minnovation is valuable in the start-up phase, it can be even more valuable in the scale-up phase, particularly when one of those engines comes crashing to the floor. When your product isn't selling, your market isn't growing, or your idea isn't taking hold around the water cooler, there's a temptation to scrap the playbook and throw a Hail Mary in a desperate attempt to score a game-changing touchdown. Yet a massive move may not be what's called for. Sometimes a small pivot is all you need.

In 1957 Wilbert "Bill" Gore, a chemical engineer at DuPont, was part of a skunk team that discovered a new application for the synthetic polymer PTFE, the basis of Teflon. But DuPont wasn't interested in pursuing new applications, so Bill left the company. At age forty-five, with five children to support, he and his wife, Genevieve "Vieve," started a business in their Delaware basement. They incorporated on their twenty-third wedding anniversary. "All of our friends told us not to do it," Vieve said. "It's hard to describe what it's like to bring your husband home and turn him loose." Bill did the math and figured they had two years to make it, or he'd have to slink back to DuPont.

Everything Gore did was a minnovation from the original PTFE, starting with a ribbonlike cable that could be used to insulate wires and pipes. For two years the Gores tried selling the product, but nobody was buying. Their self-imposed deadline was nearing. "We came very close to calling it quits," Vieve said. One day, while Bill was running an errand, the telephone rang in the basement. Vieve, who was alone sifting PTFE powder, answered the call. It was a man from the Denver water department. He asked for the product manager. Vieve said he was out. How about the sales manager? Not here either. The president? Vieve said he couldn't be reached. "What kind of company is this anyway?" the caller hollered.

One with a pipe dream that would soon come true. The man ultimately ordered $100,000 worth of ribbon. The Gores had a viable business, but it was still a modest one. The company grew sluggishly over the next decade. It took Bill and Vieve's son Bob, who joined the company in the mid-sixties, to come up with the minnovation that changed everything.

In 1969, fearing that the wire and cable business was slowing, Bob began trying to stretch PTFE to the breaking point to see how malleable it was. An even more flexible product would reduce costs and increase profits. Each attempt failed. Fed up one day, Bob, dressed in a white lab coat and asbestos gloves, grabbed a rod from the oven and angrily yanked it. The footlong rod stretched to almost five feet. "I couldn't believe it," he said. Fearing it might be a fluke, he didn't tell anybody. The next day he re-created the experiment, then gathered his dad and colleagues and performed it publicly. "We were all very quiet," Bill Gore said. "We were all trained scientists, so we recognized the importance of what Bob had done."

What he had done was invent Gore-Tex. This minnovation, which grew out of a moment of desperation, allowed the company to pivot in an entirely new direction, breathable fabric. Gore moved quickly to exploit the new discovery but didn't abandon its legacy clients. The company had supplied cables to NASA for the first moon landing in 1969, for example; now it sold NASA the fabric that would be used in the spacesuits of the first space shuttle astronauts. Gore went on to capture 70 percent of the waterproof outerwear market (including my daughters' snow boots) and became one of the two hundred largest privately held companies in the United States. The company's string of successes, stretching across seven decades, all stemmed from a series of minnovations from a single core product.

This story shows how entrepreneurs need to be stubborn enough to keep pounding away at their initial ideas, yet open minded enough to pivot to more attractive products or markets if they present themselves. That approach perfectly captures the case of the "snail sisters."

The Endeavor entrepreneurs Maria and Penny Vlachou grew up in Corinth, Greece. In 2007, while traveling in Switzerland, Maria was chatting with Penny on the phone and complaining about the high cost of escargot—thirty-seven euros for a dozen. Looking out her bedroom window, Penny joked she could grow snails in her backyard. "I'd buy them!" Maria said. Within months the sisters had opened a snail farm and started selling escargot to shops and restaurants. But they couldn't keep too many snails on hand because they easily spoiled, so they pivoted and recruited a network of farmers from whom they could buy on demand.

When we first met the snail sisters, I was skeptical. "Aren't we about *high-impact* entrepreneurs?" I asked. Then Adrian Gore, Endeavor South Africa's chairman and one of the toughest number crunchers I know, told me, "Linda, I've been trying to poke holes in their business model, but I can't." A top auditor from EY said, "That's it, I'm quitting my job and starting a snail farm!"

What everyone most admired was how Penny and Maria had tweaked their strategy to survive do-or-die moments. When the sisters realized that consumers didn't have time to prepare live snails, they began selling canned escargot. When the Greek financial crisis wiped out the domestic market for luxury molluscs, the sisters looked abroad. "Our sales in Greece wouldn't increase," Maria said, "so we turned to other countries. Every problem has a solution." Today 70 percent of the sisters' revenue comes from exports to Spain, Italy, and France. Impressing a South African executive is one thing, but Penny and Maria managed to sell Greek escargot to the French: *Vive la minnovation!*

Finding new uses for old products is another way to demonstrate flexibility in the face of crises. Executives from Kimberly-Clark were touring Europe in 1914 when they discovered a cotton substitute called creped cellulose wadding. They sold it to the U.S. military to use as filters in gas masks in World War I. Stuck with a huge surplus after the war, they could have shut down that line. Instead they marketed the product to women as a sanitary cold cream remover. Women wrote back that while the product worked fine, they were annoyed that their husbands and kids kept swiping the cold cream removers to blow their noses. The intraprenuerial skunks inside Kimberly-Clark took note. The company repositioned the product as a tossable hankie and rebranded it as Kleenex.

Yet another way to minnovate involves how you market your product. In 1959 the Mattel cofounders Ruth and Elliot Handler introduced a new doll at New York's annual toy fair. The doll was modeled on a German adult entertainment toy named Lilli, known for her large breasts and sexy clothing. The Handlers toned down the makeup but kept the bosom. If she was going to be a role model for little girls, Ruth said, "it was a little stupid to play with a doll that had a flat chest." The Handlers named the doll after their daughter, Barbara. They called it Barbie Millicent Roberts.

The Handlers' plan had been to do what toy companies had always done: market Barbie to moms. But when moms took one look at the "shapely teenage model," they revolted. Her body was unrealistic, they said. (And they didn't want their husbands gawking at the doll.) This was the Handlers' engine-on-the-floor moment. Instead of panicking, they pivoted and did something previously unheard of in American business: They advertised the product directly to children. Barbie's first appearance was in a televised ad on *The Mickey Mouse Club* in 1959. The company sold 351,000 Barbie dolls that year.

The twentieth century's ultimate minnovator in chief will always be Henry Ford. With the Model T, he upgraded the transmission of existing cars, improved the engine, and elevated the suspension. He also developed a new kind of steel that was significantly lighter and three times as strong. As he said, "I invented nothing new. I simply assembled into a car the discoveries of other men behind whom were centuries of work." (The most significant of Ford's minnovations was his decision to relocate the steering wheel from the right side of the car to the left. Before, drivers worried about steering into a ditch, so they wanted to eye their outer wheels. Ford correctly anticipated that in the future drivers would be more anxious about oncoming traffic and would prefer to sit closer to the middle of the road.)

I tell my entrepreneurs: "Stop trying to shoot the moon all the time." In make-or-break situations sometimes the smarter move is to make an incremental adjustment. Innovation may capture more headlines; minnovation captures more markets.

— 4. DROP THE PENS —

But don't minnovate to the point of distraction. Resist the urge to launch dozens of different products and scores of niggling side projects. Focus.

In 2011 a business accelerator in California set out to understand which start-ups went big, which fell flat, and why. One question it examined: Is there a right or wrong amount to pivot? To get at that dilemma, researchers looked at the number of adaptations a company made to its product line. Researchers compared start-ups that made no changes, start-ups that made one or two changes, and start-ups that made more than two.

Their discovery: Start-ups that *pivoted once or twice* raised two and a half times more money, had almost four times more user growth, and were 50 percent less likely to scale prematurely than start-ups that pivoted either more than twice or not at all. The takeaway: Be open to change, but not *too* open.

In 2010 Sugianto Tandio took over his wife's family's plastics company in Indonesia. For four decades the firm, Tirta Marta, had sold flexible packaging products, but Sugianto had other ideas. Trained at 3M, he immediately took the company in a new direction. He refocused Tirta Marta on "eco-friendly" innovation. His most daring was a plastic polymer made from tapioca—yes, tapioca—that became the first "Fair for Life" certified bioplastic in the world. It had the dual benefit of improving the environment and giving local farmers a livelihood. Retailers pounced, and the company's plastic goods gained 90 percent of the local market. By the time Sugianto applied to become an Endeavor entrepreneur, he was building a strong green company.

But our business experts uncovered a flaw. "He's a great promoter for Indonesia, and he can solve a world problem," one said, "but he has too many business models and too many products." Joanna Rees, an Endeavor board member, said, "He spends a lot of time talking about making branded pens, which is a completely different business. He needs to focus."

The deliberations lasted over an hour, but the panel ultimately decided he deserved to be supported. When the judges were asked if they had any advice, Joanna didn't hesitate: "Drop the pens!"

A year later Tirta Marta was focusing on expanding abroad and developing an eco-friendly home shopping bag. Not on its horizon: a biodegradable pen.

Joyful exuberance can be an entrepreneur's greatest strength, but it can also lead to crippling distraction. Many entrepreneurs make the mistake of expanding to a new region before their brands have momentum in their own neighborhoods. Or they'll start new product lines when their initial business is just taking off.

Compare two iconic companies. The first is Apple. Steve Jobs was a strict proponent of discipline and focus. He first learned this philosophy while working the night shift at Atari as a college dropout. Atari's games came with no manual and needed to be uncomplicated enough that a stoned college freshman could figure them out. The only instructions for its Star Trek game were: (1) Insert quarter. (2) Avoid Klingons.

When Jobs returned to Apple in 1997, after a decade away, the company was producing a random array of computers and peripherals, including a dozen different versions of the Macintosh. "Which ones do I tell my friends to buy?" Jobs asked. After a few weeks of review, he'd finally had enough. "Stop!" he shouted during a strategy session. He grabbed a Magic Marker, padded in stocking feet up to the whiteboard (yes, a whiteboard; he thought they promoted focus), and drew a two-by-two grid. He labeled the two columns "Consumer" and "Pro" and the two rows "Desktop" and "Portable." Your task, he told his team, is to focus on four great products, one for each quadrant. All other products should be canceled. There was a stunned silence.

But Jobs did not stop there. Next he asked his top managers, "What are the 10 things we should be doing next?" After much jockeying, the group identified a list. Jobs then slashed the bottom seven and announced, "We can do only three."

As Jobs said, "Deciding what not to do is as important as deciding what to do. That's true for companies, and it's true for products."

Contrast this approach with Sony. As the *New York Times* pointed out in 2012, Sony, once a beacon of innovation, had not turned a profit in four years. A former Sony executive acknowledged this, saying, "Sony makes too many models, and for none of them can they say, 'This contains our best, most cutting-edge technology.'"

The lesson for entrepreneurs: Don't muddy up your brand with too many peripheral products or services. Focus on what you do well, and exploit it fully.

Consider one of the most iconic toy companies of all time. In 1932 a struggling Danish carpenter named Ole Kirk Christiansen started making wooden toys: piggy banks, yo-yos, pull toys, cars. He held a contest among his staff to name the company, offering a bottle of homemade wine as a prize. Two finalists emerged; Christiansen chose his own entry, Lego, a variant of the Danish expression "play well." (Presumably he also kept the bottle of wine!)

During World War II Danish parents bought up Lego toys as a

distraction for their children, but the war also created a wood short-age. So in 1947 Christiansen bought a plastic injection molding machine and came up with a line of interlocking, stackable blocks. Customers hated them, preferring the wooden toys. Over the years the company improved the quality, and the firm grew modestly. In the 1970s, when busy baby boomers became parents and saw the blocks as educational, demand surged, and Lego's profits doubled every five years.

But by the 1990s Chinese knockoffs were flooding the market, crippling sales. In response, Lego went on an innovation spree. Designers dreamed up blocks in every color, tie-ins with *Star Wars* and *Harry Potter*, even Lego jewelry. The number of Lego pieces ballooned from 7,000 to 12,400. And it nearly killed the company. By 2003 Lego, like one of those Frankenstein-like creatures a four-year-old makes that can't stand up, was on the edge of bankruptcy. "We almost did innovation suicide," a senior executive said. So the Christiansen family brought in a former McKinsey consultant to be CEO. He sold a chunk of the company, slashed jobs, and outsourced production. He also issued strict orders to go back to the brick. Every Lego had to go up for a vote among designers. The selection shrank back to seven thousand.

Lego's sales soared, growing by almost 25 percent a year. In 2012 the firm reached a valuation of $15 billion, passing Mattel (and Barbie!) to become the world's most valuable toy company.

Experimenting, exploring, expanding are all part of entrepreneurship, but sometimes you have to do the opposite. Sometimes the best thing is to turn away from the shiny new thing. Ignore the distraction. Stop creating more trouble for yourself. Your engine didn't just fall on the floor; you let it fall by not keeping your eye on what really mattered. Don't worry, you'll have plenty of time to expand later on. For now drop the pens and go back to the core ideas that got you here in the first place.

— 5. DREAM BIG BUT EXECUTE SMALL —

It was the kind of out-of-the-blue gift from the PR gods of which entrepreneurs dream. In December 2012 the *Slate* columnist Farhad Manjoo wrote a piece in which he called the hooded sweatshirt sold by San Francisco–based start-up American Giant the greatest hoodie ever made. "There is really no comparison between American Giant's hoodie and the competition," Manjoo wrote. "When you wear this hoodie, you'll wonder why all other clothes aren't made this well."

The story went viral. ABC News, NPR, and the BBC did follow-ups. Within thirty-six hours, the company had sold out of hoodies. "We were down to the bare shelves," Bayard Winthrop, the company's founder, said.

What an inspiring story of well-deserved success, right?

Hardly. The company could not cope with the demand. Those shelves remained bare for nearly *six months*. As one disgruntled customer commented on *Slate*, "The company may in fact make the world's best hoodie (I'll judge for myself if mine ever comes), but they obviously completely suck at scaling up to meet the demand created by this article."

The flub was even more painful because Winthrop, before starting the company, had been an expert in scaling. He was the guy companies called when they needed to grow but couldn't. Now he was facing the opposite problem. "Inventory planning, your systems, your ability to scale . . . that's all great in theory," Winthrop said. But when your execution doesn't meet your planning, you have what one reporter deemed a catastrophic success, a business whose overnight fame propels it to overnight doom.

Dreaming big is admirable, but if you can't execute small, don't expect your vision to come true.

In 2011 a group of entrepreneurs, VCs, and academics in Silicon Valley, who called themselves Blackbox, set out to identify what they called the genome of tech start-ups. "More than 90 percent of startups fail," the group wrote in a document titled "The Startup Genome Report," "due primarily to self-destruction rather than competition." Even those that do succeed, they said, experience several near death experiences along the way.

Blackbox created a database of 3,200 high-growth Internet start-ups and received in-depth feedback from 650 companies. Their number one conclusion: Premature scaling is the most common reason for start-ups to fail. Three-quarters of start-ups fail for this reason, they said. Think about that: The gravest threat to success is not bad products, poor design, or lack of funds. The biggest hindrance to going big is trying to go big too early. Or as the report put it, entrepreneurs "tend to lose the battle early on by getting ahead of themselves."

Some of the most common reasons these companies failed:

- Building a product that didn't solve a problem

- Spending too much on acquiring customers and not enough on perfecting the product

- Plowing forward without getting feedback from the users

The common theme here: Don't get ahead of yourself. As one interviewee said, "Scaling comes down to making sure the machine is ready to handle the speed before hitting the accelerator." The genome report even put a number on it. Firms that approach going big in a step-by-step way grow twenty times faster than the norm.

I've seen that in our network. When Mark Chang opened Job Street.com in Malaysia in 1997, he assumed his company, a recruitment site akin to Monster.com, would bring him a steady paycheck, but not much more. "I really thought it would be a mom-and-pop thing," he said. But as soon as he gained traction, everyone asked, "*Why aren't you expanding across Asia? What about listing on the NASDAQ?*" "People were just handing out cash in those days," Mark said. "Ignoring their advice was exhausting."

Innately conservative, Chang instead focused on writing software, including custom tools for Shell and Dell. He also hired a seasoned CEO to complement his engineering skills. He avoided rapid expansion. The result of all this plodding? Chang survived the dot-com bust of 2000, which wiped out many of his competitors. He also weathered the 2008 downturn. Today Chang sits on the board of Endeavor Malaysia and JobStreet is considered among the most successful Internet companies in Southeast Asia. In 2014 it was acquired for $524 million. Chang greeted the news with characteristic understatedness. "We only know the 'kerbau way,'" he said, referring to the Indonesian water buffalo. "Work hard and wait for the rain."

Now there's a mascot for the execution-oriented entrepreneur: Be a water buffalo. Work hard and wait for the rain.

The Mexican entrepreneur Miguel Angel Dávila knows how hard it is to actually do this, especially when everyone is out to squash you. A Harvard-trained MBA, Dávila felt Mexico was ready for an alternative to the "brick and stick" model of going to the movies, meaning "You bring a brick to sit on and a stick to beat away the rats." So he and some friends opened Cinemex, a chain of comfortable movie houses with cutting-edge projection, surround sound, and stadium seating. His biggest asset, he told me, was a minnovation: putting lime juice and chili sauce on the popcorn instead of butter.

His biggest challenge, though, was something far less glitzy than Hollywood: Mexican unions had a seventy-year lock on the theater business with arcane rules, such as one that said anyone who sold soft drinks could not sell food. When the unions boycotted his opening day, Dávila fought back at the labor board, which ultimately sided with Cinemex. The union was replaced with a modern workforce. Dávila worked hard to satisfy both employees and customers, and a decade later came the rain: Cinemex sold for $300 million.

Dávila, who serves on Endeavor Mexico's board, counsels entrepreneurs not to try to compete with stories of lightning-fast, hockey-stick growth. "Those things are Halley's comet," he said. "They come around once every hundred years." Instead, "figure out something people need and find a way to execute it better than everyone else."

The lesson: Don't go from zero to sixty too fast. Dream big, but execute small.

— 6. EAT THE ELEPHANT ONE BITE AT A TIME —

One day I was leaning my whiteboard against the wall when I realized something: These ideas, which had sprung from a hundred different conversations and a dozen different scenarios, all had one theme in common. It's the same theme that united my advice in the start-up phase.

We think of entrepreneurship as being a big, scary thing, involving terrifying leaps of faith and sweeping acts of disruption. In fact, it's something quite different. It's about building up your emotions to take on the status quo, then tamping down your emotions once the problems start to hit. It's about taking courageous actions to destabilize the world but doing so through a series of judicious moves that won't destabilize you. It's about both embracing risk and mitigating risk.

It's about achieving daring dreams through prudent steps.

The lesson here is to act in the opposite way of everyone around you—and perhaps counter to your own instinct. When your path seems smooth and secure, unsettle it. Push yourself to imagine something fresh, to drum up a dangerous idea, to startle the everyday. As I've said, zig when everyone else zags.

But when your path is rough and unsure, I urge you not to cut and run. Stay calm; narrow your options; get the right people on board (and get rid of the wrong); make targeted changes; fulfill your promises.

Keep going.

The journalist Ben Sherwood spent years talking to people who survived extraordinary circumstances, from plane crashes to lion maulings. In his bestseller *The Survivors Club*, he says that many survivors share a mind-set. "In a crisis, they're alert, engaged, and aware. They think—they plan—and they take action." What they don't do is panic, freeze, or feel overwhelmed.

In air force survival school, Sherwood explained, people are taught to conquer moments of confusion with a memorable axiom: *You eat an elephant one bite at a time.* Survival is a big, ornery animal. If you try to eat a fifteen-thousand-pound pachyderm in one sitting, you'll either give up or get sick. Instead, the key to survival is to take it slow, Sherwood concluded. "Take one small bite. Chew. Swallow. Then take another."

The same applies to entrepreneurs. Reid Hoffman delivered a similar message to our founders at an Endeavor summit. Lots of gurus compare entrepreneurship with running a marathon or riding a roller coaster, he said, but he rejected those analogies. Instead, Reid compared the challenges of starting and scaling a venture with what pioneers faced in settling the American West. "In charting the new frontier," he said, "they didn't scale the plains in a day. They broke up the trip into many legs. Step by step, day by day, they got closer to their dream."

Going big doesn't always mean going fast. Surviving the onslaught of tests during the scale-up phase often requires slowing down at points. As Henry Ford put it, "Nothing is particularly hard if you divide it into small jobs."

From his experimental department to mine: The next time a piece of your dream comes crashing to the floor, take a breath, pick it up, go back to work. And chalk it up as your Model T moment.

CHAPTER 6

Leadership 3.0

About four years after cofounding Endeavor, I was fired by my assistant. I was on a trip to Cambridge, Massachusetts, where I was addressing the first-year class of Harvard Business School. The occasion was the unveiling of the first business case study about Endeavor. (It was the same day I was introduced as the stalker.) Afterward I was feeling pretty high. The day felt like a milestone in my own entrepreneurial journey, and I was pumped. Then my assistant, Belle, called.

"Linda, did you remember to authorize this month's payroll?" she asked.

"No, but I'm sure someone else did," I said. "Now can I tell you what happened today?"

"Someone else!" she said. "You're the CEO. No one else is authorized to pay everybody." Belle paused. "That's it." She continued. "You're fired. You're no longer in control of payroll. You may not realize this, but your employees need to pay rent."

"Employees?" I thought. *"I don't have employees."* In my mind, the eight people who then worked in Endeavor's New York office were my teammates. I wasn't their boss; I was their partner. There were no

hierarchies, no bureaucracies, no processes. We were a start-up, and we were all in this together.

It took Belle, one of the youngest employees in my organization, to teach me one of my most grown-up lessons. I wasn't just a founder, a teammate, and an entrepreneur. I was a leader, too. And I had better start learning to lead or I wasn't going to have a team to rely on.

In the years since that blunt awakening, I've seen many entrepreneurs falter on the same terrain in the course of going big. Having gotten their start-ups up and running, founders sometimes forget they actually have to run them. Whereas once they worked in their pajamas, tinkered in their garages, or sent e-mails in the middle of the night, now they have proper offices, proper employees, and proper meetings, and they continue to operate in crazed start-up mode because they don't know how else to lead.

But while seat-of-the-pants is no way to lead, high-and-mighty doesn't work either. Most leadership books bulge with research drawn from august generals, Olympic champions, and corporate titans, most of which is incompatible with running a lightning-fast, hyperwired organization. Jack Welch has about as much in common with the modern everyday entrepreneur as an aircraft carrier has with a surfboard.

I wanted to identify the "Goldilocks rules" for leading like an entrepreneur—not so "hard" that they apply only to button-downed organizations; not so "soft" that they apply only to T-shirted start-ups. Leadership 3.0 is what I call these new skills. They're a blueprint for remaining nimble in the midst of growth, navigating the rush of social media, and taking the measured risk of exposing yourself to your team.

Everyone I meet is searching for these rules. High-jumping gazelles certainly need them. Leadership development comes up constantly when we ask the Endeavor entrepreneurs what they need most in order to take their businesses to scale. Mission-driven dolphins and lifestyle-focused butterflies are equally baffled. At school drop-off I talked to a mom who had been running a design shop from her living room and was about to hire her first employee. "What if they don't do what I say?" she asked.

But to my surprise, even intrapreneurial skunks and top corporate executives—the ones I would have thought had leadership figured out—are seeking guidance. In recent years I've been invited to a number of Fortune 100 companies to run Leadership 3.0 workshops. At first I wondered what veterans of big business, with their five-year plans, could learn from quicksilver start-ups, whose plans change every five minutes. Turns out these captains of industry view their elaborate infrastructure and grinding deliberations as more detriment than asset nowadays.

For corporate leaders, the greatest risk is not being nimble enough.

With so many start-ups eating the lunch of big corporations, these executives find themselves borrowing the famous line from the deli scene in the film *When Harry Met Sally*: "I'll have what she's having."

So what are successful entrepreneurial leaders doing right? In my view, they have four attributes in common. They are:

Agile

Accessible

Aware

Authentic

The Three R's might be fine for the classroom; for the office it's the Four A's. I'd like to go through them one at a time.

— AGILE —

One night a few years ago my husband came into our bedroom and announced he wanted to turn us into an agile family. I'd never heard the word "agile" used in this way before. With the passion of a convert, he launched into an explanation.

In 1983 Jeff Sutherland, the chief technologist at a financial firm, was appalled by the dysfunction of software development. Companies followed the waterfall model, in which executives issue from above orders that trickle down to frustrated engineers. Eighty-three percent of projects failed. Sutherland became a skunk entrepreneur. He designed a new system in which ideas don't flow from the top; they percolate from the bottom. In his model, which came to be known as agile, workers are divided into small teams, meet daily to review progress, experiment liberally, and succeed or fail quickly.

Today agile is standard practice in a hundred countries, and its techniques also have flooded into management suites, from Google to Facebook to TED. Many Endeavor entrepreneurs rely on it. Wences Casares, the onetime Patagonian sheep farmer, told me using agile was the best leadership decision he ever made. It reminded him that he wasn't always right and that good ideas can come from anywhere in his organization. (Meanwhile, ask Wences his best *life* decision, and he'll tell you it was marrying Belle, the fiery assistant who fired me!)

As it happens, my family did adopt some agile techniques, including a new way to reduce chaos in the mornings and a weekly family meeting to review progress, from eating more vegetables to less screaming. (And yes, that includes the parents.) The team at TED became so enamored of the idea that they asked my husband, Bruce, to deliver a TED talk, "Agile Programming—for your family."

More important, I began to see why agile is so relevant for entrepreneurs. While the approach has many tools, three in particular apply to leaders: (1) constant experimentation, (2) small, self-governed teams, and (3) embracing failure.

First, agile leaders don't issue rigid five-year plans. They encourage their teams to adjust and experiment constantly. Consider the Chinese appliance manufacturer Haier. In 1993, when Zhang Ruimin took over as CEO, the stodgy refrigerator company had barely averted bankruptcy and had little chance of competing against the global brands GE and Whirlpool. Zhang divided the company into four thousand teams and encouraged them to become more autonomous and customer focused. The team at the struggling call center took note. They vowed to answer calls within three rings and dispatch technicians within three hours.

Not long after, a technician took a call about a clogged washing machine in rural Sichuan and quickly discovered that the owner had been using the machine to clean mud off his newly harvested potatoes. Instead of blaming the farmer, the response team sent the story back to Haier's engineers, along with research showing that millions of other Chinese had been clogging their washing machines with dirty produce. The engineers responded by inventing a machine that could not only wash potatoes but also peel them. They also developed a model for Mongolian herders to help churn yak milk into butter. All this experimentation led to the holy grail of laundry, a washing machine able to wash clothes without detergent. In 2013 Haier ranked as the number one global appliance brand in the world for the fourth year in a row.

Second, agile leaders organize their workers into small, self-managed teams. Bountiful evidence shows that the tighter the working group, the better the work. The legendary advertising executive George Lois, the image guru behind Xerox, Tommy Hilfiger, and MTV and the inspiration for *Mad Men's* Don Draper, insisted that team size is a key to success. "If you had ten incredibly bright people—nothing could come out of it," Lois said. "You could have Nobel laureates in the room, and you'd have big trouble." How large should teams be? "Nothing great can come of more than three people in a room," he said. *"Nothing."*

Jeff Bezos agrees. He instituted a two-pizza rule at Amazon: If a team can't be fed with two pizzas, it's too big. At a company retreat where someone suggested that employees start communicating better, Bezos stood up and declared, "No, communication is terrible!" He preferred a decentralized, even disorganized company where independent ideas flourished over groupthink. Today 90 percent of Amazon is run with agile.

Third, agile leaders are not afraid of the *F* word: failure. Being willing to tolerate failure has always been critical to the start-up phase of being an entrepreneur. Thomas Edison famously said of his iterative lightbulb experiments, "I have not failed 10,000 times. I have not failed once. I have succeeded in proving that those 10,000 ways will not work. When I have eliminated the ways that will not work, I will find the way that will work."

But as important as failure is to leaders getting started, it's even more important to leaders going big. Many of the most innovative ideas in larger organizations never come to the surface because the skunks behind them are too afraid of losing out on promotions, making their bosses look bad, or getting shown the door. A 2013 survey of five hundred U.S. companies found that nearly 40 percent of the executives surveyed cited anxiety about being held responsible for mistakes or failures as their greatest impediment to taking initiative. Better to just keep quiet and continue doing your job.

These days more and more companies are pushing back and finding ways to create a free-to-fail zone. For one such business, failure is inherent to the brand. In 1953 Norm Larsen, the head of the fledgling Rocket Chemical Company in San Diego, was trying to solve a long-standing problem of the aerospace industry, rust. General Dynamics, a leading defense firm, was working on America's first intercontinental ballistic missile, but the weapon's outer shell kept corroding. Larsen thought a water displacement solution could keep moisture away from the steel skin.

His first formula didn't work. Neither did his second. His third, fourth, and fifth iterations were equally ineffective. On thirty-nine tries, Larsen kept coming up short. But on his fortieth attempt, he hit on a cocktail of oil and hydrocarbon that could repel water.

General Dynamics bought the first batch, and it worked so well employees began sneaking the solution home in their lunch pails to fix rusty car parts and squeaky doors. This gave Larson an idea: Why not sell directly to the public? He packaged his secret formula into aerosol canisters, and soon the blue and yellow cans popped up across the United States. Larsen called the product WD-40, his abbreviation for what he had recorded in his lab book: "Water Displacement, 40th formula."

Today the WD-40 Company is still based in California. In deference to its origins, the CEO, Garry Ridge, has made failure central to the company's daily operations. All of the firm's three hundred employees are encouraged to share both the positive and negative outcomes of every situation. "There is no penalizing for lack of success," he said, no whack-a-mole culture where the minute someone tries something new and comes up short, he or she is beaten down by others. "At WD-40 Company, we don't make mistakes," Ridge said. "We have learning moments. We give people permission to have a conversation about things that go wrong."

One thing going wrong was that customers complained for years they were losing the red straw that came with the WD-40 can. A team was established to solve the problem but couldn't. The group reached out to an external design firm, which came up with a "smart straw" built directly into the cap. The new device added $1.25 per can, but customers were thrilled. One wrote: "It's about damned time." From a base of $130 million in revenue when Ridge took over the company in 1997, revenues topped $300 million a decade later, while employee retention grew to three times the national average.

One fierce advocate for this new style of mistake-tolerant leadership is Scott Cook, the cofounder and executive committee chairman of Intuit. He told an *Economist* conference in 2011 that in thirty-five years in business, he had completely altered his view of leadership. "My father learned leadership in the U.S. military in the Second World War," he said. "In his time, leaders were those who framed the options, made the decisions, and told people what to do. Very much like Eisenhower planning D-Day." In our day, Cook continued, leaders must be more like Thomas Edison. "The new skill in leadership is leadership by experiment."

Cook cited a five-skunk team from TurboTax as an example.

Their hypothesis: If people could fill out tax forms on their cell phones, they wouldn't have to pay tax consultants to do it. The group's first experiments failed, but its second ones surprised them. When customers snapped photos of their W-2s, accuracy improved. Snap-Tax was released nationally in January 2011; within two weeks it was the number one finance app on both Android and iOS with over 350,000 downloads.

"When the bosses make the decisions," Cook said, they're made by "politics, persuasion, and PowerPoint." When leaders empower self-directed teams, the best idea wins.

And it's never too late to embrace failure. India's iconic business leader Ratan Tata became a convert in the twilight of his career. The seventy-five-year-old executive ran a conglomerate of over a hundred companies, from software to steel to tea that generated $100 billion annually. In his last year as chairman, Tata instituted an unconventional competition: a prize for the *best failed idea*. "Failure is a gold mine," he said. It's the only way to foster innovation, keep the company fresh, and reward employees for trying new things.

Take it from one of the most iconic names in global business: Don't fear the *F* word.

Instead, go agile. Drop the long-range planning in favor of constant adaptation; slash bureaucracies in favor of two-pizza teams; and create a culture that prizes experimentation and occasional disappointment over mindless repetition.

And every now and then go out of your way to give someone an A for getting an F.

— *ACCESSIBLE* —

It was a four-star panel. Marc Benioff, the founder and CEO of Salesforce.com, was hosting a discussion with the retired general Colin Powell and the GE chief executive Jeffrey Immelt. The setting was the 2012 Dreamforce conference; the subject was leadership.

Powell went first. "I was born analog," he said, "and I've been desperately trying to keep up with the digital world." (Benioff pointed out that he was doing pretty well. The former secretary of state had nearly three million followers on Facebook.) Powell said that with so much technology, leaders risked being disconnected from their teams. "Young people are digitally wired, so you have to keep up with them," he said. Leaders can no longer sit back and wait for problems to come to them. They have to reach out and engage people at all levels.

Immelt agreed. "In my world, I'm always fighting size and bureaucracy," he said. Immelt had initiated a major effort to return GE to its entrepreneurial roots. Quoting "the great philosopher" Mike Tyson, Immelt suggested that large companies like GE ought to be more nimble: "Everybody has a plan until they get punched in the mouth." A big part of that change fell on executives like him, who needed to become more responsive to employees. Technology helped.

"What social media does for me is it gives me access to customers and employees," Immelt said. Through digital platforms, he now got raw data from his sales force in the field. He'd use this to press managers up the corporate chain, saying, "What's going on here, guys?" Also, social media obliged him to be more open as a leader, he said. "You have to be willing to share more, and you better just deal with it." In Immelt's case, that meant keeping an internal blog for GE employees. "I've been doing it for two years. It's just my voice. It's my message, my way." He added dryly that he doesn't let his general counsel see it.

Immelt isn't alone. A 2012 Weber Shandwick survey of executives in ten countries found that "sociability" among CEOs had doubled in the prior two years. Two-thirds of CEOs post to a company Web site; half post to a company intranet. Like the heads of Marriott and Zappos, some corporate leaders blog; like Rupert Murdoch, Marissa Mayer, and Richard Branson, others tweet; like the founders of Google, still more hold in-person Q&As with employees. Garry Ridge, of WD-40, sends his employees a daily inspirational quote and promises to address each grievance within twenty-four hours.

However you choose to interact, your team will eat it up. Half the employees in the Weber Shandwick survey said they felt more inspired when their CEOs engaged social media.

I had to learn this reluctantly. In the early years of leading Endeavor, I had the reputation of a bad delegator. I was deemed mercurial, meddling, and reluctant to give up control. Worse, I had no clue how to manage a growing team. If I was serious about going big, I had to follow the same advice I give to entrepreneurs and bring in experienced senior managers.

So I hired a chief operating officer. After less than a year she complained that everyone was going around her and coming directly to me. She quit. A year later I hired a second COO. It quickly became clear that the team didn't respond to him. "He's too corporate for our culture," they said. I had to ask him to leave. By this point I had made a bad situation worse. The whispers that I was a prima donna became more like a loud din. Even when I hired several impressive senior VPs from Dell, Bloomberg, and Silicon Valley the clamor continued.

By this point we were reaching a crisis. Whereas once our whole office could survive on one pizza, now we needed a delivery truck to feed us all. Endeavor was nearing three hundred full-time team members worldwide. I needed a partner. So I called up Fernando Fabre, an economist and for six years the managing director of Endeavor Mexico. He was adored by our entrepreneurs and respected across our network. He'd also become the point person for anyone worldwide who had an issue to pick with me. (This kept him quite busy!)

"Hey, Fer, how are you?" I said.

"Good, and you?"

"Excellent. How would you like to become the COO of Endeavor?"

There was silence on the other end of the phone.

I went on. "You know we're scaling the organization. I'll need to focus externally. So we need someone strong to take over day-to-day management. I thought you—"

He cut me off. "Linda, I get it," he said. "But I won't take the job with that failed COO title. If you're willing to bring me on as Endeavor's president, then I accept."

I was, and he did. Fernando moved to New York, and our new era began. At which point I promptly blew it again. Not with Fernando, but with everybody else. I thought that with a new president and other senior executives we were beginning to feel like a mature organization, so I did what I thought mature organizations did: I convened senior management meetings.

They backfired. First, Fernando was forced to hold countless planning sessions before these meetings and numerous debriefs afterward. "My calendar was filled with meetings about meetings," he said. Second, the meetings were chipping away at our culture. Before, Endeavor had been a communal organization; now the "cabinet" was meeting in a conference room with glass walls, so that everyone else could see they hadn't been invited. I clearly needed a new way to lead.

The solution was social media. At the suggestion of several younger members of our team, Endeavor had recently installed Salesforce Chatter, a social network for the workplace that enables employees to post questions, comments, and concerns. Fernando launched an all-out effort to get everyone hooked. He offered various incentives for team members to post a weekly wrap-up (including, in a nod to his Mexican roots, a bottle of tequila). Fernando himself started commenting on soccer matches; I challenged him to a "Chatter throwdown" over who could accrue more "likes."

The plan worked. Our entire global team gravitated to Chatter, sometimes preferring it to e-mail. Ideas got stoked; new connections bloomed. Endeavor had returned to its start-up roots as a collaborative company. As for the cabinet meetings, they're done.

Perhaps the ultimate example of how leaders have to step outside their bubbles is the one who lives in the biggest bubble of all, the president of the United States. When Barack Obama was elected, he fretted, like all his predecessors, about disappearing behind the oval curtain. He fought to keep his BlackBerry, for example, to let friends and aides reach him directly. (He was denied an iPhone for security reasons.)

During the 2008 campaign, one of those aides, a twenty-five-year-old Pentecostal pastor named Joshua DuBois, sent an unsolicited e-mail directly to Obama's BlackBerry during a particularly difficult time. The e-mail contained a meditation on the Twenty-third Psalm. Now that's a skunk move: pushing preaching on your boss. "I didn't know how he would respond," said DuBois, the faith outreach director. "But in just a few minutes, he got back to me and said the message helped him, and he'd like me to continue each day." The e-mails wove together Scripture, history, jazz, and current events, and Obama enjoyed them so much he asked DuBois to keep writing them once he moved to the White House. "Every morning I get something to reflect on," the president said.

Presidents, like all leaders, don't communicate with just their teams but with the larger world as well. Here, too, Obama has experimented with accessibility. He held the first Twitter town hall and an online chat about housing on Zillow. He even went open kimono on a Reddit "Ask Me Anything" session. In 2012, while Republicans were holding their convention in Florida, Obama stepped into a nondescript back room in a Charlottesville, Virginia, arena furnished with a desk, a floor lamp, and a MacBook Pro.

Obama typed out, "Hi, I'm Barack Obama, President of the United States. Ask me anything." Two hundred questions flooded in during the first nine minutes. They ranged from the serious—"Are you considering increasing funds to the space program?"—to the silly—"What color is your toothbrush?" Obama's digital chief was supposed to filter the questions, and a speechwriter was there to transcribe the president's answers, but the plan didn't last. Obama refused to abandon the keyboard. "I'll just keep going," he said.

So off he went. On work-family balance: "The big advantage I have is that I live above the store—so I have no commute!" On the White House beer: "I can tell from firsthand experience, it is tasty." On the toughest decision of his term: "The decision to surge our forces in afghanistan." (Little details, like forgetting to capitalize "Afghanistan," actually increased the president's credibility.) Nearly three million people visited the Web page during the forty-five minute session; over the next twenty-four hours, another two million stopped by.

No matter what kind of organization you're in, all leaders today must make themselves accessible—to their closest partners, their lowest employees, their far-flung constituents. They must act, in other words, like entrepreneurs. And guess what? Most leaders who leave the bubble enjoy the fresh air. As the president typed at the end of his first AMA, "By the way, if you want to know what I think about this whole reddit experience—NOT BAD!"

— *AWARE* —

A few years ago I was giving a speech about the state of Endeavor to around five hundred of our supporters, mentors, and entrepreneurs. I showed a draft to my husband, Bruce. His response: "Too much Superman, not enough Clark Kent." He went on to explain (lovingly, but *still*) that he thought I was spending too much time touting our successes and accomplishments and not enough time discussing our challenges and needs. "When you make yourself sound invincible, you don't sound real," he said. "Plus, you're not inviting the listener in." His insight got me thinking. Now that we're in an age when leaders have to come down off the summit, what posture should they adopt with their employees, clients, and customers?

One answer emerging from a new generation of scholars and thinkers is that leaders need to be much more open about their own shortcomings and assertive about taking responsibility. They need to be aware.

Two stars in organizational behavior, Alison Fragale of the University of North Carolina and Adam Grant of the Wharton School, both found overwhelming evidence of the perils of being omnipotent in how you present yourself. In his bestseller *Give and Take*, Grant lays out the case for what he calls powerless communicators, those who "are more inclined toward asking questions than offering answers, talking tentatively than boldly, admitting their weaknesses than displaying their strengths, and seeking advice than imposing their view on others." Whereas powerful communicators put people off with their seemingly superhuman qualities, powerless ones draw others in with their imperfections and self-awareness.

Effective leaders, in other words, are less super, more human.

I heard a term that encapsulates this idea perfectly: "flawsome." A combination of "flawed" and "awesome," "flawsome" is a way to say something is great but imperfect. In business the term has come to mean an awareness of, and a willingness to admit, your shortcomings. This includes your products, your workers, and your organization.

In April 2009 two employees at Domino's made a video of themselves sticking cheese up their noses and waving meat under their rear ends (subtle!) before adding it to food being delivered to customers. The video went viral, garnering a million views on YouTube. Though the offending employees were fired and arrested, the company still had a PR nightmare. Domino's took forty-eight hours to respond—forever in social media time—then issued a perfunctory video apology from the company head, Patrick Doyle.

But to his credit, Doyle didn't let the story end there. The crisis revealed that Domino's had an image problem that went far beyond rogue pizza makers. The company spent months soliciting feedback. One survey ranked its pizza the worst in flavor, tied with Chuck E. Cheese. Doyle made the unusual decision to embrace the critics. Nine months after the initial crisis, Domino's released a brutally honest video entitled *The Pizza Turnaround* to announce that it was scrapping its old recipe. The video featured Domino's employees talking about how much people hated their product. Doyle appeared first, wincing at a consumer's saying, "How hard can it be? There doesn't feel like there's much love in Domino's pizza." Doyle responded, "You can either use negative comments to get you down, or you can use them to excite and energize your process." One employee added, "It hits you right in the heart. This is what I've done for twenty-five years now." Another started crying.

When the new recipe appeared in stores, Domino's added a Twitter feed to its Web site (#newpizza), showing both positive and negative responses. It also introduced an online pizza tracker, which asked consumers for feedback. Responses were delivered in real time to employees and broadcast on a billboard in Times Square. Word of mouth exploded, and sales soared. Even more important, the effort boosted company morale. With Domino's back in the news for positive reasons, employees were "proud to come to work every day," one executive said. CNBC named Doyle the best chief executive of 2011.

Two Endeavor entrepreneurs went even further in embracing their critics and restoring employee goodwill. Mario Chady and Eduardo Ourivio were the Brazilian childhood friends who built the line of pasta bars featuring juggling chefs. Their focus on fun-loving service brought the company back from bankruptcy; within a few years Spoleto was running three hundred restaurants. Then one day in 2012 a wildly popular Brazilian comedy troupe called Porta dos Fundos ("Back Door") released a YouTube video that spoofed the chain's fast-talking chefs.

"Good morning," said the customer.

"Good morning," said the chef.

"I'd like the penne with—"

"Penne!" the chef shouted into the kitchen. "What sauce?"

"I'd like the tomato sauce."

"What toppings?"

"I'll have some corn."

"Corn. What else?"

"H—"

"Ham. What else?"

"Ummm . . ."

"Speak up."

"Give me a second."

"WHAT ELSE DO YOU WANT?"

At the end of the video the chef tosses hearts of palm at the customer, the customer pleads, "I just want to eat lunch," and the chef explodes, "Nobody told you to come eat lunch in hell!"

The video scored, topping nine million views. Though it was titled only *Fast Food*, everyone knew its target was Spoleto. The comedians braced for a call from the company's lawyers. Instead, when the phone rang, it was one of the company's founders. "We want to take you out for a beer," Eduardo said.

Over the objection of Spoleto's PR and legal teams, Mario and Eduardo went forward with the rendezvous. Beers were drunk, jokes were exchanged, then Mario and Eduardo came clean about their real intention: First, they wanted to sponsor the troupe's YouTube channel; second, they wanted the comedians to change the title of the video to *Spoleto*; and third, they wanted to pay the troupe to make a sequel.

Why would the company's founders go out of their way to make fun of themselves?

"We were simply acting according to our culture," Eduardo told me, "not taking ourselves too seriously, always searching for the silver lining."

In the second video, the ill-tempered chef is fired and finds himself working at a call center. He returns to Spoleto and appears wearing an apron that reads, "In Training!" When he insults another customer, he's finally let go for good. The screen reads: "This should never happen, but sometimes it's beyond our control. If you receive bad service at Spoleto, tell us and help us improve." An e-mail address appears.

The spoof of the spoof racked up four million views, but even more valuable, it pumped up employees. "The chefs loved it," Eduardo said. The exposure helped attract new talent. "When we recruited, forty percent of candidates listed the two videos as one of their primary reasons for applying," Eduardo told me.

These days it's awesome to work for a company that's flawsome.

The lesson for leaders is that in an age when social media magnifies and leaves a permanent digital trail of your flaws, how you respond to them becomes even more critical. One entrepreneur I know has made how he responds to mistakes the signature of his entire brand.

Danny Meyer is the celebrated New York restaurateur behind Union Square Café, Gramercy Tavern, and Shake Shack. He and his restaurants have won an unprecedented twenty-five James Beard awards. Born in St. Louis, Danny visited Europe as a teenager and later worked as a tour guide in Rome. It was during those trips that he first became enamored with the culture of gracious hospitality. "The hug that came with the food made it taste even better," he said. That realization led to what he calls his core business strategy, enlightened hospitality. As he describes it in his leadership manifesto, *Setting the Table*, "Hospitality exists when you believe the other person is on your side."

Danny's test as a leader was to take his vision for service (which he honed in his first restaurant, where he could be present around the clock) and figure out how to translate it across a growing collection of establishments spread throughout the country. Even as he went big, he still wanted to feel small. And he wanted his customers to feel cared for.

I've gotten to know Danny a little over the years, and his answer to this challenge is to accept that everyone will not be happy with every meal and prepare his team to react appropriately. He starts at the hiring stage, with an idiosyncratic job application that includes questions like "How has your sense of humor been useful to your service career?" "What was so wrong with your last job?" and "Do you prefer Hellmann's or Miracle Whip?" His explanation: In hospitality there must be a certain amount of fun involved, and those questions give him an idea of whether applicants can join in.

Second, he trains all employees on what he considers the difference between hospitality and service. Service, he says, is mindlessly giving customers more choices and empty chitchat. He cites the

Ritz-Carlton, whose workers say a rote "my pleasure" in response to everything. "Hearing 'my pleasure' over and over again can get rather creepy after a while," Danny said. "It's like hearing a flight attendant chirp 'Bye now!' and 'Bye-bye!' two hundred times as passengers disembark from an airplane." Service is the mechanical act of delivering a product, Danny said. "Hospitality is how the delivery makes the recipient feel."

Finally, Danny put his views on paper. He wrote a step-by-step manual for how employees should treat mishaps. Some of his tips:

- Spill a bowl of soup on a customer? Offer to pay for dry cleaning and send out a dish for the customer to enjoy while others are dining.

- Make a mistake? Never make an excuse. Say, "I am sorry this happened to you," not "We are short-staffed tonight."

- Something goes wrong during a meal? Have the kitchen send out a complimentary dessert or beverage as an additional generosity.

Above all, he said, employees must write a "great last chapter" to every incident. When Bob Kerrey, the former senator and a regular customer, cheerily informed Danny over lunch at Eleven Madison Park that one of his tablemates at Gramercy Tavern the previous night had found a beetle in his salad and the staff had handled it perfectly, Danny felt embarrassed. He was also determined not to let a near-eaten bug be the end of the story. So he sent a complimentary salad to the senator's table adorned with a piece of paper that said, "RINGO." The server said, "Danny wanted to make sure you knew that Gramercy Tavern wasn't the only one of his restaurants that's willing to garnish your salad with a Beatle."

Leadership today is not simply about making yourself look good; it's also about how you respond when you look bad. Even Superman isn't Superman around the clock. To be an effective leader, be aware of how others perceive you and cop to your flaws every now and then. Embrace your inner Clark Kent.

— *AUTHENTIC* —

The final lesson of entrepreneurial leadership may be the most challenging and most important of all. Expose yourself. Allow yourself to be vulnerable.

Be authentic.

In late 2005 the Indianapolis Colts were undefeated through thirteen games. If the Colts kept up their streak, the head coach, Tony Dungy, would become the first African American to lead his team to a Super Bowl title. Dungy had always been a different sort of leader. A deeply spiritual man, he was open about his faith.

Dungy translated his values into a compassionate leadership style, something rare in his profession. While he was coaching in Tampa, his place kicker started missing crucial field goals. Instead of cutting him, as most coaches would have done, Dungy asked if something was wrong. He was told the player's mother had recently died of cancer. Dungy reassured him: "You're a part of our team." The next week, the kicker nailed the game-winning score. He said of Dungy, "What he did was relieve the pressure from me. A lot of other coaches would have just let me go."

As the 2005 season neared its climax, Dungy gave his team off for Thanksgiving, a rare treat. The eldest of Dungy's five sons, Jamie, who was attending college in Tampa, flew in to visit his father. At the end of his short stay, Jamie hurried to catch a plane. There was no time for a good-bye hug. "I knew I'd see Jamie again at Christmas and get my hug then," Dungy wrote in his memoir, *Quiet Strength.*

The next month the Colts finally lost their first game. Three days later Dungy's phone rang at 1:45 A.M. "I hope one of our players isn't hurt," Dungy thought. But it wasn't one of his players. Jamie had been found in his apartment in Tampa after hanging himself. "As the nurse was speaking to me, I frantically began to pray for Jamie," Dungy wrote. "But as her words sank in, it became increasingly clear that we were beyond that point. Jamie was gone."

Beyond the pain he faced as a father, Dungy also faced a leadership challenge. The entire Colts organization flew to Tampa for the funeral. Dungy addressed the team in his eulogy. "Continue being who you are," he said. "If anything, be bolder in who you are, because our boys are getting a lot of wrong messages today about what it means to be a man in this world."

The owner of the Colts told Dungy he could take the rest of the season off. Dungy discussed it with his family and decided to return to the sideline. With the Colts assured of a play-off spot, the last game didn't matter, but it mattered to the team. The game came down to the final play, a quarterback sneak from the opposing team. When the Colts held, the hometown crowd erupted. "Even though we hadn't needed to win the game," Dungy said, "the players had wanted to win it for me and my family."

The Colts lost in the opening round of the play-offs that year. The next season Dungy became the first African American coach to win the Super Bowl.

There was a time when leaders could keep personal tragedies like this away from the teams they led. That time is gone. The same forces that are obliging leaders to be more agile, accessible, and aware— social media, a younger workforce, a greater need for employees to feel invested in their work—also require today's leaders to be more open about their own lives. Vulnerability, once the antithesis of the strong leader, has become almost a requirement.

The leading voice of vulnerability these days is Brené Brown, a professor at the University of Houston and the author of *Daring Greatly*. Even though "soft" topics are usually considered the provenance of Oprah, Dr. Phil, and the like, Brown's message has been embraced by the business community. Speaking at an *Inc.* magazine leadership forum, Brown said entrepreneurship is all about the courage to open yourself up. "To be an entrepreneur is to be vulnerable every day," she said. It's a mix of uncertainty, risk, and emotional exposure. But while people often seek vulnerability in others, she said, they tend to conceal it in themselves. The challenge is to accept that vulnerability is not a weakness but the "absolute heartbeat of innovation and creativity."

Of all the qualities of Leadership 3.0, this one, being vulnerable, raw, authentic, has been the hardest one for me to learn. But it's also the one I learned most viscerally.

In 2008 my husband was diagnosed with a rare, aggressive form of bone cancer. Doctors found a ten-inch osteosarcoma in his left femur. Our daughters were three at the time. For six months Bruce endured more than a dozen rounds of brutal chemotherapy, during which he was hospitalized on multiple occasions. He then had a seventeen-hour surgery in which doctors removed his femur and replaced it with titanium, relocated his fibula from his calf to his thigh, then cut out half his quadriceps. Only two people had survived this surgery before him. Afterward he returned for four more months of chemo. For more than a year Bruce was in and out of the hospital, walking on crutches, losing his hair and body weight, and fighting for his life.

Bruce's cancer arrived in our lives at the exact moment when Endeavor had decided to rapidly expand, doubling the number of continents and countries we served and aggressively spreading our model. I was initially paralyzed about how to handle this situation. I was determined to go to every chemotherapy session and doctor's appointment, and I needed to provide stability for our daughters. But my demands were also increasing at work. My instinct as a leader, especially a female one, was to do what I had been trained to do: hold it together, compartmentalize, put on a brave face. Never let anyone see you sweat or, especially, cry.

But the truth is I had no choice. No poker face could hide the struggle. So I did the opposite. First I told my board. I telephoned our chairman, Edgar Bronfman, Jr., the one who'd pushed hardest for our expansion plan, and described my situation. The board would step into the breach, he said. Edgar's continuous displays of emotional intelligence and grace had helped me through many stressful situations, so in one sense I wasn't surprised by his reaction. Nor did it surprise me when the Endeavor team blossomed in my absence, with everyone adjusting and taking on slightly different roles. The expansion continued.

But what happened next did surprise me. By mid-2009 Bruce had been declared cancer-free and I returned to work full-time. But the experience had changed me. And so I let down my guard, dismantling the wall I'd built to separate Endeavor issues from personal ones. I kept the team informed of Bruce's progress. I shared how the twins were responding. I even broke down on occasion. Rather than freak teammates out and distance me from them—Would they know what to say? Would they consider me weak?—my vulnerability drew us closer.

And it changed me as a leader. By showing my true self, by revealing that I needed other people, by communicating through every meeting, e-mail, and, yes, the occasional tear that I wasn't invincible, I allowed people—especially employees—to relate to me as they never had before. By indicating that I needed help, I received it in ways I never would have otherwise.

And our organization's culture was transformed. Several younger team members came up to me and admitted that before my family crisis, while they'd admired my passion and entrepreneurial pluck, they hadn't found me, well, relatable. Now that they thought they knew who I was *as a person*, they said they were more willing to follow me anywhere.

I had always thought I needed to be invincible as a leader, that we must mimic the stone-faced expressions of the marbled leaders we grew up admiring. But those unfeeling faces are exactly what's become outmoded. Because a core tendency of entrepreneurs is to be forces of creative destruction, entrepreneurial leaders need to creatively destroy old-fashioned leadership styles. The risk is that you may make yourself a little more exposed; the reward is a deeper bond with your team.

Leave the marble and bronze for the Caesars, Lincolns, and Pattons. Today's leaders must display a much wider emotional breadth. You can begin by embracing the four A's of Leadership 3.0: Be agile, accessible, aware, and authentic.

And in so doing, kick some A.

CHAPTER 7

A Circle of Mentors

They call him the Nerd Whisperer. The Gipper. The Coach. He's one of the most influential people in Silicon Valley, yet few people outside a small circle have ever heard his name. He likes to hug. He likes to tease. He likes to curse. And he's quietly amassed a reputation as the most effective, behind-the-scenes adviser in American business.

Bill Campbell is the ultimate example of an entrepreneur's best friend. He's a mentor. Eric Schmidt said of him: "His contribution to Google—it is literally not possible to overstate." Danny Shader, the CEO of PayNearMe, said: "Outside of my father, he's the most important male figure in my life." Steve Jobs, who used to take weekly walks with Campbell and who put him on Apple's board, said: "There's something deeply human about him."

Born and raised in Pennsylvania steel country, Bill Campbell was a failure at his first major job. As the coach of the Columbia University football team he was 12-41-1. His fatal flaw, he said, was that he wasn't tough enough to ask players to put football first. He went to work in advertising and became vice president of sales at Apple, where he helped get the company's famous "1984" ad past naysayers and onto the air during Super Bowl XVIII. Later he ran a failed start-up and served as the chief executive of Claris and Intuit.

But it's Campbell's role as an informal adviser that generated his greatest impact. With a style that *Fortune* likened to a mash-up of Oprah, Yoda, and the college football coach Joe Paterno, Campbell became the man top entrepreneurs in Silicon Valley called when they got into a jam.

His first client was Jeff Bezos. Amazon's board brought Campbell in to ensure that the former Wall Streeter had the "operational chops" to run a business. At Google, Campbell was recruited when Schmidt joined as CEO to smooth the transition with the company's cofounders. Schmidt's initial reaction: "I don't need any help." But soon Campbell was helping him tweak everything from how he hired senior executives to how he ran board meetings. As Schmidt put it, "I'll say, 'What should we talk about at the meeting?' and he'll say the three most interesting things and the tone." When Google acquired YouTube, Campbell was dispatched to offer the same guidance to the CEO Chad Hurley.

What does Campbell believe he's offering? "Since I've been around a little bit, I give a little advice here and there," he said. "How fast they should grow, how fast they should hire, how they should raise money, how they should use the money, and when they should bring in financial people." And what does he charge for his services? "My fees are well known," he told the *New York Times*. "Zero. Nobody has to negotiate with me." At Google he did get a coveted parking space.

Few ideas in business conjure up more vivid images of bold individualism than the do-it-yourself entrepreneur. Entrepreneurs go it alone, the mythology insists. Even when working in pairs or small groups, entrepreneurs are considered swashbuckling mavericks, bucking the establishment, tilting at windmills. The philosopher Ayn Rand captured this ideal in her novels *The Fountainhead* and *Atlas Shrugged*, and today she's often celebrated in entrepreneurial circles for glorifying the morality of individual achievement. The economist Friedrich

Hayek championed the idea that societal changes are wrought by creative lone wolves.

That image of self-reliance is irresistibly romantic, deeply entrenched, and completely misleading. Far more than others in business, entrepreneurs need help. Lots of it. A survey we did of Endeavor entrepreneurs showed that the most valuable contribution to their success—outside of their team—came not from those who provided financing but from those who gave good advice. As one entrepreneur put it, "There's lots of money out there, and it's all worth the same. But there's not a lot of good advice."

In this chapter I'll tell you the best way to get that advice. From the beginning, mentorship has been a big part of our model at Endeavor. In our first fifteen years, our volunteer mentors provided over a million hours of counseling to our entrepreneurs. Tom Friedman, in *The World Is Flat*, called us "mentor capitalists." What I've learned is that nearly everything people think about mentors is wrong. For starters, forget that notion that you have to spend years finding and wooing the "right person" to settle down into a lifelong relationship with. A mentor as your soulmate?

Not anymore. These days, you need one set of mentors early in your career and a different set later. You need mentors for leadership, mentors for brand building, and mentors for dealing with that pain-in-the-butt colleague who's holding you back. You even need mentors who are *younger* than you to help you see what's coming.

In our hyperfast age, mentoring relationships are no longer marriages that go on for a half century. If you want to go big, you need a team of mentors. As Kathy Kram, the leading expert in the field, said, "The advice used to be, 'Go find yourself a mentor.' Now the advice is to build a small network of five to six individuals who take an active interest in your professional development." Save monogamy for your private life; in your work life, you want to be polymentor-ish.

So what does that configuration look like? To me, the right model is a 360-degree approach: a circle of advisers who can give you a rotating mixture of tough love, specialized advice, fresh insights, and clear direction. This circle of mentors is as disruptive to the traditional workplace as entrepreneurship is to the traditional economy. And not surprisingly, entrepreneurs are leading the revolution. Here's what you need to do to join.

— GET YOURSELF A SIMON COWELL —

The first myth I want to explode about mentors is that they're your protectors whose chief job is to shield you from harm and make you feel good. They're not. They're bearers of the truth—or at least should be. But that raises the undeniable question: Can you handle the truth?

The English word "mentor" is derived from Homer's *Odyssey*. In the classic epic poem, when Odysseus goes off to fight in the Trojan War, he puts his young son, Telemachus, under the care of his friend Mentor. The surrogate father figure is supposed to be wise and encouraging. In actuality, Mentor does his job poorly (he robs the boy), and Telemachus grows up to be too timid to stand up to the unwanted suitors courting his mother. The goddess Athena, disguised as Mentor, steps in. "Forget the pastimes of a child," she tells Telemachus. "You are a boy no longer." Athena urges Telemachus to man up, confront the suitors, and go abroad to find his father. This is the tough love he needs. Telemachus heeds the advice, kills the suitors, reunites with his father, and becomes the epitome of perseverance.

This tradition of tough love is still alive in the land where the Trojan War was fought.

The döner is to Turkey what the hot dog is to the United States. A popular street food made from sliced meat and served on the go, the döner is a symbol of Turkey's deep roots as a hub of travel and trading. But as the country became more prosperous, a new generation of Turkish families was turned off by eating food from street vendors. The entrepreneurs Levent Yilmaz and Feridun Tunçer saw an opening. They would create a casual restaurant chain specializing in Iskender döners, those drenched in tomato sauce and yogurt but served in a clean, sit-down environment. They called their company Baydöner ("Mr. Döner") and focused on the new wave of shopping mall food courts, vowing to make their restaurants meet international standards.

Levent and Feridun were ambitious. As soon as they opened their first restaurant, they registered the Baydöner brand in twenty other countries. They believed they could quickly open two hundred stores across Turkey and would soon have a Baydöner in every food court in the Middle East and Europe. And they got off to a promising start: Their flagship restaurant broke even within a year, and over the next five years they opened forty stores across Turkey.

Still, when the fast-moving founders joined Endeavor, our mentors quickly offered sobering advice: Go slow. First, the entrepreneurs faced real estate challenges because mall construction was slowing. Second, wages were already beginning to creep up, pressuring their bottom line. Finally, expanding to new markets would be hard. Customers might have different tastes and workers different skills. A Saudi mentor said expansion would require more training because local employees wouldn't know how to make a döner. Sami Khouri, the head of a Lebanese conglomerate, was blunter: "You should go big in Turkey before going abroad."

For the empire-minded entrepreneurs, the advice was hard to hear. But a year later Levent told me it was the best advice he ever received. "Sami was right. We were not even at seventy stores in Turkey, and our aim was two hundred and fifty. Before we expand internationally, we have to finish our national expansion. Then we can try for the world."

In my experience, what entrepreneurs think they want from a mentor is wrong. They believe they're looking for a wise elder statesman who will eagerly open doors and gingerly offer encouragement; instead, what they need is a tough-talking truth teller. In lieu of a warm bath, most entrepreneurs need a cold shower.

The best mentor-mentee relationships I've seen follow this path. They thrive on painful honesty. The Internet pioneer Kevin Ryan is a frequent Endeavor mentor. Kevin is a serial entrepreneur whose ventures include Gilt Groupe, Business Insider, and 10gen. His natural instinct is to encourage entrepreneurs. Yet he's learned he's most effective when he's delivering his harshest advice. In 2009 Kevin met Amin Amin, a young Jordanian who was attempting to improve education in the Middle East. Amin formed a company to train teachers. Kevin, who serves on the board of Yale, loved the concept. "I'm more passionate about education than anything else," he said.

But a year later the company was stalling, and Amin was feuding with his investors. Kevin was the one to deliver the harsh assessment. "I love the field you're in," he told Amin, "but this company is not worth your time." As Kevin told me later, "For many people, tough love is hard to hear. That's why it's called tough love! But in Amin's case"—Kevin continued—"it was not a difficult message to give because in many ways it was an inspirational message. Because he is so good, I thought he should and could launch a company from scratch."

A year later Amin formed another educational reform company, ASK, for Attitude, Skills, and Knowledge. Within two years the company employed over ninety-five people and generated revenues of $4 million. More important, its programs were showing results. Amin told me, "I was stuck in the details of my conflict with the investors. Kevin made me understand that we are stuck only when we make ourselves stuck."

Finding the right mentors and getting the right advice are hard enough. But the even bigger challenge is following the advice once you receive it. My experience has led me to a simple maxim: Listen especially closely to suggestions that you initially most disagree with.

This is particularly true for people who are already flying high. The bigger entrepreneurs get, the more closed their ears become. In 2009 Twitter was a rapidly growing start-up with what seemed like an unlimited upside, but its organizational structure was a mess. The cofounder Evan "Ev" Williams was the CEO, but there was no CFO, CTO, or COO. The board kept pressuring Williams to fill those positions, but he couldn't make up his mind. The founder of several start-ups and coiner of the term "blogger," Williams liked to surround himself with friends—people he trusted and who would not question him. But by inviting only yes-men into his inner circle, Williams had no one willing to speak truth to power.

So the board intervened. It decided to bring in—you guessed it— the Nerd Whisperer, Bill Campbell. As Nick Bilton reported in *Hatching Twitter*, Williams asked in their first meeting, "What is the worst thing I can do as CEO to screw the company up?" Campbell's response: "Hire your friends." The coach then launched into a ten-minute rant about the perils of mixing friendship and business. (Fire your mother-in-law!) The founders of Twitter had never drawn such a distinction. Office meetings were social occasions, and nights out often morphed into brainstorming sessions. Campbell called this approach a recipe for disaster. Williams took notes.

And then the CEO proceeded to do exactly what the mentor had warned him against. Williams put his sister in charge of procurement for the company kitchen and hired his wife to redesign the company's office. He also brought in vanloads of friends from Google, including Dick Costolo, who had recently sold his start-up to the search giant. Williams ran into his old pal at a party and asked him on the spot if he would become COO. Costolo later tweeted, "First full day as Twitter COO tomorrow. Task #1: undermine CEO, consolidate power."

A former professional improv comedian, Costolo was joking, though his tweet proved prescient. Williams and Campbell had begun meeting weekly by then, and though @ev was always willing to listen to Campbell's advice, he seemed loath to execute it. This made Twitter's board members unhappy. They believed Williams's indecision was creating an organizational pileup. Costolo, meanwhile, was excelling as COO, including brokering $25 million in deals with Microsoft and Google. Faced with a CEO who would not take advice from either his formal board or the best mentor in the industry, the board stepped in. Williams was asked to step down. His replacement: his old friend @dickc.

Just because you have the vision and moxie to get an initiative going doesn't mean you can make the tough decisions to help it go big. The skills are quite different, and knowing the moment to pivot is almost impossible to detect. You need someone to provide honest advice, and then you need to act on it.

A colorful example of why truth telling can be more effective than sweet talking is Simon Cowell, the acerbic music executive who skyrocketed to infamy in the early 2000s by dispensing withering critiques on *American Idol*. Among his most notorious zingers:

"You sound like a cat jumping off the Empire State Building."

"It was a little bit like a chihuahua trying to be a tiger."

"Whoever your voice coach is, fire her!"

Cowell's antics inevitably produced a backlash. When Maroon 5 lead singer Adam Levine was recruited to mentor young singers on a rival show, *The Voice*, he told producers, "We're not going to make fun of these people. We're not going to sit there and criticize them in a mean way." But while *The Voice* is a fun show and a ratings success (OK, I admit it: I watch), it has yet to produce a breakout star. Cowell, meanwhile, helped launch at least a half dozen multiplatinum acts, including Kelly Clarkson, Carrie Underwood, Susan Boyle, and One Direction. "It's not about winning a silly trophy," Cowell said. "It's about mentoring someone to become a star."

If you want someone to make you feel good (or even someone who's good to look at), find yourself an Adam Levine. But if you want to go big, get yourself a Simon Cowell.

— CUT THE CORD —

The second big myth about mentors is that you find them when you're getting started and keep them for the rest of your career. Wrong. For starters, you need a different set of mentors with each successive set of challenges you face. But even more important, the mentors you acquire early in your career may give bad advice, grow bored with you, become your rival, or otherwise outlive their usefulness. You have to find a way to move on and get the help you need.

There comes a time when you have to cut the cord.

As a boy growing up in Jordan, Ala' Alsallal loved books. He loved them so much he couldn't wait to read the latest Harry Potter volume in Arabic. But the lag time was usually eight months, so Ala' translated the books himself and posted them online. His lag time: three months. While his pluck was admirable, his business was unlawful, as he learned soon enough, when the books' publisher shut him down.

But Ala' would not be squelched. While doing graduate work in computer science, he crafted a plan to open the first online bookseller in the Middle East. This idea was foolhardy in a number of regards: (1) Internet access was still a luxury in the Arab world, (2) fearing fraud, customers were reluctant to enter their credit cards, and (3) Amazon had a twenty-five-year head start and was known for crushing competitors. Ala' didn't care. He registered the domain name Jamalon.com ("top of the pyramid") and wrote a business plan. Then he stalked potential mentors.

His initial target was the perfect early-stage mentor, Fadi Ghandour, the founder of the global logistics company Aramex, the first Arabic company to go public on NASDAQ. Fadi, also an Endeavor board member, loves entrepreneurs. And he's a truth teller. "Ala' was kind of a pain in the ass, in a good way," Fadi said. "I knew the first time I met him that he was special." But his business model wasn't ready. "I told him to finish his degree, go back, and work on it," Fadi said.

Two years later, degree in hand, Ala' launched Jamalon.com out of his family's home with a $2,000 investment. When an order would come in, Ala' would buy the book from the publisher and ship it to the customer. To promote his brand, he painted the family van purple and drove it around town. After two months Ala' scored a $15,000 seed investment from Fadi and the same from another backer. Everyone else turned him down. "Amazon will slaughter you," people said.

Ala' entered the Endeavor network two years later, and while his growth had been steady, we had the same concerns. So we did something radical. We telephoned Diego Piacentini, the head of international business at Amazon. If Amazon were going to swallow up Jamalon, Diego would be doing the swallowing. But Diego was also Endeavor Mentor of the Year in 2011. "I envy entrepreneurs," Diego told me. "Early in my career I became a company executive. I'm inspired by people who start their own ventures."

At first the two were allies. Diego advised Ala' to change his business model. Instead of ordering books on demand, Jamalon started warehousing its fifteen thousand most popular titles, allowing for quick delivery. Diego also brokered a deal between Jamalon and Amazon that would fulfill Jamalon orders outside the Middle East. For Ala', working with Diego was helpful—and tactical. "I like maintaining a good relationship with competitors," he said. But then Jamalon started growing, and Diego realized that Ala's model overlapped too much with Amazon's; he could no longer give impartial advice. "I can't wear two hats in this situation," Diego said.

Ala' wanted to maintain the lifeline, but I told him it was time to cut the cord. Diego and Ala' maintained a personal relationship but parted ways professionally.

Another way you might outgrow your mentor is if you enter a new profession. After you cut the cord with your old life, you need a midwife to your new one. This is especially true for butterflies who choose to become entrepeneurs after pursuing more traditional paths. This need has become so widespread a novel solution has emerged.

Gerry Owen was a fiftysomething assistant pastor at a megachurch in Garland, Texas, when he retrieved the prayer box from the sanctuary one Sunday afternoon. Inside, he found a card: "Pray for me. I need to sell my coffee shop." Owen turned to his wife: "Can we do this?" Gerry and Melissa had been married several months before (in a coffee shop!), and Melissa had been dreaming of opening a similar place for years. But they had no experience. Melissa was an operating room nurse; Gerry had been an executive at Frito-Lay before entering the ministry. They needed a mentor, and they found him through the Internet.

In the early 2000s Duncan Goodall was a Yale grad and management consultant who hated his life. He was working one hundred plus hours a week and traveling all the time. "I was a virtual stranger to my wife," he said. So he quit and bought a coffee shop in New Haven, changed its name to Koffee on Audubon, and started a catering operation. He became known as Yale's "professor of coffee shops."

Eventually Goodall enlisted to become a mentor on PivotPlanet, one of a handful of new Web sites designed to hook up those dreaming of opening a business with experienced entrepreneurs. "The money is nice, but that's not the real reason I do this," he said. "On a deep philosophical level, I believe people are more happy and free if they have their own business."

The Owens found Goodall's profile on the site. For $2,000, they got to tail him for two days and get tutorials on everything from pouring espresso to arranging a pastry shelf. Goodall gave them some tips for going big:

- Employees are your greatest source of joy and frustration.

- Money is made by attention to the smallest of details (and the "right" details).

- If you try to be everything to everyone, you become nothing to everyone. Choose a specific customer niche and be everything to them.

Two years after reading the prayer request, Gerry and Melissa opened the Fourteen Eighteen Coffeehouse in downtown Plano. (The first thing Goodall had said to them: "Don't buy the shop for sale; start your own.") The new shop was shabby chic, with comfy couches, games, and live music. Inspired by Goodall, Owen distributed a manual that urged employees to "ADJUST," to keep tweaking what they did until they got it right.

The main lesson from these examples is that mentorship is like a revolving door. Whether you're starting the climb to go big or starting to climb a new ladder, get the advisers you need at each new phase of your career. And if your old mentors are no longer helping, continue to show your gratitude, but otherwise cut the cord.

— *PHONE A FRENEMY* —

The third myth about mentors I'd like to shatter is that they have to be more experienced than you. Sometimes the sharpest tips come not from someone who went through what you're experiencing in a different era but from someone who's going through it right now.

I've gotten to know a group of Turkish tech entrepreneurs who are bonded by equal parts friendship, business, and mentorship. They play poker together, go clubbing together, vacation together. At thirty-six and forty-five, Nevzat Aydin and Sina Afra are the senior members of the group. They met in the 2000s, when Sina was starting a flash sale Web site similar to Gilt and Nevzat was running an online food delivery business similar to Seamless. Their Turkish elders had no idea what they were doing. "We both had Internet businesses, which no one else understood, so we coached each other," Sina said. "As a young entrepreneur you can get information everywhere. The most valuable guidance comes from people who are dealing with the same challenges and pushing for the same transformational change."

One advantage of sideways mentors is that the relationships are often less formal and more frequent, allowing your peer to see through the more polished image you present to others. That's what happened to this group. Nevzat brought along another young entrepreneur,

Hakan Baş, who ran an online jewelry store. He easily fitted in. The buddies partied together and followed one another on Twitter. One day Hakan tweeted about attending a panel at a university, one of several speaking commitments he had accepted. Nevzat tweeted back, saying Hakan should stay in his office and do his day job. "He made the tweet sound so funny," Hakan said, "but it was also good guidance."

The next year Hakan made headlines when he became romantically involved with a model. Nevzat called him up. "People now know you as someone dating a model rather than the CEO of your company. Your personal life is overshadowing your professional life." Hakan was jolted but grateful. "Nevzat explained that he was not telling me to do anything in particular, but he just wanted to let me know what was happening. He cares about my image. Lots of people give me advice about business; he's more focused on coaching me as a leader."

Contrary to the conventional wisdom, sometimes the best mentoring advice comes not from the wizened sage sitting in his armchair but from the guy swaying next to you on the dance floor. New research backs this up. Kathy Kram, the mentorship scholar, and University of Virginia professor Lynn Isabella compared peer-mentor pairs with more traditional relationships and found greater reciprocity when the two were at the same stage in their careers. Peers "can coach and counsel," they wrote. "They can provide critical information; and they can provide support in handling personal problems and attaining professional growth.

This is the philosophy behind groups like YPO, Entrepreneurs' Organization, and peer support networks like the one British Telecom started. "We found that 78 percent of our employees preferred to learn from their peers," a BT executive explained. "But little money or attention was focused on this." So the company launched Dare 2 Share, a podcasting platform that allows employees to share knowledge and advice.

But what happens if the peers are competitors? That actually may enhance the advice. Kathryn Mayer, an executive leadership coach and the author of *Collaborative Competition*, argues that mentoring relationships can be even more fruitful if there's a touch of rivalry between them. "Frenemies" can also be your friends.

Consider two of the most high-profile rivals in modern technology. In 2001, when Google was just a few years old, its cofounders, Larry Page and Sergey Brin, met Steve Jobs. The trio went for long walks, and Jobs gave them advice. He even recommended his personal life coach, Bill Campbell, as a mentor.

But in 2008 Page and Brin were the recipients of one of Jobs's legendary tirades, which quickly led to one of Apple's equally legendary lawsuits. The subject: Google's foray into iPhone's turf with Android. And while I would like my young daughters to read this book, I think it's worth quoting in full what Jobs told Walter Isaacson about the incident: "Our lawsuit is saying, 'Google, you fucking ripped off the iPhone, wholesale ripped us off.' Grand theft. I will spend my last dying breath if I need to, and I will spend every penny of Apple's $40 billion in the bank, to right this wrong. I'm going to destroy Android, because it's a stolen product. I'm willing to go to thermonuclear war on this. They are scared to death, because they know they are guilty. Outside of Search, Google's products—Android, Google Docs—are shit."

Okay, Mr. Potty Mouth, you made your point. But get this: Only three years later, with Page set to return as the CEO of Google, he went to see the one figure in Silicon Valley who had made a similar move back to the helm of a company he'd founded. Page said Jobs requested the meeting. "He was quite sick," Page said. "I took it as an honor that he wanted to spend some time with me." But in Isaacson's recounting, it was Page who asked Jobs if he could drop by. Jobs wasn't thrilled. "My first thought was, 'Fuck you,'" he told his biographer. But then Jobs remembered that the HP cofounder Bill Hewlett had once guided him and thought it best to pay it forward. "So I called Larry back and said sure."

Page dropped by Jobs's Palo Alto home. The two lived fewer than three blocks apart. They spent their time discussing Google's future.

"The main thing I stressed was focus," Jobs said. "Google is now all over the map. What are the five products you want to focus on? Get rid of the rest, because they're dragging you down. They're turning you into Microsoft. They're causing you to turn out products that are adequate but not great."

A short time later Page gathered employees and told them to focus on just a few priorities, such as Google+ and Android, and to make them "beautiful," the way Jobs would have done. The following year Page announced that Google would discontinue some products and that he intended to focus on unifying customers' experience, the strategy that made Apple the largest company in the world. This time, though, there would be no accusation that Page had "ripped off" the playbook from Apple; Google's strategy had come straight from Steve Jobs.

— NOT ALL MENTORS HAVE GRAY HAIR —

Why would John Donahoe need any help? The tall, tastefully gray-haired, conventionally handsome fifty-four-year-old carries himself with the élan of someone who's been at the head of his class his whole life. And he has! He was an econ major at Dartmouth, earned an MBA from Stanford, and worked at Bain for nearly twenty years, including six as CEO. When we sat down to have dinner, he was the chief executive of eBay, credited with rejuvenating the e-commerce giant. John struck me as one of the few people in Silicon Valley who didn't need Bill Campbell's advice (though the two are friends). Surely he didn't need to learn anything at this stage of his career.

But I was wrong.

That night John told me a story that perfectly captures the way mentorship is being disrupted in the age of entrepreneurship. In 2012, when eBay had a market value of around $40 billion, John called the influential VC Marc Andreessen and asked for an introduction to the best young founder in Silicon Valley. John believed eBay's site was stodgy, and he wanted some advice on how to spruce up its design. Andreessen introduced him to Brian Chesky, the thirty-year-old founder and CEO of Airbnb, the white-hot online platform that allows individuals to rent anything from an extra bedroom to an entire house.

John drove over to Airbnb's offices and grilled his much younger "colleague" about how he satisfied customers' need for change, how he tweaked his design, how he updated his products. "I was furiously taking notes," John said. After two hours John got up to leave. "Oh, no!" Chesky said. "You don't get to do that. Now I get to pick your brain." The graduate of the Rhode Island School of Design then started quizzing the management guru on how to reorganize his team, how to centralize operations, how to lead. The two have been meeting regularly ever since. John said, "I got to tutor him on the timeless principles of leadership. He's been my mentor on how to run a more nimble entrepreneurial company."

These days it's not enough to have seasoned advisers to give you tough love and peers who are willing to give you direct feedback. You also need to have mentors who are younger than you. The reasons are not hard to fathom. First, younger people have access to the tastes, habits, and customs of their generation. If you're over forty, did you see twerking coming? Would you have guessed that an app that deletes images from a recipient's phone within ten seconds would be worth billions? Second, younger people know technology; they're digital natives, not digital trespassers. Finally, they're eager to help. Unlike trying to get on the calendar of an esteemed elder stateswoman, snagging a meeting with the social media whiz kids is a breeze. Just send them a Snapchat.

Some people call these relationships reverse mentoring, but I prefer upside-down mentoring. Jack Welch is often given credit for legitimizing the idea. In the late 1990s he ordered five hundred top-level executives to reach out to people below them to learn about the Internet. The concept has been gaining momentum ever since, picked up in places like GM, Unilever, and the Wharton School. In a rare academic study of the idea, Sanghamitra Chaudhuri and Rajarshi Ghosh found that upside-down mentoring was particularly effective in today's entrepreneurial economy because it forces companies to abandon their hierarchies and take the best ideas from wherever they come.

The biggest upside to these programs, Chaudhuri and Ghosh found, is that they keep boomers engaged and millennials committed. Merrill Lynch started a program to teach executives how to lead diverse employees; Lockheed Martin used one to boost morale among young people. One of the oldest companies in America, 176-year-old Procter & Gamble, used upside-down mentorship to tackle an especially dogged problem: the absence of women in top management. In 1992 only 5 percent of vice presidents and general managers were women. "There have been meetings where you look around at thirty people in the room, and they're all men," said CEO John Pepper. "This is screwy," he added, especially when the topic being discussed was feminine hygiene products.

So P&G launched a Female Retention Task Force and named the Tide executive Deborah Henretta its skunkette in chief. The first thing she did: changed the name of the group to the Advancement of Women Task Force. (Um, memo to anyone who's never been pregnant: "Retention" means something totally different to women. . . .) Next Henretta did market research to find out why two-thirds of employees who were leaving the company were women. What she discovered is that they weren't leaving to have children, as the company had expected. Forty-eight out of fifty were leaving for other high-stress jobs where they worked even more hours. They didn't mind working; they just minded working at P&G.

Henretta's solution? A program called Mentor Up in which senior managers would become the protégés of younger, female employees. The idea was greeted with skepticism on both sides. When the twenty-nine-year-old brand manager Lisa Gevelber was paired with the forty-three-year-old vice president Rob Steele, she thought, "What could I say to Rob that would teach him something new?" Steele was even harsher. "Do I really want this?" he thought. But over time their mentor relationship thrived. Gevelber explained that women felt passed over for promotions and looked down on for being moms. Mothers even felt that taking a sick child to the doctor in the middle of the day was frowned upon at P&G.

In the program's first five years the number of female VPs and general managers increased sixfold; by 2012, 43 percent of managers worldwide were women. As for Henretta, *Fortune* magazine included her on its Most Powerful Women list for six years in a row, and in 2013 she was named president of P&G's global beauty group. It took a skunk to put lipstick on a dinosaur.

In her bestseller *Lean In*, Sheryl Sandberg credits *Fortune* magazine's Pattie Sellers with conceiving a new metaphor for modern-day professional paths: "Careers are a jungle gym, not a ladder." The same may be said for mentoring: Instead of simply looking upward a few rungs for someone to pull you along, try looking above, alongside, below, anywhere you can to find someone to give you the gentle push you need.

– FEED THE LITTLE FISH –

Once you've gotten yourself a circle of mentors, there's one more step to make the circle complete: Become a mentor yourself.

In 2001 I was invited to visit a group of wealthy Mexican businessmen in one of the country's most exclusive clubs. As I was walking through the halls, I asked if I was the only businesswoman in the building. "No," said my escort. "There is one other."

I had been brought here by Pedro Aspe, Mexico's former finance minister, who was interested in encouraging entrepreneurship in Mexico. He offered to introduce me to some "key businessmen." When I walked in the room, I realized he had undersold the group: Ten percent of the country's GDP was represented, including Carlos Slim, who for a time was the "world's richest man."

Slim started off. "Linda, we don't understand. We're starting to see young entrepreneurs in Brazil, Argentina, and Chile. Why not in Mexico?"

"With all due respect," I said, "you are the big fish. Here in Mexico you tend to *eat* the little fish."

The men stared at me with blank faces. There was silence, which I promptly filled with anxious laughter. I glanced at Pedro, who nodded at me to continue. "If you want entrepreneurship to thrive here," I said, "why don't you think of building an aquarium, where the big fish— that's you—learn to *feed* the little fish?"

A year later we launched Endeavor Mexico, with Pedro as our founding chairman and four others in the room on the board. Over the next decade we set up offices in nine Mexican states and supported more than eighty high-growth companies. In 2012 Mexico's leading business magazine published an article about the country's thriving entrepreneurial ecosystem. The headline: BIG FISH FEEDING THE LITTLE FISH. The source: one of the men in that room.

Over a number of years Endeavor has done extensive research that demonstrates the ripple effect of mentoring. When entrepreneurs mentor other entrepreneurs the spirit of entrepreneurship spreads. Wences Casares, for example, the Patagonian sheep farmer turned Internet entrepreneur I met in the early days of Endeavor, sold his e-trading platform in March 2000 to Banco Santander for $750 million. The news electrified young entrepreneurs across the region. "If Wences can do it, I can do it too," they said. Even more important, Wences turned his attention to helping others. He became an angel investor, he joined Endeavor's board, and today he still devotes an hour a day to mentoring the next generation.

If Wences can do it, *you* can do it, too.

Scholars who've studied how phenomena like happiness and divorce spread have identified what they call social contagion theory. The idea is that when one person embraces a life-changing philosophy, he or she eagerly passes it on to others. The spirit of chance taking, change making, and dream chasing belongs on that list. Entrepreneurship is contagious. The chief way it spreads is mentoring.

When I first started helping entrepreneurs, I would not have placed mentorship that high on a list of things they needed most. Surely money would be number one. But two decades later I realize I was wrong. I've heard the same thing from so many different entrepreneurs that I now believe it's true: Mentor capital is even more valuable to them than financial capital.

Why? Part of it comes down to what I experienced when I was trying to take Endeavor to the next level. We had a growing organization and a wonderful idea. I had passion and desire. But I kept hitting walls. I would reach a tricky place and feel isolated, scared, and exposed.

At every juncture, the way I escaped was to turn to someone for help: colleagues in the nonprofit world, veterans of fast-growing companies, the first generation of working moms. I especially turned to my board. When Edgar became chairman, he unwittingly became *my* mentor, both guarding my back and pushing me forward. And he did it without any recognition. One reason mentorship has become so central to who I am is that I'm forever trying to help others who find themselves in situations similar to those moments when I felt most alone and someone stepped into the breach to help me.

Which brings me back to what I said at the outset of this book: The biggest barriers to success in the entrepreneurial age are not physical, financial, educational, or national. They are psychological. The keys to unlocking success are believing in yourself and finding others who believe in you. That last one may be the hardest of all, which is where mentorship comes in.

Everything in the life of the entrepreneur is conditional. If the work isn't interesting or fun enough, the employees leave. If the profit or impact isn't great enough, the funders leave. If the product or service isn't effective enough, the customers leave. Even your family's support is often conditional. The entrepreneur is always dangling on the precipice, at the risk of feeling abandoned, on the cusp of falling over.

That's why you need such a large circle of mentors. Mentors keep you balanced.

But how do you find them? That may be the most surprising lesson of all: Chances are you already know them—or someone who does. In my experience, the real problem in getting the right support is that nobody knows you're looking. It's been a common theme in all these discussions about going big. Sometimes the most important thing you can do is to admit you're vulnerable and need help in the first place.

It's like the old Taoist saying "When the student is ready, the master appears." Want to find the right mentor? Reach out. Tell those around you what you need.

Open the door, and the mentors will walk through.

PART III

Go Home

CHAPTER 8

The Purpose-Driven Workplace

*E*arly one evening when my daughters were in third grade, Tybee and I were walking to school to see Eden's class perform *The Tempest*. Tybee started excitedly telling me about a book she was reading, a girls' self-esteem manual I had somewhat heavy-handedly placed in their bedroom. She was particularly animated about a spread on fashion and body image through history.

"Mommy, can you believe all the things women used to do to look fashionable?" she said. "Some removed their ribs so they could pull their corsets tighter!"

"Oh, really?" I said.

"And did you know that in the 1920s, women started bandaging their breasts so they would have more boyish figures?"

"Actually, I didn't know that until recently," I said. "But I was just reading a book about how entrepreneurs don't just try to make money, they also try to make the world a better place. And I learned about the woman who undid those bandages!"

Then I told Tybee this story.

Ida Kaganovich was born in Belarus in 1886. Her father was a Talmudic scholar, so her mother supported the family by running a small grocery store. Ida moved to Poland as a teenager to study math and Russian, as well as to apprentice as a seamstress. While there, she became a socialist, dedicated to the idea that capitalism could not provide justice for women. Back at home, she met a fellow revolutionary, William Rosenthal.

In 1905 Ida and William, facing persecution, fled to Hoboken, New Jersey. Unwilling to take a factory job, Ida bought a Singer sewing machine and launched her own dressmaking business. "Why risk it?" friends said. "Because I don't want to work for anyone else," she answered. The dyed-in-the-wool socialist had become cotton-and-crinoline capitalist.

But Ida's figure-flattering dresses clashed with the undergarments of the times. By the 1920s, the bodice-squeezing corset of the Victorian era had fallen out of favor, replaced with a strip of fabric that flattened breasts against the rib cage. The bandeau, as it was called, was said to be necessary because it allowed women to dance the Charleston without their breasts falling out. For the fashion conscious, the goal was to look boyish.

Ida didn't have a boyish figure. She was buxom, and she designed dresses for "real women" like herself. "Companies used to advertise, 'Look like your brother.'" she said. "Well, that's not possible. Nature made women with a bosom, so why fight nature?"

Ida and William started designing an alternative—dresses with fitted brassiere cups. At first, these mesh cups were built into the dresses, but the cups proved so popular that Ida and William began selling them as add-ins for a dollar. To contrast with "boyish form," they sold them under the name "Maidenform."

From their shop on 57th Street, the accidental entrepreneurs launched a revolution. They took advantage of another hallmark of the new era: advertising. Their signature "I dreamed" campaign showed women, topless except for a Maidenform bra, working in an office or throwing a baseball, with the line, "I dreamed I went to work in my Maidenform bra" or "I dreamed I opened the World Series in my

Maidenform bra." One showed a woman in a red skirt and white bra, surrounded by ballot boxes and fireworks, with the slogan, "I dreamed I won the election in my Maidenform bra."

A Maidenform in the Oval Office: Now that's dreaming big!

By the 1930s, Maidenform was selling half a million bras a year; by the 1970s, it was selling 100 million a year. Ida's comfortable, affordable products liberated millions of women. But what interests me about this story, I told Tybee, is that it shows how not just fashion but entrepreneurship, too, has changed over time. In the old days it was enough for entrepreneurs to say they were benefiting society by offering innovative products, generating profits, and handing out steady paychecks. By these measures, Ida Rosenthal was a barrier-smashing success.

But times have changed. Products, profits, and paychecks are not enough anymore. These days, society cares how you treat your own workers. Customers want to know you promote the same values inside your walls as you do outside; job hunters want to know you care about them before they send in an application. Your culture is your brand.

And on that score, Ida fell short. A devotee of modern management techniques, the chain-smoking CEO sped up her assembly lines, browbeat her union workers, and argued that her seamstresses should be able to work longer since they got less fatigued because their breasts were "uplifted." The only place women didn't dream of working, it seems, was Maidenform itself!

In the first two sections of this book I've talked about what it means for entrepreneurs to get going and go big. But there's a third component to living like an entrepreneur. It begins when you focus on a series of larger questions: What purpose am I trying to achieve? What's the meaning behind what I'm doing? What type of life do I want to live?

I'll spend the next two chapters addressing those questions. Everything up to now might be thought of as the nuts and bolts of entrepreneurship. Now it's time for the spit and polish. I sometimes think of this part as the *art* of entrepreneurship. I call it "going home."

The first topic is how to build an organization that doesn't just maximize efficiency but is infused with values. Today, entrepreneurs are at the forefront of a new era in which organizations put talent at the heart of their business models. And they have no choice. Having grown up surrounded by entrepreneurial freedoms, workers expect flexibility. They insist on collaboration. They demand meaning.

I've watched leaders struggle with these issues for years (and struggled with them myself). Here's what I've learned: If you want to build a cohesive organization, it's no longer enough to think about your own leadership style; you need to spend an equal, if not greater, amount of time thinking about how to satisfy and nurture talent.

Leadership, as hard as it is, may be the easier side of that equation. At least you can control your own behavior. Creating an environment that brings out the entrepreneurial instincts in your workforce—a worldview we might call "employeeship"—now that's tricky.

Here are some ideas that can help.

— *PSYCHIC EQUITY* —

Look around any major city and you'll see the names of the biggest corporations plastered on the grandest buildings. Scores of companies from Dubai to Dallas have made their glimmering headquarters the public face of their economic might. The bigger the building, the more clout the brand.

But look around Buenos Aires and there's one name you won't see on a skyscraper.

Globant is a technology company started by four friends in a bar in 2003. From their base in Argentina, the scrappy founders set their ambitions high. "Our goal is to be the world leader in creating innovative software products," they said. Boosted by A-list clients like Disney, American Express, and Coca-Cola, Globant quickly spread to eight countries, its annual revenues topped $150 million; its workforce swelled to three thousand people.

As Globant's reach grew, the founders faced a familiar decision. They needed to expand their operation and rally their workforce for a new phase of growth. The easiest way to do that would be to consolidate everyone in a flashy, state-of-the-art headquarters. The press would write about it; competitors would take heed; the world would be on notice that a Major New Player had arrived. In short, everyone would love it.

Everyone, that is, except their employees.

Globant had made workplace culture the heart of its identity. It promoted team-building initiatives like Stellar, a peer recognition program in which workers, called Globers, could award gold stars to colleagues for promoting core values. It allowed employees to compete for new projects. When Nike invited Globant to bid for an ad campaign, the company didn't turn to its marketing team. It hosted a crowdsourcing session in which everyone in the company had a shot. One hundred Globers submitted ideas; Globant won the account, and the Glober behind the winning submission got an iPod.

Nothing tested Globant's employee focus more than the question of where they would work. The founders' instinct was to assemble everyone in a downtown tower. But when they plotted employees' addresses on a map, they quickly discovered that almost no one lived downtown. Forcing employees to waste time in long commutes would rob them of personal time and violate one of the company's core values: Globers set their own schedules. So the founders took the opposite tack: They built three smaller offices whose locations were chosen to minimize travel times.

The story of Globant's invisible headquarters perfectly captures the first major issue I feel you need to consider when focusing on today's workers: You have to know what motivates them. If you think it's primarily money, think again. The biggest single change in the workforce of the entrepreneurial age is the list of priorities workers bring to the job. Paycheck is on the list, but it's increasingly crowded out by a host of new considerations: impact, freedom, quality of life.

There are benefits to this new reality—organizations with fewer financial resources can compete for talent—but there are risks as well. Fail to give workers what they want, they'll walk.

One Monday morning in 1965 Bill Gore, the former DuPont engineer who founded W. L. Gore & Associates, was taking his usual stroll through his Delaware plant. But that morning he noticed something unusual: He couldn't name everyone. Instead of making him happy (business was booming!), the discovery made him upset. He quickly dashed off a memo: No Gore facility would have more than two hundred employees. Also, each facility must be interdisciplinary—no isolating the PR department or "siloing" the engineers. Everyone must be able to know everyone else's name and be in position to work with everyone on the team.

More memos followed, as Gore developed a philosophy he called the Lattice Organization. He wrote: "Most of us delight in going around the formal procedures and doing things the straightforward and easy way." Gore introduced an informal, nonhierarchical approach that unleashed individual creativity. His company had no titles and no job descriptions. There were also no "employees" or "bosses." Instead all workers were "associates" who were guided by "sponsors" and who organized themselves into self-managed teams. Gore's approach became known as unmanagement, and it helped turn his company into one of the most innovative in the last fifty years, succeeding in such wildly varying fields as medicine (heart patches), clean energy (air pollution filters), dentistry (Glide dental floss), and music (Elixir guitar strings).

Unmanagement did not work for everyone. Gore once said that for those who can't adapt to the amorphous structure, "it's an unhappy situation." The current "un-CEO," Terri Kelly, admitted that many workers still need more external direction. "Some people want to see a road map," she said. But the vast majority of Gore associates relish the freedom. They become designers of their own work lives, entrepreneurs within a collective of entrepreneurs. As one said, "This company trusts you as soon as you walk in the door to make good decisions." Today turnover at Gore is 8 percent, less than half the industry average. And it is one of the few companies to have been included on the *Forbes* Best Places to Work list every year since the magazine started the ranking in 1984. In 2004 *Fast Company* named Gore "pound for pound the most innovative company in America."

In an economy where companies compete on service as much as they do on quality and price, finding ways to unleash creativity is becoming increasingly crucial. Research from the Hay Group found that companies with highly engaged people have 50 percent higher employee retention, 89 percent higher customer satisfaction, and 400 percent higher revenue growth. Retail stores that scored higher on employee satisfaction generated $21 more in earnings per square foot. Still, most companies do a poor job at engaging their teams. A Gallup survey of companies worldwide found that only 13 percent of employees are engaged at work.

So what can you do to invigorate your team members? It turns out what you might think is the most obvious answer—give them more money—is not the complete answer. When Endeavor surveyed entrepreneurs and employees at our sixty fastest-growing companies in 2013, we discovered that they all used a number of strategies with employees that were similar to Gore's lattice. These include nonhierarchical structures, open and frequent communication, ways for employees to submit and implement ideas, and creative reward systems. As Nemr Badine, a digital marketing entrepreneur from Lebanon, said, "At the end of the day, monetary incentive is nice, but you have to cater to people's emotional needs. Make them feel like they are a part of something bigger."

It's what I like to call psychic equity.

A growing body of research shows that employees need more than the carrots that have long been dangled before them. Duke University economist Dan Ariely, a pioneer in this field, has done a number of studies to test the effectiveness of financial incentives. This research is tricky, he admits, because academics don't have the resources to do these tests on Wall Street. He did his first test in India. He asked eighty-seven participants to perform simple tasks, then offered them rewards ranging from fifty cents (a day's labor) to five dollars (a month's labor) to fifty dollars (five months' labor).

Conventional economics would hold that the participants' performance should improve commensurately with the size of the bonus. Ariely found the opposite. The lowest bonus group performed no better than the middle bonus group. Even more surprising, the highest bonus group performed worst of all. When Ariely replicated the study at MIT, offering sixty-dollar and six-hundred-dollar rewards to students, he found the same thing. In eight of nine times that Ariely did similar experiments around the world, he found that higher financial incentives led to worse performance. His conclusion: Human beings are naturally happy to do things but not when they're paid to do things.

Ariely is not saying that people should not be paid to work; nor am I. What he's saying is that thinking your employees need only a paycheck is out of date. Entrepreneurs understand this better than most because they're often cash squeezed at the outset. Without the ability to fall back on money, they're forced to find innovative ways to motivate employees. One technique: Rethink job titles.

The Endeavor entrepreneurs René Lankenau and Luis Garza realized that Mexico had a problem. There were too many babies and not enough day care. To address this pain point, René and Luis started their company, Advenio, to provide on-site child care at corporations, beginning in Mexico City. As Advenio expanded to new cities, the founders grew concerned they'd lose quality control, so they took an unusual step for a start-up. They hired a dedicated person to monitor company culture. Her title: chief mom. She in turn hired a dream manager to help workers achieve their goals. Not only were these job titles fun and empowering, but they also sent a message that each employee's success was key to the company's success.

Dolphins, because they work in nonprofits, have long understood the need for nonfinancial incentives. Nancy Lublin runs Do Something, a nonprofit that encourages young people to take action through social change. Each year it recruits more than two million volunteers. Nancy is the CEO, though she lists her job title as chief old person. One of her ideas: Give out job titles that make people proud. "People aspire to the higher title, so why not give it to them?" Nancy wrote in her book *Zilch*. "Better yet, you can make up a new title that makes employees feel valued."

Plenty of for-profit businesses are following suit. Pinterest designers are called pixel pushers. The owner of a candy store chain styles himself chief gummy bear. One ad agency calls its administrative assistants first-impressions officers.

Make a good impression with your employees: Let them have a say in picking their titles.

Another step is to follow Globant's playbook and give workers more autonomy. For years companies have been giving employees chunks of time to work on pet projects. At 3M, it was 15 percent of their time; at Google, it was 20 percent. LinkedIn has an initiative to let employees pursue an approved project for up to three months; that's 25 percent of the year.

But forget the arms race of percentages for a second. Quicken Loans has a program called Bullet Time that allows independent projects every Monday afternoon after one. Facebook runs a programming marathon called Prototype Forum that encourages employees to develop experimental products. One winning idea was Facebook Wi-Fi, which offers people free Wi-Fi at cafés anywhere in the world if they log in and give the company their coordinates.

Butterflies operating small businesses are also finding creative ways to grant employees more self-expression. At Artists Frame Service in Chicago, framers are assigned their own color screws. Jay Goltz, the founder of Artists Frame, explained the impact of the signature screws this way: "It creates pride of ownership." Also, the frames' quality significantly improved once autonomy replaced anonymity.

"When the wire on a frame falls off and it comes back, we know who did it," Goltz said.

The days when entrepreneurs could rely on their natural charisma and brilliant ideas to compensate for creating brutal places to work are over. Employees today have higher expectations. As Dan Pink pointed out in *Drive*, the best way to tap into people's intrinsic motivations is to give them freedom, mastery, and purpose. In my frame, these are components of psychic equity. They're especially crucial for the book-end generations—older workers and younger workers. Neither generation rates money as the most important form of compensation. Instead, Pink wrote, "they choose a range of nonmonetary factors, from a 'great team' to 'the ability to give back to society through work.'" And if they can't find that package, they'll leave. In other words, make your workplace more entrepreneurial or find your workers fleeing to launch enterprises of their own.

— CULTURE CLUB —

Every other year Endeavor holds a summit at which our founders meet high-profile business leaders to discuss strategy, trends, and how to make their organizations thrive. In 2013 one of the speakers was Jenn Lim, the CEO and chief happiness officer of Delivering Happiness, the company she cofounded with Zappos CEO Tony Hsieh. Jenn's mission is to inspire others to follow the example of the online retailer and make joy a core business strategy. At Zappos, workers are called "Zapponians" and they take "zolidays." Every year the company publishes a *Zappos Culture Book* with entries from employees.

Jenn's message to our entrepreneurs was that since your culture is your brand, your employees are your chief asset, so you'd better make sure you have the right assets on board. About halfway through her talk, Jenn said something that jumped out at me, because it captured what I and many of our entrepreneurs have learned: Successful leaders "hire slow and fire fast."

The first half of that equation involves your taking the time up front to not cost you time and money later. Zappos holds two sets of interviews. First, the team hiring asks candidates questions about experience and skills. Then the HR department grills them to gauge cultural fit. Zappos is so serious about culture that it offers $4,000 for new hires to quit after their first week, so as not to waste resources training someone who doesn't gel with the group. Think about that: Zappos will pay you to walk away after five days if you don't fit in with its culture!

What resonated with me about Zappos is that workers today aren't just recipients of your culture; they are ambassadors for it. They can't project your values if they don't embody your values. That's why you have to screen them carefully.

No one understood that better than Debra Jane Sivyer. Debbi was a high school graduate who found work as a foul ball girl for a baseball team and as a water ski performer. At eighteen, she met the economist Randy Fields; the two were married the following year. As a housewife Debbi baked cookies for her husband's office. Everyone liked them, so she thought of opening a store. "I knew my disadvantages," she said. "I was young, had no college credentials, came from little means. I was blond and people figured I had no brains." Her husband said her idea was "loony"; her father balked. "The thing that really got me going," she said, "was when my mom said I would fail."

The first Mrs. Fields Chocolate Chippery opened in August 1977. At three o'clock she had not sold a single cookie, so Debbi loaded up a tray with cookies and walked down the street, giving them away. By day's end she had lured enough people back to the store to make seventy-five dollars. By 1980 she had 15 stores; by 1986, 350 stores. (By then she was also buying 10 percent of the world's supply of macadamia nuts.) But she had a problem: how to hire people who embodied her upbeat personality and could re-create the "Mrs. Fields experience." Debbi remembered all of her customers' birthdays, for example, and expected her employees to do the same. So she devised a creative hiring strategy.

First, she brought out a tray of cookies and asked applicants to taste them, so she could gauge their enthusiasm for the product. Next, she asked candidates to take trays of cookies out onto the street and give the samples away, to test how outgoing they were. Finally, she asked them to sing "Happy Birthday" in the store, as they would be required to do if they were hired. "I wasn't trying to see how well they sang," she said. "I was looking to see would they be willing to do what I asked them to do to make the customer happy. When you're trying to build a business and make customers happy, you have to do anything it takes." Debbi called the process the three S's: sampling, selling, and singing.

As important as it is to hire slowly, it's even more important to fire fast. In *Good to Great*, the management expert Jim Collins talks about the dual importance of getting the right people on the bus and moving the wrong people off the bus. Collins says great bus drivers (read: great leaders) begin not with "where" but with "who." "They start by getting the right people on the bus, the wrong people off the bus, and the right people in the right seats."

Kevin Ryan, the serial entrepreneur who led DoubleClick from a twenty-person start-up to a global company with over fifteen hundred employees, calls this process addition by subtraction. He told me, "Part of building a great team is learning to recognize when individuals aren't working out and then letting them go." His advice: "Don't let a bad situation fester."

One reason I became obsessed with finding the right way to let the wrong people go is that for a long time I was not so good at finding the right people in the first place. To put it another way, I used to be bad at hiring, so I had to become good at firing. But while I agree with Jim Collins and Kevin Ryan in general—letting people go is necessary— my experience with entrepreneurs has led me to believe that there are better and worse ways of doing this.

First, working with founders in emerging markets, I learned that most people live and work in small worlds. Your employees are also your former classmates, your neighbors, the children of your mom's best friend, the kid who looked up to you down the block. You can't cruelly fire somebody and expect to do business, eat lunch, or go to the grocery store without incurring some bad karma.

Second, in the age of social networks, even an ex-employee is still a spokesperson for your brand. That person you just let go is posting about his or her experience on Facebook, broadcasting his or her views on Twitter, and leaving a digital trail of complaints that's forever available to the next recruit who types your company's name into Google. There are even sites, like Glassdoor.com, that serve as open bulletin boards for gossip about hours, working conditions, and who's got the worst boss. Forget the revolving door; these days the bigger threat to entrepreneurs are walls that talk. There are no secrets anymore.

All this has put more pressure on the art of letting people go. Nothing defines your culture more than how you treat people you no longer need or want around. The classic scene from the movies, one that's far too real for many people, involves employers cutting off their employees' e-mail, taking their keys, keeping their contact lists, and sending them on a perp walk with a lone cardboard box filled with droopy plants and water-stained photos of their kids. This kind of draconian action may be necessary in a few rare situations, say, at banks or security firms, where sabotage is an issue. Yet for nearly every entrepreneur I've ever met, this way of firing people is not only unnecessary but self-destructive.

There is a better way. You can move people out gracefully. Just because you make a swift decision to discharge people, that doesn't mean you have to rush their exits. You can allow them to use your office to find future work. You can offer to be a reference. You can let them notify others themselves. I'm not naive: It's still awkward and uncomfortable. I've practiced lots of termination speeches in the mirror. I've seen lots of tears. Anyone you force out is not going to leave singing your praises.

But if you handle yourself thoughtfully, people won't leave cursing you either. And in many cases, they'll thank you for the transition time. In today's hyperconnected world, that's vitally important. Our experience with entrepreneurs shows that when you're building a company, minimizing detractors may be even more critical than maximizing promoters.

This new way of letting people go is so crticial that even my daughters picked up on it. One day, when my girls were six, they were singing a silly song with some friends. The song was to the tune of "Happy Birthday."

> *My mommy hates work*
> *She fired a jerk*
> *She hired a monkey*
> *Who ate my homework*

At the end of the song, Tybee turned to her friend and said, "Well, actually, my mommy doesn't fire people. She just tells them they'll be happier elsewhere."

— *IF YOU CAN'T BEAT 'EM, YOU KNOW, LIKE, JOIN 'EM #FOMO* —

One summer morning on the fifth floor of the iconic Puck Building in New York's SoHo district, a swarm of new employees from the fashionable eyewear brand Warby Parker gathered for their weekly company-wide meeting. "This is actually our biggest number of hires," said Neil Blumenthal, one of the founders. At thirty-three, he was probably the oldest person in the room. "Come on up," Blumenthal called to a recruit. "Give us your fun fact!"

Fun facts are a Warby Parker tradition and one of many ways the company has designed its workplace to fit the temperament of its youthful workforce. Younger employees are different. They don't like to wait; they don't like to pay dues; they don't like to do drudgery. And it's not enough to roll your eyes and insist they do it your way. Your way needs to adopt some of their ways, the most important of which is: Their work needs to matter—to them and to the world.

At Warby Parker, one way that message is conveyed is to make the workplace more collegial. One of the company's eight core values: "Inject fun and quirkiness in everything we do." Fun facts are an attempt to do that. While no one has topped an early hire's revelation that she once held Michael Jackson's infant son, Blanket, today's entries are eclectic and, more important, bonding. Kate, from product strategy, is a champion rodeo barrel racer. Natalie, from customer service, was a fan dancer for Beyoncé in the Super Bowl halftime show. Julie lost her sense of smell crowd surfing at sixteen.

Warby Parker sells cheap eyewear over the Internet and in a handful of retail stores. By the standards of contemporary business, its young employees should be undervalued. Instead, they are empowered, upbeat, and engaged. "I know that technically it's like a call-center job," said Mikayla Markrich. (Fun fact: She was a Segway tour guide in her native Hawaii.) "But it doesn't feel that way. You think of the call-center stereotype: The people are old; they're miserable; it's kind of a dead-end job. Here everyone is so young and so smart. And we aren't treated as though we're just the customer service representatives. We're viewed as part of the team."

What Blumenthal realized was that to succeed, he and his partners needed to give their young employees more than just safe jobs with good benefits; they needed to give them a feeling of belonging. Every new hire gets a gift certificate to a Thai restaurant (the cuisine of choice during the founding); a copy of Jack Kerouac's *The Dharma Bums* (Warby Parker is an amalgam of two Kerouac characters); and a free pair of glasses, whether they need them or not. Every week all employees tell their manager their happiness rating on a scale of zero to ten. Blumenthal surveyed employees asking why they were attracted to Warby Parker and why they stayed. "And to both of those questions, compensation was dead last," he said. "It was culture and opportunity to learn and have an impact."

Warby Parker's employees are mostly millennials, a term that describes anyone born between 1982 and 2000. They are the most intensely studied of contemporary workers in part because they're the fastest-growing group—millennials are now 36 percent of the American workforce and will reach 46 percent by 2020—but also because they're so baffling to older employees. Researchers have found that millennials display three fundamental qualities that distinguish them from others.

First, they came of age in an amped-up, always-on world, so they expect the same at work. They are consumed with speed; they want it yesterday. The good news is, they've never known nine to five, so they aren't bound by old-fashioned time clocks; they're much more willing to work at odd hours and to crash to get a job done.

Second, millennials care more about their personal brand than the company's. One lesson millennials definitely absorbed from their parents: They can achieve whatever they desire. If they can't find personal fulfillment at your company, they'll search for it elsewhere. In one study, millennials indicated they were deciding whether to stay or quit a new job within weeks. Boomers, by contrast, expect to spend up to four years in a job before moving on.

Because of this, younger workers want to believe they *matter*. A 2012 survey by Net Impact found that 72 percent of college students said that a job that allowed them to make an impact was very important to their happiness. Their parents may have been content with putting in long hours at a corporate office, then giving back at the PTA bake sale or the year-end charity drives. But millennials don't see the boundaries between their work and their service to society, and they don't want to work for anyone who does.

The FAA, the fifty-year-old Washington agency charged with overseeing aviation, learned this lesson reluctantly. For years the agency's recruiters used a pitch familiar to the federal government. As Ventris Gibson, the agency's head of HR, put it, "Our message has always been that you should come to work at the Federal Aviation Administration, become an air traffic controller or aviation safety inspector, and you will earn great benefits. To be honest, for my generation of Boomers, that message worked just fine."

But for new recruits the refrain fell flat. Younger workers were looking for meaning, not benefits, and they saw the agency as a stale bureaucracy. With a generation of veteran air traffic controllers reaching retirement age, the FAA faced a recruitment crisis. In 2008 the situation was so dire the agency resorted to hiring high school seniors to fill its ranks.

Then it dawned on Gibson and her team: The FAA wasn't a stodgy bureaucracy; it was the foundation of a functioning society. Nearly two million passengers a day board domestic flights in the United States. Aviation brings families together, expands individuals' horizons, and allows nearly every business in the country to thrive. The FAA is the backbone of the U.S. of A.

So Gibson introduced a new recruiting message. "Now we really hammer home the idea that if you come to work at the FAA, you can be part of changing the agency that will change aviation," she said. "We talk to millennials about how they can lead the aerospace industry and make their mark." The agency's Web site boasts, "Working at FAA offers a unique opportunity to experience a career where your impact not only reaches throughout the aviation industry but around the world as well." The new frame worked. "It used to take us a lot longer to recruit the best and the brightest," she said. "Now that we have changed our value proposition, they land on our doorstep."

Finally, millennials need to be connected with others at all times. Having grown up in homes where their families were teams, having gone to schools that had students work in teams, when they get to work they expect to be part of a team as well. Millennials aren't bothered by flow charts and chains of command. One department faced with a rapidly approaching deadline? They'll happily volunteer to help finish the job. They also want to feel as if they have a finger in every pot and a voice in every decision.

One way to handle this is transparency. At Warby Parker the entire team comes together on Wednesdays to hear updates from every department. At Endeavor, Fernando and I had to go a step further, adopting a technique we saw our entrepreneurs use: job rotation. Our employees were always antsy about what everyone else was doing, so we instituted a career path rotation. New hires start on our search and selection team; after twelve to eighteen months they move over to service our entrepreneurs; a year later they may move on to launch new countries or other departments. Thomson Reuters was having a hard time retaining recruits because the newbies wanted to understand the whole company and were unhappy about specializing. So now the recruits rotate through three positions for nine months each. Retention rates of associates at Thomson Reuters soared to 95 percent.

Another millennial device gaining popularity is the hackathon. Started in the software industry in the late 1990s, a hackathon (the word is a combination of "hack" and "marathon") is an around-the-clock, caffeine-fueled binge, usually lasting a day or two, in which workers come together in a mad dash to complete a project. Facebook was an early adopter, having hosted over thirty hackathons since 1996. The "like" button, chat, and video functions all grew out of hackathons. These events are the ultimate way to crowdsource a problem, a cross between *The Social Network* and *Animal House*.

Or at least they were. Nowadays they've gone mainstream and often involve a competition, with different teams vying for a prize.

- In 2013 British Airways assembled one hundred Silicon Valley luminaries (including the Endeavor entrepreneur Vinny Lingham) and tasked them with designing solutions to increase the number of women in STEM—science, technology, engineering, and math. The hack? They had to do it while thirty thousand feet in the air. The event took place aboard BA flight 9120 from San Francisco to London. After they landed, participants presented their ideas at an innovation summit.

• That same year a group of skunks inside Boston Children's Hospital approached MIT about collaborating on a hackathon to improve pediatric care. Over the course of a weekend doctors, nurses, clinicians, dieticians, engineers, and coders came together. Among the proposals that emerged: RightByte, a mobile platform that assembles recipes for families facing food allergies; eNgage, a dancing robot that reminds kids when to take their medicine; and the Comfy Ball, a "smart" ball children can squeeze to signal pain.

What's important about these hackathon occasions is that they break down traditional time sheets and appointment calendars. They create a spirit of teamwork and collective problem solving. They do things, in other words, on millennial time.

And millennial time and values are spreading beyond their own demographic. Take DreamWorks, where employees' average age is thirty-six. The studio releases only around three movies a year, and its stock fluctuates on box office performance, so the founders, Steven Spielberg, Jeffrey Katzenberg, and David Geffen, thought hard about how to cultivate workplace culture. The DreamWorks campus has the normal Southern California mix of breezy pathways, picnic tables, and Ping-Pong. Employees are grouped into two-pizza-size pods. The company runs classes on everything from yoga to improv.

But more important, DreamWorks has adapted its culture to meet the expectations of millennials, who constitute 20 percent of its workforce. The company avoids dividing employees into silos. Anyone is allowed to contribute to any creative endeavor. The company even trains every employee on how to deliver effective pitches to senior executives. That means the accountants can comment on plot twists in an animated movie, and assistants can recommend songs for the sound track of an Oscar contender. To prove the point, the company lists every employee in the credits of every film. These policies have helped DreamWorks maintain a loyal workforce, with a turnover rate under 5 percent. As the head of human resources explained, "Each employee is encouraged to be their own CEO."

And that's the point. Millennials are to other workers as entrepreneurs are to the rest of the economy: Their energy, zeal for disruption, and drive for collegial creativity are infecting everyone around them. These ideas may have begun in the hoodied crowd but they increasingly apply to everyone. You can't beat 'em, so you might as well, you know, like, join 'em.

#Withit.

— PUT OUT YOUR FAMILY PHOTOS —

My final hard-earned truth about how to elevate your employees is equally simple in theory yet hard in practice: Tell them to get a life, or even better, get a life yourself and set a good example. And by life I mean a personal life that doesn't revolve around work.

About three years into Endeavor, after working around the clock for years, I went to visit our team in São Paulo, Brazil, where our managing director was even more driven as a leader than I was. She was running the most efficient office in our network. Her team was skilled; their productivity, off the charts. My first day hosted by Endeavor Brazil, I called everyone together to tell them how impressed I was. Afterward several team members pulled me aside. "We need to talk to you," they said. "Will you tell our boss to take a lunch break every once in a while? None of us ever leaves our desk. We're too afraid."

When I returned home to Endeavor's headquarters in New York, the first thing I did was book my first vacation in three years. I realized my team hadn't taken their vacations because they saw me working all the time and thought I expected the same of them. I noticed the difference immediately, with people returning from time off feeling refreshed and energized. I hadn't realized the signaling effect I had as a leader.

Today I make it known that I drop off my kids at school each morning and am home by dinnertime almost every night; if there's a ballet performance or a curriculum night, I will attend; I schedule regular family vacations. I may get up early; I may send e-mails before going to bed. But I prioritize work-life harmony. And my team can, too.

This lesson of setting boundaries is especially important in the always-on world of today. Americans receive an average of fourteen vacation days a year but take only ten, leaving nearly 600 million unclaimed vacation days a year. By contrast, the French get thirty days, they take all of them, and 90 percent still complain they feel "vacation deprived."

For the first time in my life I see evidence around me that Americans are growing more serious about stepping away. Zulily is an online deals site for parents and kids. Founded in 2009 by Darrell Cavens, a forty-year-old father of two, the site grew in its first five years to more than eight hundred employees. Cavens quickly learned that two things draw anxiety from team members: their paychecks and their chairs (specifically, where the chairs are located). "Don't screw up either," he said. But it took him longer to learn that a third thing was causing them anxiety, too: his around-the-clock schedule. Working on Saturdays? Check. Skipping vacations? Check. Sending e-mails in the middle of the night? Check. He did them all.

Until his wife made him stop. As he wrote in *Inc.* magazine, Cavens finally realized he was driving himself—and his team—into the ground. Now he leaves work early on Fridays and goes with his family to his wife's native Ireland every summer. "I've actually gotten better about not being attached to my phone over the weekend," he wrote. "That makes my wife happy, and it's been good for the team as well." Cavens continued: "Our chief merchant once admitted that getting emails I'd sent in the middle of the night or over the weekend gave her anxiety, because she felt pressure to respond." His effort to prioritize family time did not stand in the way of his company's growth. Zulily went public in 2013 at a market cap of $5 billion.

In recent years there's been a robust debate about the evolving relationship between work life and private life. By almost every measure, workers today value things that bring them joy and meaning. Foremost among these are friends and family. Younger workers especially may like to be "on" all the time, but they also like to turn off when they want. Two-thirds of millennials say they would like the ability to shift their work hours or occasionally work from home. And the clamor for flextime grows even louder as people grow older and have children. Among workers in the thirty-six to forty-two age range, 72 percent say that flexibility is key to their quality of life.

Going off the grid is the new status symbol.

That includes men. A 2013 study from BabyCenter, the leading parenting Web site, found that 79 percent of dads are involved in their children's bedtime routines, 61 percent put their families before work, and 75 percent make it home for dinner as often as they can. And these numbers are growing. The number of dads under thirty who say that being a father is important to them is twenty points higher than dads over forty.

While dads are coming out of the closet at work and declaring their love of family, women are too often still forced to conceal their interest in their families for fear of being passed over. In a study we did at Endeavor, the top three reasons women cited for leaving corporate jobs to start their own companies were: (1) need for more flexibility; (2) experiencing the glass ceiling; and (3) being unhappy with their work environments. One thing they especially disliked about their old workplaces: Their offices made working moms feel like second-class employees.

The two skunks at Clorox who combined their jobs into one, Suzanne Sengelmann and Mary Jo Cook, told me their company's willingness to offer flexible hours was a big reason they could attract top female candidates. "We discovered we had a competitive advantage by allowing women, particularly ones with children, to maintain a career while also spending more time with their children," Suzanne said.

This competitive advantage talk came as a surprise to me, given

Clorox's Bay Area location, which means that it competes head-on with the hottest Internet companies. But Suzanne explained, "Women were being recruited for dot-coms, which were seen as more creative, sexy, progressive, and entrepreneurial companies, but they insisted you work six days a week. We were able to maintain talent by focusing on quality of life."

In 2012 I gave a speech at a prestigious Wall Street firm. Before my talk, I was asked to lead a roundtable with thirty top female executives. These women expressed surprise when I told them that as an entrepreneur and CEO I fully integrated my family calendar and my work calendar, that my girls were regular fixtures around the Endeavor office, and that I often made references to Tybee and Eden in my speeches and annual letter to our network. This seemed completely alien to their experience on Wall Street. The most shocking thing several of these women told me: They didn't dare have photographs of their children in their offices for fear that it would make them seem less loyal to the firm.

Putting employees first means realizing employees are people first. That may be the most important point of all. At the end of the roundtable discussion, one of the women asked if I had any advice to pass on. "Yes," I said. "Put your family photos out!"

Until recently companies designed work environments to suit their needs and forced employees to adapt. These days, egged on in part by a new generation of employee-focused start-ups, companies are looking first at the needs of their workers and adapting their work environments to suit them. The smartest organizations are realizing that leadership is not the only key to a well-functioning enterprise. Something else is equally important.

It's employeeship. And it's time you got on board.

CHAPTER 9

Go Big AND Go Home

Dear Eden and Tybee,

As you know, I've spent a lot of time recently working on this book. I wrote it for anyone who dreams of trying something new. I wrote it for people who are joining companies, leaving companies, starting companies, or changing companies from within, and many who will never set foot in companies at all. I wrote it for anybody who wants to take risks but wants to do it without risking it all.

But deep down I was secretly writing it for you. I wanted you to know what I've been doing all these years and what I've learned along the way. I especially want to prepare you for the world you're about to enter. So as the writing draws to a close, I want to devote this final chapter to answering those questions directly.

First, a little background. As I sit down to write this letter in our Brooklyn home, you girls are downstairs, making rubber band bracelets. For the past few months you've been busy taking orders from friends, arranging your unsold wares on toilet paper tubes to make them look more presentable, and devising a discount pricing scheme: a dollar for one bracelet, 25 percent off for two. I suggested you raise your price, but you rebuffed the idea. "We want a lot of customers," Eden said. "People won't buy from us if we charge too much money."

At first, you called your enterprise KAO, for Kids Accessories Organization, but you decided you didn't want to suggest you weren't interested in profit, so you formed a company. You invited three friends and became BEETS Kids Crafts (BEETS being an acronym from the first initials of your names). You then developed a plan for a Web site and added a second product line, laminated bookmarks. You even asked for a Square Reader for your ninth birthday so you could accept credit cards! (I embraced your moxie, though when you tried to set up a table to hawk your merchandise in the playground nearby, I told you you couldn't do that without a permit.)

In short, you've become entrepreneurs.

Your timing couldn't be better. You are growing into a world that's quite different from the ones your grandparents and even your parents grew into. When your grandparents were your age, in Rhode Island, Maryland, and Georgia, they could expect to graduate from college and hold the same job for the next fifty years. Even when your dad and I were just starting out, people talked about following a career path, climbing the ladder, joining the rat race.

Today those paths are no longer straight; those ladders have tumbled; those rats are less willing to run someone else's race. As Tom Friedman said, "My generation had it easy. We got to 'find' a job. But, more than ever, our kids will have to 'invent' a job." Instead of following a course set by others, more and more people today have the opportunity to decide a course that they want to follow, then change it if that doesn't work, and pivot again if they choose. Rather than think of your life as following a single career track at all, you might be better off viewing your life as attempting to master a set of skills.

We don't yet have a good name for those skills. But we do know where they come from. They come from a group of outsiders who are committed to looking at the world a little differently and overturning traditional ways of doing things. They come from a collection of

"Davids," to use Malcolm Gladwell's term, who take on entrenched "Goliaths." They come from people who are not bound by convention, precedent, or habit but are committed to disruption, adaptability, and reinvention.

They come from entrepreneurs.

What I most want to tell you is that these skills will form the foundation of whatever path you choose to follow in your lives. It doesn't matter whether you start an enterprise, work for someone else, go into public service, or join a cause. (Or as is more likely, you mix and match among these.) As your mom I'll support you in whatever direction you choose (within limits, of course). What does matter is that you understand that accepting the world as it is will likely lead to a life that's, well, acceptable. If you want to have a more fulfilling life, you'll look at the world around you not as it is but as it can be. And then you'll take a step or two to turn that vision into a reality.

I have been helping dreamers do just that for most of my adult life, more than twenty years now. And I've picked up a few ideas for how to increase your odds for success. In the next few pages, I'd like to share with you what I believe are three key things you need to know to help your dreams come true. And because I'm your mom, I'm also going to remind you of what many entrepreneurs I know seem to forget: to find time to enjoy what you build with someone you love.

— GET GOING —

A lot of people will tell you the first step to starting something new is to have an idea. I don't agree with that. To me the first step starts long before that. It's a commitment to looking at the world through rainbow-colored glasses. A rainbow, as you know, is a refraction of sunlight through rain. When the light comes from the sun it's white, but when it hits raindrops, it disperses into a spectrum. You long ago memorized the colors: red, orange, yellow, green, blue, indigo, violet— ROY G. BIV, an acronym, just like BEETS.

An entrepreneur is like a drop of rain to a beam of light: You take something that looks one way and transform it into something else entirely, something that makes the world around you more beautiful and everyone else say, "Wow!"

My favorite story lately is one you taught me. Sure enough, it involves rainbows.

By day Cheong Choon Ng crashed cars. A test engineer at Nissan, Ng spent hours hurling vehicles at hard surfaces: walls, concrete barriers, other vehicles. By night the Malaysian immigrant with a graduate degree in mechanical engineering tried to bond with his two adolescent daughters. He found it tough. One evening the girls were making bracelets out of small rubber bands. Ng thought he could use his design experience to impress his girls, but his fingers were too chubby. So he fetched a wooden board from the basement of their Detroit home, studded it with push-pins, and used a dental hook to crisscross the rubber bands. The result was a long, colorful braid, like a bike chain, only thinner and more flexible. To turn the chains into bracelets, he fashioned fasteners out of cut-up credit cards.

His daughters were suitably impressed, and soon the neighbors' daughters were as well. His girls urged him to sell the gadgets, but his wife said, "No way!" The couple had saved up $11,000 in an education fund for their daughters, and she wanted to preserve it. So he used his jerry-rigged contraption to weave his wife a ring (smooth!), and she relented. Ng spent $1,000 registering his invention, $5,000 having it manufactured in China, and $5,000 on colorful rubber bands. He called his creation the Rainbow Loom.

But as soon as the orders began arriving in the summer of 2011, the crash expert hit his own wall. The rubber bands came covered with a grimy dust, so Ng washed them, first in his bathtub, then in the washing machine. The hooks came in the wrong shape, so he spent hours fixing them with a hammer, one by one. There were good days and bad days, he told *Entrepreneur* magazine. "But most of the times, they were bad days." Soon those days got worse. Retailers had no interest in the odd-looking gizmos, and selling them online fizzled. Then he realized why: No one knew how to use the things. So Ng and his daughters posted a handful of explanatory videos on YouTube.

Finally a call came: The owner of a Learning Express franchise in Alpharetta, Georgia, wanted twenty-four looms. Two days later she called again and ordered forty-eight more. A week later she placed an order worth $10,000. Ng said, "My wife and I were looking at the computer where the orders came in. We were staring at it for three minutes." It was a year after he had made her the ring, and the couple had already earned back their daughters' college fund.

The Learning Express owner quickly spread the word to her 130 fellow franchisees. The crafts store Michaels caught wind of the trend. And in the summer of 2012 Rainbow Loom went viral at girls' overnight summer camps. As one retailer said, "The last time parents were this hot and heavy over a toy, it was Beanie Babies." Ng quit his job as a crash tester and went to work on Rainbow Loom full-time, as did his wife. Eventually they rented a seventy-five-hundred-square-foot warehouse. In 2013 the company sold 3.5 million units with a retail price of $16.99. You certainly did your share, girlies: You each have your own looms, and you've given and received more than a dozen more as gifts. As parents Dad and I like them because they're creative and social, and they keep you off electronic devices. Even better, the Ngs' entrepreneurial vision has inspired your own.

For his part, Ng said he was overwhelmed that Rainbow Loom had tapped into a generation. "I am still waking up every morning and asking myself and telling myself at the same time: 'Is this for real?'" His answer: "This is real. This is a dream come true."

Sometimes seeing things differently leads to starting a company, as Ng did. Sometimes it's taking anything that's been done the same way for a long time and upending it.

One of your favorite singers, Beyoncé, is a great example of how everyone, even those who are already on top, needs to take risk these days. Pop stars usually release albums with standard playbooks. They flood the radio with singles, pose for magazine covers, appear on TV chat shows, and partner with major retailers. This predictable buildup also comes with a downside: leaks, bootlegs, and digital piracy. Beyoncé did none of those obvious things (and faced none of those downsides). Instead, around midnight, ten days before Christmas, she simply wrote "Surprise!" to her more than eight million followers on Instagram, and her entire "visual album," containing fourteen songs and seventeen videos, appeared for sale on iTunes.

The stunt assured that the release was an event. The news generated 1.2 million tweets in twelve hours, helped by artists like Lady Gaga who were eager to further undermine traditional media. Katy Perry tweeted, "Don't talk to me today unless it's about @Beyoncé." Owning the album became a status symbol. One journalist wrote, "I like Beyoncé, but she's not my favorite artist. There's probably something else I could have done with the $15 I dropped on this. But because the availability of the album was a surprise, it became an impulse purchase." And the no publicity gambit assured that the publicity would follow. As one fan tweeted, "Beyoncé doesn't need publicity. Publicity needs Beyoncé."

The move wouldn't work for every artist, but that's not the point. The point is that by embracing measured risk, Beyoncé overturned the long, steady decline in record sales (hers included) and generated something rare—a pop culture moment. Her entrepreneurial creation was a new way of doing things. "I didn't want to release my music the way I've done it," she said. "I am bored with that."

And it succeeded, wildly. The album went to number one in ninety countries. It sold 80,000 units in its first three hours, enough to crash iTunes. It reached 430,000 copies on its first day, more than her first week's sales two years earlier. And it topped a million in its first week. One DJ said, "It's an instant classic, a game changer." He was right. Entrepreneurs don't reflect the world; they remake it in their image.

That's really the message I want to leave you with. The first step to acting like an entrepreneur is to look not at the writing on the wall but at the spaces between the writing. It's in the gap between what's being said (or done) and what's not being said (or done) that entrepreneurs thrive. Costica Bradatan, a philosopher and the author of *Dying for Ideas*, wrote that there is always a void left between what we are and what we can be. "Whatever human accomplishments there have been in history, they have been possible precisely because of this empty space," he said.

I wish for you girls the ability to see the gaps and the desire to fill the empty space.

But I also warn you: This will come with a backlash. Many will not understand. Some may even call you crazy. And you know what I say: If they *don't* call you crazy, you aren't thinking big enough.

If you don't want to hear this lesson from me, then hear it from Katrina Markoff. After graduating from Vanderbilt University with degrees in psychology and chemistry, Markoff traveled to Europe to pursue her love of food. She studied at Le Cordon Bleu and worked at the molecular gastronomy restaurant El Bulli under Ferran Adrià. He encouraged her to backpack around the world. Two things happened during Markoff's travels. First, she ate a beignet filled with frozen chocolate ganache. "That experience of eating this doughnut-crusty exterior and, when you bite down, this molten explosion of chocolate started piquing my curiosity about chocolate," she said. Second, she accumulated a suitcase full of exotic spices.

Back in the United States Markoff moved to Dallas and went to work for her uncle's mail-order catalog. He asked her to find an up-scale candy bar, and she quickly decided that there was little innovation going on in the world of chocolate. The global market was huge: $100 billion, with 20 percent of sales coming from the United States and most of those from women. (And if we're talking dark chocolate, count me among them!) But Markoff thought that "everything was just loaded with sugars and artificial flavorings and extracts and wax, and there was no story."

One evening she came home wearing a necklace from the Naga

tribe in India. "I was researching a little bit about the culture," she said. "Then for some reason I went into my kitchen and made a curry and coconut milk chocolate truffle and called it Naga. That's when it hit me that I could use chocolate as a way to tell stories about cultures, art, people, and the world."

That night Markoff ended up making twenty different flavor profiles, all based on her travels: saffron with white chocolate and sugar crystals to represent Gaudí's architectural masterwork in Barcelona; a Hungarian paprika and chocolate ginger. But she could find no one who shared her quirky taste. "Dallas in 1997 was still very much a BBQ town," she said, "and these people were like, 'I'm not trying that curry thing.'" Finally she found one woman who was willing to try her sushi special—chocolate with wasabi. "She took a bite and her face went from disgust and worry to awe and surprise to 'Oh my God, this is actually good.'"

That glint of encouragement was worth its weight in cacao. Markoff opened her first store in Chicago in 1998, and she now sells chocolates in two thousand outlets worldwide. Her annual revenues top $35 million. Besides her freshman class of curry, saffron, paprika, and wasabi, her high-end label Vosges Haut-Chocolat includes such mixins as olives, wattleseed, Himalayan sea salt, and bacon. She started a line called the Groove Collection influenced by African-American music and another inspired by *The Hunger Games*. She also developed a more mass-market all-American label called Wild Ophelia that sells four-dollar bars with classic American flavors like beef jerky, barbecue potato chips, and peanut butter and banana. It's now sold in Target and Walgreens.

To me, what Markoff represents is the fearlessness of the entrepreneur. About her offbeat flavor combinations and quest for good ingredients, she said, "Nothing is totally sacred to me. If I find a wattleseed supplier who has better wattleseed than Australia, I'll gladly go there. I'm constantly trying to innovate. I want to evolve. The recipe today will probably not be the same recipe ten years from now."

This bravado is especially important for women, Markoff said. "I think it's really important for women to have confidence in her individuality and not try to conform to being someone she thinks she needs to be." I would certainly love you girls to internalize that.

But mostly what I want you to learn is the courage to take your dream out of your head and put it to the test in the real world. Don't just think it; act on it. This notion may be best captured in a song we used to sing around the house. It comes from the ultimate candy bar story: *Willy Wonka and the Chocolate Factory*. And it's Willy Wonka's classic theme song, "Pure Imagination." "Come with me," he sings, into the land of pure imagination. There is no better life than the one you can conceive. "Want to change the world?" he asks. "There's nothing to it." Simply look around and imagine a better life.

As Willy Wonka says, "Anything you want to, do it."

— GO BIG —

The second key skill you'll need to bring change to the world will really test your creativity, as well as your sanity, your patience, and your resolve. It has to do with how to take your dream and make it as real as possible. That may mean turning your accessories partnership into a worldwide craft-selling platform or starting an organic asparagus farm (if you ever eat asparagus) or rethinking the PTA or writing experimental music or inventing a cancer drug. It doesn't really matter what your dream is, "going big" means doing it to the utmost.

To do that, you need one thing: other dreamers to share your dream.

I've spent years helping risk takers think bigger, and from what I've seen, the biggest single mistake they make is not learning how to work effectively with others to refine their ideas, adapt them, pick them up after they fall to the ground, raise them to the sky so they can soar again, then let their success shine on everyone who's touched them.

Dreamers are good at motivating themselves. They're not always so good at motivating others. I know this because I had to learn it myself. And what I've come to believe is that in this era, when entre-preneurship is everywhere, a new type of leadership is emerging. When I started out, I had internalized an old-fashioned notion of what it meant to be in command: Leaders are strong, steady, domineering. Today that's changed. Instead of being invincible, leaders are open, at times even vulnerable. Instead of being rigid, leaders are nimble. In-stead of bellowing from on high, leaders encourage creativity and in-fluence to bubble up from below.

You've seen the fruits of this in your own lives. When you were born, you received a Radio Flyer wagon as a gift. On your first birth-day, we put the wagon in the middle of the dining room table and filled it with flowers, diapers, pop-up books, and photos. Later you held the bar and pushed it around our house. You both loved that wagon, and it was incredibly durable, but the company that manufactured it nearly didn't endure. How it survived is a wonderful example of how to thrive in the age of reinvention: Make your dream a team effort.

Antonio Pasin was sixteen years old when he moved to the United States from Italy in 1914. The son of a cabinet-maker, Pasin started a similar business in Chicago, but the customers were more interested in the wooden wagon he built to carry his tools. They wanted wagons like it as toys for their children. So like any good entrepreneur, Pasin pivoted. The auto business was booming at the time, and he used some of the scrap metal that became plentiful to build a steel wagon. He called it Radio Flyer after two recent inventions, the radio and air travel. Helped by the 1933 Chicago World's Fair, Radio Flyers became a household staple. The business had sold nearly 100 million wagons by the time Pasin's grandson Robert took over in 1997.

The company was also at risk of going under at the time. Cheap plastic wagons were overtaking the market, replacing their steel an-cestors. Radio Flyers had become as trendy as Saturday afternoon ra-dio serials and Pan Am wings. Robert said, "We were a manufacturer, a steel stamper, and that's what we were good at. We weren't asking moms what they wanted in a new wagon."

This was Robert's leadership test: He could retool the company and survive or remain nostalgic and fade away. What he chose to do is instructive: First, he sat the entire team down and explained the situation. He let them know how serious things were but also provided reassurance, saying, "We're going to keep treating people here as well as we possibly can." Then everyone in the company joined in a year-long review. The process led to a decision to manufacture a plastic wagon and eventually to stop making the steel ones. Even more vital, it led to a rethinking of the company culture.

By the time I met Robert nearly a decade later, Radio Flyer was thriving. He was known as Chief Wagon Officer and had set up smile squads to organize team-building exercises like heritage days and company-wide volunteer efforts. Employees could nominate colleagues for Little Red Rule Awards for upholding the company motto, "Everytime we touch people's lives, they will feel great about Radio Flyer." Internal classes, called Wagon U, offered lessons on business. Robert himself taught one titled "Reinventing Radio Flyer Through Goof-ups, Growth, and Gratitude."

By reaching out to others instead of retreating, Robert remade the century-old company. Sales quintupled to $100 million, and Radio Flyer reached number thirteen on *Fortune*'s "Top 50 Best Small Places to Work." (He also started listening to moms. That wagon from your birthday party? Robert sent it to me and asked for feedback. I suggested a wagon that could hold more than one toddler, so you wouldn't have to take turns being pulled around. The next year he sent a Double the Love twins wagon.)

Radio Flyer's lesson about the need to actively engage employees and customers applies to all entrepreneurs, whether you're running a small company, redesigning a homeless shelter, or making letterpress invitations in your basement. It even applies when you're inside a big business. Some of the boldest entrepreneurial ideas these days come from within corporations. And to succeed, they, too, need buy-in from the group.

In 2009, three years before Taco Bell would celebrate its fiftieth anniversary, CEO Greg Creed was worried. "Our target audience is in their 20's," he told *Fast Company*. "Turning 50 makes us sound old, and I didn't want to sound old." He didn't want a celebration or a cake, he told his team. He wanted a new taco.

Tacos, with their bendable-breakable corn shells stuffed with ground beef, lettuce, tomato, and cheese, were simple but stale. Creed said, "If you look at all the buns the burger boys sell, and the bread at Subway, they are forever coming up with a new bread bun. The crunchy taco: It was yellow and made of corn. We sold a couple billion of them, but there was no innovation."

Creed's task was similar to Robert Pasin's: Reinvent something most people didn't think needed reinventing. And he took the same tack. He sat his team down and called for a group approach. Creed gave his team just under thirty-six months to reinvent the taco. The group began with an all-day brainstorming session at the company's headquarters in Irvine, California. Ideas included importing elements from burritos and nachos. But the wackiest idea was the one that broke through: Make a taco shell out of Doritos. The company's marketing director said, "It was like 'Holy crap!' Nobody had ever done this before: turning a Dorito into a taco shell."

But turning that idea into reality proved to be a nightmare. Problem number one: getting the flavoring onto the shell. The first thing the team members did was go to Home Depot and buy a paint spray gun, which they used to spray the orange dust onto the existing yellow taco. They quickly realized that wouldn't work because it would produce a nacho-cheese nuclear winter in the factory. The seasoning would have to be baked in. Problem number two: Doritos are made to be crunchy; taco shells are made to be malleable. Early prototypes were too fragile, too soggy, or too unevenly flavored. Problem number three: What did the public think? The first consumer taste test bombed. The team went back to work, then for the next round invited individual fans and bloggers, including an Arkansas man who had started an online campaign calling for Doritos tacos. This time the response was more encouraging. Finally, after forty recipes, the company rolled out a prototype. Customers went crazy. One Taco Bell addict drove nine hundred miles from New York to Toledo, Ohio, to taste it.

The company was eager to launch, except for problem number four: It had no formal contract with Doritos' parent, Frito-Lay. That would take months. So Creed invited the company's CEO to his office. The Taco Bell chief said, "We both realized that if we let the lawyers get involved, this thing would get slowed down and bogged down. So we did a handshake deal. Everyone was like, 'You can't launch without a contract.' And we were like, 'Just watch us.'"

Doritos Locos Tacos went on sale in early 2012. The company sold 100 million of them before the contract with Frito-Lay was signed. The product was so hot that Taco Bell had to hire fifteen thousand new employees to meet demand—two or three people per store. In year two the company introduced a second flavor, Cool Ranch. That year revenues from the Doritos line reached $1 billion, with more products on the way, including a burrito with Fritos in it. As Taco Bell showed, sometimes the key to going big is not thinking outside the box; it's getting more people inside the box and letting them think and solve problems together.

In school you girls learned about safety in numbers. When I asked what this meant to you, Tybee said, "When you have more people on your side—like a revolution or a new idea like BEETS Kids Crafts—you have better chances of winning." Well put.

Want to go big? Don't go it alone; go with others.

— GO HOME —

And then the most important lesson of all: Go home. Make time for the ones you love.

The easiest thing to think about living like an entrepreneur is that these skills apply to only one part of your life: your job. That's a mistake. In the same way that entrepreneurs are redefining many of the traditional rules of the workplace, they're also helping to break down one of the most stubborn boundaries of all: the one between work and family. While it's popular to say you can have either a successful career or a meaningful personal life, I'd like to suggest you can aim for both.

I didn't always believe this; you girls taught me this lesson. Now it's one of the things I stress most to entrepreneurs. To make my point, I often use a twist on a familiar phrase.

In the early 1990s a small company in Southern California that specialized in motorcycle parts started making oversize exhaust pipes called Porkers Pipes. To capture their bravado, the package designer recommended the slogan "Go Big or Go Home." He later wrote, "Everyone from the company owner on down asked the same question, 'What does this mean?' My reply was, 'It doesn't mean anything.'" But the meaningless phrase entered California's hot rod culture and from there jumped to extreme sports. Soon it embodied the swagger of a new generation. (The designer, by the way, was like the woman who initially got only thirty-five dollars for designing the Nike swoosh. He received just fifty bucks for coining the catchphrase of a culture.)

For years I delivered this message to entrepreneurs and tried to follow it myself. Whatever happened, I pushed harder, faster, louder. "Go Big or Go Home!" I blared. I was like an X Games skateboarder, addicted to the thrill of the stunt. I occasionally retreated, like when Endeavor tried to expand to India and we encountered some resistance. I invoked Go Big or Go Home, and we pulled out. But in general, I knew one direction: higher.

Then I was on a business trip to Austin, Texas, and I called your dad. "I think I ate some spoiled guacamole," I said. "I threw up twice in the bathroom tonight." Well, it wasn't the guacamole. It was you! A few weeks later Dad and I went to see a doctor, and we learned we were having identical twins. We were overwhelmed, but we had little time to react. The next day I boarded a seventeen-hour flight to South Africa. Several months later my doctor put me on bed rest. "Tushie on the cushie," your dad cried out as I sat in our living room, two babies in my belly, two phones on my ear. I stayed that way until you arrived, at thirty-eight weeks and over six pounds each.

That's when I began to realize I would need a new slogan. I couldn't choose between my work or my family. But I couldn't give one up either. I would need to find a way to do both.

In *Built to Last*, Jim Collins and Jerry Porras say successful companies do not oppress themselves by what they call the Tyranny of the OR. Collins and Porras mention certain examples of such tyranny:

You can have change OR stability.
You can have low cost OR high quality.
You can invest for the future OR do well in the short-term.
You can create wealth for your shareholders OR do good for
    the world.

Instead, highly visionary companies liberate themselves with the "Genius of the AND," the ability to embrace two extremes at the same time. "Instead of choosing between A *OR* B," Collins and Porras argue, "they figure out a way to have both A *AND* B."

Entrepreneurs have the ability to do the same thing in their overall lives, I believe. It's one of the ways they can lead society at large. Instead of choosing career *OR* family, they can choose career *AND* family. Instead of aiming for work-life balance, they can strive for work-life integration.

Instead of choosing to Go Big *OR* Go Home, they can choose to Go Big *AND* Go Home.

Now, I'm not deluding myself. I know life is full of trade-offs. I know there are important work events I've skipped to be home helping you with your homework. I also know there have been times when I've wanted to make sure you were brushing your teeth and instead have glanced at my smartphone. (And you know it, too. One of your favorite ways to taunt me is to chant, "Mommy! Mommy! Mommy and her e-mails!") And I know I'm very lucky when I head off on a day-and-a-half trip to Dubai that your dad works from home.

I'm not perfect, but I do believe one of the benefits of being an entrepreneur is that it forces you to look at all aspects of your life as laboratories for reinvention. You keep trying. And if you make a mistake, you try even harder.

That's even more true today, when technology has opened up unimaginable new ways to time shift, delegate, share, and rejigger. I see more and more moms and dads scheduling early morning meetings or doing work late at night so they can be more present with their kids during the day. I see flextime, working from home, taking sabbaticals as ways for people to have fulfilling careers while spending more hours with their children. I see people giving up comfortable jobs in corporations to start risky ventures because they're no longer willing to work around the clock. I see the genius of the AND gaining favor all around.

Some people will tell you that you can't go big because you're women. I need you to know that they are wrong. Women have always been, and will always be, entrepreneurs. They're also daughters, sisters, wives, aunts, mothers, and grandmothers. Forget this notion that you have to "balance" these competing aspects. That term suggests some sort of fifty-fifty equilibrium, where you inevitably do each side poorly.

In the world of Go Big AND Go Home, you are called to manage both sides the best that you can.

Fortunately, there are role models. Tina Fey, the actress, comedian, writer, producer, and mom, wrote a book, *Bossypants*, mining the question of how working moms can survive in a male-dominated workplace. She fiercely defended the idea that women can go big. When she became an executive producer of *30 Rock*, she wrote, people asked her, "Is it hard for you, being the boss?" and "Is it uncomfortable for you to be the person in charge?" Fey added cheekily, "You know, in the same way they say, 'Gosh, Mr. Trump, is it awkward for you to be the boss of all these people?'" Her response: "I can't answer for Mr. Trump, but in my case it is not."

The secret to being a good boss, she continued, is hiring the best people and getting out of the way. "Contrary to what I believed as a little girl, being the boss almost never involves marching around, waving your arms, and chanting, 'I am the boss! I am the boss!'"

But what resonated most with me about what Fey shared is the extreme efforts she made to be successful at work AND at home. When her show first launched, she had doubts. "I now had an eight month old at home," she wrote, "and I wasn't sure that this new seventy-hour-a-week job was, as disgraced politicians say, 'in the best interest of my family at this current juncture at the present time.'" So she made adjustments. She had breakfast with her daughter, acted during the day, spent the evening with her daughter, then invited the writing team to her house until two in the morning, while her husband sat in the pantry writing the score for the show. And she would sometimes disappear into the kitchen and break down.

She wrote: "Of course I'm not supposed to admit that there is a triannual torrential sobbing in my office, because it's bad for the feminist cause. It makes it harder for women to be taken seriously in the workplace. It makes it harder for other working moms to justify their choice." But she also had friends who stayed home with their kids, and they also had triannual sobs. "So I think we should call it even." Fey's conclusion: She didn't want to give up her work; she didn't want to give up her family; she would have to find a way to have both AND.

These days more and more men are realizing that they, too, want to Go Big AND Go Home. The fashion designer Kenneth Cole is married to the filmmaker Maria Cuomo; they have three daughters. One day Cole was working in his home office when his youngest daughter, then eight, arrived home from school.

"What are you doing?" she asked.

"I'm working," he responded.

"Who gives you the work?"

"Well, I give it to myself because I have to get it done."

"Well, aren't you the boss?" she asked.

"Yes, that's why I give myself the work, and that's why I have to make sure it gets done."

His daughter strolled off, but the next day, at the exact same time, she walked into his office again. "What are you doing?" she asked. "Who gives you the work?" The two had the same conversation, then repeated it again two days later.

Not long after, Cole was telling the story to a friend. "She's a smart girl, but she just doesn't get it," he said.

His friend replied, "Or *you* don't. She spent a week trying to teach you a lesson, and clearly, you still haven't learned it."

When you're an entrepreneur, Cole concluded, it's especially important not to succumb to the temptation to work around the clock. "I've learned that I can't win 24 hours a day," he said. "I've learned that life is about finding a working compromise." Most of all, he learned not to subtly value his job over his family. And that's what I want you to remember.

Fortunately, you're the ones who taught it to me. One day, when you were five, I had just finished packing and was preparing to leave for a business trip. As the taxicab pulled up, Eden tugged at my leg and said, "Remember, you can be an entrepreneur for a short time, but you're a *mommy* forever."

I can't say it any better myself. Go big if you choose, girls. But don't forget to go home. (And come visit me and Dad every now and then.)

— *WHEN YOU WISH* —

Nearly two decades ago I ventured out into the world to find dreamers who needed a little help making their dreams come true. Along the way I met a woman named Leila. She had been trained to sell hamburgers at a McDonald's in Brazil but wanted to help her neighbors in the slums of Rio, where she grew up, feel better about their hair.

The first time I met her, she was soft-spoken, timid, and intimidated by the world around her. She looked as if she might break. But with every barrier she crossed, every person she hired, and every milestone she achieved, she grew stronger. Today she runs an international company nearing $100 million in annual revenues, provides jobs for over twenty-three hundred people, and is a role model for entrepreneurs.

I saw Leila recently. She was beautiful, confident, and brimming with new ideas. She's already picked out the location for her first U.S. salon, in Harlem. And this time, when I looked at her, I thought of you, girlies. I thought of all the opportunities that people in your generation will have that so many generations, in so many places around the world, never had before.

If Leila can do it, you can, too.

Walt Disney, who had one of the greatest imaginations of the last century, used as his theme song, "When You Wish upon a Star." It captures the essence of being an entrepreneur, which is to be empowered by fantasy: to live within your own illusions, then strive to make them real. Anyone can see things others don't. The entrepreneur does that and so much more, making the ultimate leap from conjuring to creating to changing lives. And as Jiminy Cricket told Pinocchio, these days "it makes no difference who you are."

Take chances, girls. Take the journey with others. And don't forget to take time to enjoy what you create with those you love.

But mostly, believe that what you imagine can come true. Because it can.

But not if you don't try. So when you're ready, take the advice of Willy Wonka: Hold your breath. Make a wish. Count to three.

Jump.

I'll be cheering you on.

Love,

Mommy

TEAM CRAZY

I want to begin by thanking the one thousand Endeavor entrepreneurs around the world. Your passion, enthusiasm, and doggedness inspire me every day. My goal has been to build a movement of, by, and for entrepreneurs—and you've done that. Special thanks to the many entrepreneurs (along with board members, mentors, and other supporters) who appear by name in this book, for sharing your stories, missteps, and triumphs.

Peter Kellner is a pioneer, partner, and friend, and his vision continues to shape Endeavor. Bill Drayton gave me the knowledge and push to start something on my own. George and Bicky Kellner never stopped believing. Stephan Schmidheiny, Peter Brooke, Bill Sahlman, Eduardo Elsztain, Beto Sicupira, and Jorge Paulo Lemann supported me before it was practical, or even rational. Jason Green and Gary Mueller were founding board members and steadfast guides. Kimberly Braswell was my ally and co-conspirator for many years.

I often speak of two eras at Endeavor: "Before Edgar" and "After Edgar." Since Edgar Bronfman, Jr., became our global board chair in 2004, I have been elevated by his mentorship, judgment, and camaraderie. A heartfelt hug to his incomparable wife, Clarissa.

I simply could not have built Endeavor—or written this book—without the breathtaking commitment from an extraordinary group of board members. You coached me, prodded me, schooled me, let me cry in front of you, gave tirelessly to our entrepreneurs, and took ownership of our idea. Beyond those already mentioned, thank you to Michael Ahearn, Matt Bannick, Nick Beim, Matt Brown, Wences Casares, Michael Cline, Paul Fribourg, Fadi Ghandour, Bill McGlashan, Arif Naqvi, Joanna Rees, Nicolás Szekasy, and Elliot Weissbluth. A hearty tribute to Reid Hoffman, who has steered me tirelessly through the publishing odyssey.

I am deeply grateful to Endeavor's partners: Bain, Barclays, Dell, EY, GE, SAP, Knight Foundation, World Economic Forum, Harvard Business School, and Stanford Graduate School of Business. A personal thank you to Pierre Omidyar and the incomparable Omidyar Network, and to the all-star team at ABRAAJ Capital. Without you, my dream would have stalled.

The heartbeat of Endeavor is the thousands of individuals in more than twenty countries who devote themselves to spreading the spirit of entrepreneurship. Led by an amazing squad of managing directors, these trailblazers serve on our boards, sit on our selection panels, spend countless hours mentoring entrepreneurs, and fervidly commit themselves to the idea that business can be a force for good. Though I am unable to thank you all by name, your passion infuses these pages.

I love coming to work every day and feeding off the enthusiasm of our 350 team members. They are smart, talented, opinionated, and exceptionally dedicated. They are led by a truly effortless commander, the incredible Fernando Fabre, who took the risk of moving his family from Mexico City to New York in 2011. (In February, no less!)

A number of those team members worked overtime as part of an Entrepreneurship Lab I set up at the outset of this book. Many thanks to Larry Brooks, Brian Chen, Joanna Harries, Julia Kaplan, Lucy Minott, Meghan Murphy, Beth Robertson, Todd Stone, and Tanvi Vattikuti. Teo Soares contributed to every chapter. Tyler Gwinn is my spirited and indefatigable chief of staff.

I am grateful for the inventive research of Endeavor Insight, led by Rhett Morris and Michael Goodwin. A robust thank you to our talented partners at Bain & Company, particularly Chris Bierly, Vikki Tam, Eric Almquist, Chris Zook, Paul Judge, Paul Markowitz, Ned Shell, and Lily West.

Others who helped bring this book to the world include Bianca Martinelli, Walt Mayo, Dustin Poh, Alphonse Tam, Allen Taylor, Daniela Terminel, and most especially David Wachtel.

David Black is an unwavering friend and an unrivaled agent. Every conversation with him packs the motivation of a great locker room pep talk. Thanks also to Sarah Smith and the gang at the David Black Literary Agency.

The moment I met Adrian Zackheim I knew my book had found its home. Adrian runs a creative and entrepreneurial (!) operation at Portfolio, and at every turn he lifted this project with his deep knowledge and incisive ideas. Maria Gagliano edited this book with precision and emotional intelligence. She pushed me to be more revealing, and I am so thankful that her voice helped shape my story. Will Weisser tenaciously and enthusiastically buttonholed everyone he could to enlist them in Team Crazy. Allison McClean became our spiritual leader, encouraging us all to be bolder. My gratitude also to Justin Hargett, Elizabeth Hazelton, and Rachel Moore.

Thank you to Goulston & Storrs, Royce Carlton, Tim Hawkins, Laura Norwalk, Chadwick Moore, and Natalia Sborovsky.

In addition to many listed above, I turned to a number of more experienced people to help me navigate the sometimes daunting process of getting this book onto the page. I am grateful for the fellowship and support of Bill Ackman, Marc Benioff, Tory Burch, Ben Casnocha, Joshua Cooper Ramo, Tom Friedman, Seth Godin, John Griffin, John Hamm, Mellody Hobson, Adi Ignatius, Van Jones, Jodi Kantor, Ron Lieber, Rob Reid, Sheryl Sandberg, Chris Schroeder, Dov Seidman,

Pattie Sellers, Dan Senor, and Whitney Tilson. Michael Dell has answered every call I've ever made, from helping our entrepreneurs to cheering me through bed rest. Ben Sherwood boosted this project for many years. Karen Kehela Sherwood lent her keen eye and big heart to sharpen these pages.

Countless times over the years, I've reached out to an unrivaled group of colleagues for advice. Thank you to Jennifer Aaker, Chris Anderson, Sunny Bates, Gina Bianchini, Matthew Bishop, Adriana Cisneros, Beth Comstock, Jonathan Cranin, Caterina Fake, Andy Freire, Wes Gardenswartz, Sal Giambanco, Deb Goldfarb, Taddy Hall, Matt Harris, Richard Hamermesh, Pamela Hartigan, Joi Ito, Dena Jones-Trujillo, David Kidder, Wendy Kopp, Cindi Leive, Simon Levene, Nancy Lublin, Sheila Marcelo, Jacqueline Novogratz, Paul Parker, Alan Patricof, Diego Piacentini, Maria Pinelli, Diana Powell, Gabby Rozman, Kevin Ryan, Garth Saloner, Lauren Schneider, Klaus Schwab, Susan Segal, Veronica Serra, Tina Seelig, Fred Sicre, and Tom Speechley.

I have friends from across my life who surround me with warmth, laughter, and love. Andrea Mail's cheerful phone calls brighten every week. I send hugs and appreciation to Nora Abousteit, Jeanne Ackman, Karen Ackman, Jenny Lyn Bader, Jonathan Baron, Piraye Beim, Karen Bloch, Carolina Brause, Campbell Brown, Marisa Brown, Belle Casares, June Cohen, David and Tracey Frankel, Melissa Glass, Mareva Grabowski, Amy Griffin, Paul Hilal, Dave Levin, Miriam Longchamp, Evie Lovett, Dani Lubetsky, Steven Mail, Rafael Mayer, the Mitchell family, Kyriakos Mitsotakis, Lia Oppenheimer, Florence Pan, Diego Panama, Rebecca Plofker, Marília Rocca, David Saltzman, Daniel Schwartz, Chip Seelig, Ken Shubin Stein, Jeff Shumlin, Devon Spurgeon, David Stemerman, Max Stier, Susan Tilson, Martin and Nina Varsavsky, Inci Yalman, Michelle Yee, and the late Joy Covey.

A shout-out to Team Brooklyn: Nuar Alsadir, Nils Anderson, Steve Bodow, Alison Carnduff, Nina Collins, Greg Dillon, Felicia Kang, David and Stacy Kramer, Liz Luckett, Andrew and Cindy

McLaughlin, Alex Posen, Katherine Profeta, JJ Ramberg, Samantha Skey, and Vince Tompkins.

Jane and Ed Feiler welcomed me as a daughter-in-law, infused me with a love for Savannah, and introduced me to the wonders of mystery weekends and Tybee Island summers. Andrew Feiler read this book in its earliest form, found every gap in logic, and loaned his extraordinary acumen to enhance the final version. Cari Feiler Bender has become a sister, and I'm so proud of her many contributions to Philadelphia. Rodd, Max, and Hallie Bender make slurp-offs and family plays more memorable and fun.

Debbie and Alan Rottenberg gave me the unconditional love that made my crazy dreaming possible. After that brief kitchen-table encounter, they actively supported my non-traditional path; and eventually, they even got what they craved: a son-in-law, grandchildren, and a (relatively) stable life for their eldest child! Rebecca Rottenberg Goldman shared this journey, and she has always been my closest confidante. Dan Rottenberg is the sage, poetic, and bighearted person every girl dreams of for a brother. My siblings-in-law (and love) Elissa Rottenberg and Mattis Goldman embody what it means to go big AND go home. Nate and Maya Rottenberg, and Judah and Isaac Goldman fill Cape House challenges and Eulinda's ice cream visits with joy.

My aunt Barbara passed away days before I finished this book. She would have enjoyed sharing news of her niece, *la chica loca*. Her spirit lives on.

In 2008, my husband, Bruce Feiler, received a life-changing call: "Your tumor is not consistent with a benign tumor." For the next eighteen months, Bruce underwent grueling, life-saving treatment, yet he still found a way to ensure that our girls knew his values and his voice. Then, once he was declared cancer-free, Bruce made another extraordinary decision: He resolved to help me find *my* voice. This dream was his before it became mine. I love you.

I wrote this book especially for my daughters, Eden and Tybee.

They stretch me, motivate me, test me, and fill me with pride on an hourly basis. They are remarkable young women, and I look forward to cheering on their crazy adventures for many decades to come. And, Girlies, I'll always remember what you taught me: I can be an entrepreneur for a short time, but I am a mommy forever.

SOURCES

*C*razy *Is a Compliment* draws heavily on firsthand conversations, meals, interviews, and mentor sessions I've held with the nearly one thousand Endeavor entrepreneurs since 1997. I've also consulted the detailed records we have on our entrepreneurs, their histories, challenges, and changes of strategy. Before joining our network, entrepreneurs must go through a year-long search and selection process. Our local boards conduct in-depth interviews with them, and our global team writes detailed profiles. Next, candidates are invited to an international selection panel, where, over the course of three days, CEOs, investors, and top business thinkers grill them and debate whether to induct them into the Endeavor entrepreneur network. The records of these deliberations, many of which I moderated, have provided deep insight into the entrepreneurial process.

In addition, our research arm, Endeavor Insight, and our partners at Bain & Company have completed numerous surveys and follow-up interviews with our entrepreneurs. All these reports helped me tremendously, and the published studies are available at www.endeavor .org/blog/category/research.

For more insight into the Endeavor process, I encourage you to read the three cases at Harvard Business School that have tracked our history, growing pains, and impact (www.hbsp.harvard.edu/product/cases). Stanford's Graduate School of Business has also studied our model; its case study can be found at gsbapps.stanford.edu/cases.

A number of the well-known entrepreneurs and business leaders who populate these pages are also members of the Endeavor network, have appeared at our events, and have provided personal guidance to me when I most needed it. They graciously shared their insights over countless conversations, telephone calls, and moments of desperation. An inadequate expression of appreciation appears in the acknowledgments section.

Finally, I have benefited tremendously from the flowering of writing about entrepreneurship in recent years and a wide body of secondary sources. To mine this literature, as well as the deep knowledge of the Endeavor network, when I first set out to write *Crazy Is a Compliment*, I assembled an entrepreneurship lab of Endeavor team members. Together, we spent more than a year scouring more than one hundred books, along with countless academic papers, research studies, and press accounts. What follows is a breakdown of the most helpful sources by chapter.

— INTRODUCTION: WHY EVERYBODY NEEDS TO ACT LIKE AN ENTREPRENEUR —

Sam Walton's "Rules for Building a Business" are detailed in *Made in America* (1992), written with John Huey. The story of Earle Dickson and Band-Aids appears in Anthony Rubino, *Why Didn't I Think of That?* (2010). For the relationship between Steve Jobs and Bob Noyce, I consulted Walter Isaacson, *Steve Jobs* (2011) and Leslie Berlin's biography of Noyce, *The Man Behind the Microchip* (2005).

Entrepreneurship Isn't Just for Entrepreneurs Anymore

Alexis Ohanian's quote "'I have a startup' is the new 'I'm in a band'" comes from an interview by Christine Lagorio-Chafkin in the October 2013 *Inc.*

Gazelles. The term "gazelle" first appeared in the chapter "Gazelle," written by David Birch and James Medoff, in Lewis C. Solmon and Alec R. Levenson, eds., *Labor Markets, Employment Policy, and Job Creation* (1994). For a more recent study, see the Zoltan Acs, William Parsons, and Spencer Tracy, "High-Impact Firms: Gazelles Revisited" (2008), available at http://archive.sba.gov/advo/research/rs328tot.pdf. The account of Michael Dell's return to his company is based on conversations I've had with Michael and Dell's chief marketing officer, Karen Quintos. For the topple rate of big firms, see Deloitte's 2013 Shift Index series, available online. For the average tenure of firms in the S&P 500, see the 2012 Innosight report "Creative Destruction Whips Through Corporate America."

Skunks. For the story of the Lockheed Corporation's Skunk Works, I consulted Ben Rich with Leo Janos, *Skunk Works* (1996). For more examples of skunks, see Scott D. Anthony, "The New Corporate Garage," *Harvard Business Review* (September 2012) and Paddy Miller and Thomas Wedell-Wedellsborg, "The Case for Stealth Innovation," *Harvard Business Review* (March 2013).

Dolphins. My conversations with Wendy Kopp began in 1989 and continue to this day. Wendy's 2012 commencement address at Dartmouth, available on YouTube, is a good source for the founding story of Teach For America. Bill Drayton was once my boss at Ashoka and remains a good friend. The quote I use in this chapter comes from an interview conducted by Gregory Lamb, *Christian Science Monitor* (May 16, 2011).

Butterflies. The latest statistics on firms with few or no paid employees are available online from the U.S. Census Bureau. The statistics on self-employed workers come from "The State of Independence in America," a September 2013 survey by MBO Partners. The 2020 number for independent contractors comes from research by the International Data Corporation, cited by Daniel Pink, *To Sell Is Human* (2013). The quote "I'm not a businessman; I'm a business, man" is a verse sung by Jay-Z in the Kanye West song "Diamonds from Sierra Leone."

For the number of species of butterflies, I consulted the *Encyclopedia Smithsonian*. The term "butterfly effect" comes from the talk "Predictability: Does the Flap of a Butterfly's Wings in Brazil Set off a Tornado in Texas?" by Edward Lorenz at the American Association for the Advancement of Science, Washington, D.C., December 29, 1972.

The Secret Sauce of Entrepreneurship

In addition to the books mentioned in this section, I'd like to highlight three contemporary books about entrepreneurship that are already becoming classics: Eric Ries's *The Lean Startup* (2011), Chris Guillebeau, *The $100 Startup* (2012), and Reid Hoffman and Ben Casnocha, *The Start-Up of You* (2012). On the theme of what it means to be a woman in business, I also recommend Katherine Graham, *Personal History* (1998), Tina Fey, *Bossypants* (2013), and Sheryl Sandberg, *Lean In* (2013).

You Don't Need a Hoodie to Be an Entrepreneur

In conceiving this book, I was also inspired by *Mastering the Art of French Cooking*, Julia Child, Simone Beck, and Louisette Bertholle.

– *CHAPTER 1: GETTING TO DAY ONE* –

I've spent countless days in conversation with Wences Casares over the years, most delightedly at his legendary *asados*, where he kindly offers me a vegetarian option! Wences has also received abundant media attention over the years, and the quote I use in this chapter comes from Wences Casares, "Teach Your Children to Be Doers," *Wall Street Journal* (June 14, 2013). I also consulted Sara Lacy, *Brilliant, Crazy, Cocky* (2011).

Jeff Bezos's story, which appears in multiple places in the book, is based on a number of sources, including Brad Stone, *The Everything Store* (2013); Richard Brandt, *One Click* (2011); Alan Deutschman,

"Inside the Mind of Jeff Bezos," *Fast Company* (August 2004); and an interview by the Academy of Achievement of Washington, D.C. (May 4, 2001), available at www.achievement.org/autodoc/page/bez0int-1.

The Distance Between Your Ears

For the story of Clorox Green Works, I conducted original interviews with Mary Jo Cook and Suzanne Sengelmann and consulted a number of secondary sources. Particularly valuable were Leonard Schlesinger, Charles Kiefer, and Paul Brown, "New Project? Don't Analyze—Act," *Harvard Business Review* (March 2012); Danna Greenberg, Kate McKone-Sweet, and H. James Wilson, *The New Entrepreneurial Leader* (2011); and Felicity Barringer, "Clorox Courts Sierra Club, and a Product Is Endorsed," *New York Times* (March 26, 2008).

Amr Shady's story comes largely from a panel we shared at the Milken Institute Global Conference in 2012.

What I'm Supposed to Be

A word about the word "entrepreneurship": When I arrived in Latin America in the 1990s, there was no popular expression in Spanish or Portuguese for what in English (and French) was called an entrepreneur. Extensive interviews of hundreds of Endeavor entrepreneurs done by Bain and Endeavor's research arm confirmed that few who started before 1999 identified what they were doing as entrepreneurship or themselves as entrepreneurs. Part of Endeavor's mission was to expose and popularize this term.

In the early 2000s we received a call from the editor of the leading Portuguese-Brazilian dictionary saying that inspired by our work, he was adding the words *empreendedor* ("entrepreneur") and *empreendedorismo* ("entrepreneurship") into the lexicon. During this same period the Spanish terms *emprendedor* and *emprendedurismo* also gained currency, in part because of the media attention given to Endeavor entrepreneurs. (The Spanish word *emprendedor* had previously been used for explorers like Christopher Columbus, as several Mexican bloggers let it be known.)

Fan the Foolish Fire

My chief sources for the Thomas Edison story were Ira Flatow, *They All Laughed* (1993), Ernest Freeberg, *The Age of Edison* (2013), Randall Stross, *The Wizard of Menlo Park* (2008), and Jill Jonnes, *Empires of Light* (2003). Here, as elsewhere, I also consulted Harold Evans's brilliant *They Made America*, coauthored with Gail Buckland and David Lefer. The quote predicting Edison's "ignominious failure" appeared in the *New York Herald* (April 27, 1879). The characterization of electric light as "death to the blonde" appears in *Gaillard's Medical Journal*, vol. 36 (1883).

Early opinions of Sam Walton's concept for Wal-Mart appear in Walton with Huey, *Made in America*. The Xbox story comes from Jeffrey O'Brien, "The Making of the Xbox," *Wired* (November 2001) and "The Xbox Story," Patrick Garrat, VG247.com (August 2011). The colleague who called Raymond Damadian's MRI project "harebrained" was Donald Hollis, a magnetic resonance expert at Johns Hopkins University Hospital. He is quoted in Evans, *They Made America*. The story of Jeffrey Braverman, of Nuts.com, comes from Ian Mount, "Forsaking Investment Banking to Turn Around a Family Business," *New York Times* (April 18, 2012).

I reencountered the quote by Niccolò Machiavelli in David Bornstein's bible for social entrepreneurs, *The Business of Changing the World*.

Stop Planning, Start Doing

Endeavor has conducted substantial research on business plans. I also consulted Julian Lange et al., "Do Business Plans Make No Difference in the Real World?" delivered at the Babson College Entrepreneurship Research Conference (2005), which cites the *Inc.* 2002 survey. Intel's original business plan is available at www.businessinsider.com/intel-business-plan-from-1968-2012-12.

For the story of Pfizer's Jordan Cohen, I consulted Arianne Cohen, "Scuttling Scut Work," *Fast Company* (February 2008); Jena McGregor, "Outsourcing Tasks Instead of Jobs," *Bloomberg Businessweek* (March 2009); Ron Ahskenas, "How to Give Time Back to Your Team," HBR.org (July 2010); Paddy Miller and Thomas Wedell-Wedellsborg, "The Case for Stealth Innovation," *Harvard Business Review* (March 2013); and Jordan Cohen's own account of the story, www.managementexchange.com/story/getting-rid-busy-work-so-you
-can-get-work.

Margaret Rudkin's story comes from Anthony Mayo and Nitin Nohria, *In Their Time* (2005). Lastly, I highly recommend Bill Sahlman's entertaining "How to Write a Great Business Plan," *Harvard Business Review* (July 1997).

— CHAPTER 2: DERISKING RISK —

For Sara Blakely's story, I consulted two pieces by the *Forbes* staff writer Clare O'Connor: "Undercover Billionaire" (March 7, 2012) and "How Spanx Became a Billion-Dollar Business Without Advertising" (March 12, 2012). Also valuable were Stacy Perman, "How Failure Molded Spanx's Founder," *Bloomberg Businessweek* (November 21, 2007), Sara Blakely's appearance in *Inc.*'s Women's Summit in January 2012 (available in videos on the magazine's Web site), and Blakely's account of her story as told to *Inc.*'s Liz Welch (February 2014).

Don't Bet the Farm

Ray Kroc's quote about risk taking has been widely documented, including Michael Masterson, *The Reluctant Entrepreneur* (2012).

Beyond Endeavor's own research on risk taking, I relied on insights from the 2013 Inc. 500 list (www.inc.com/magazine/201309/numbers-from-inc.500-companies-first-year.html0), as well as Eric Ries, *The Lean Startup* (2011) and Reid Hoffman and Ben Casnocha, *The Start-Up of You* (2012). The story of Nick Swinmurn, founder of

Zappos, comes from an interview given to the BBC (June 2010) and Dinah Eng, "Zappos' Silent Founder," *Fortune* (September 5, 2012).

The story of MTV Top Selection came from Paddy Miller and Thomas Wedell-Wedellsborg, "The Case for Stealth Innovation," *Harvard Business Review* (March 2013).

The primary source for CakeLove was Warren Brown's own telling of his story in the CakeLove Web site and through CakeLove's video podcasts. Other sources include Patrick Cliff, "Warren Brown, Cake Love and Love Café," *Inc.* (April 2005); Mike DeBonis, "The Butter Business Bureau," *Washington City Paper* (November 2005), and "From Lawyer to Baker," *Cubicle Nation* (2011).

Friends Don't Let Friends Test-Drive Their Ideas
The story of Mel and Patricia Ziegler comes from their book *Wild Company* (2012) and Adam Wren, "How One Couple Turned $1,500 into a Billion-Dollar Global Brand," *Forbes* (June 24, 2013). The account of Maiden Preserves draws on Benjamin Wallace, "The Twee Party," *New York* (April 15, 2012). The study by researchers at Babson College and IPADE Business School is discussed in Vincent Onyemah, Martha Rivera Pesquera, and Abdul Ali, "What Entrepreneurs Get Wrong," *Harvard Business Review* (May 2013).

Follow the Crowd
The story of Kickstarter is based on "In Conversation," with Perry Chen and Theaster Gates, *New York Times* (May 30, 2013); Om Malik, "Kickstarted," GigaOm.com (May 22, 2012); Max Chafkin, "True to Its Roots," *Fast Company* (April 2013); Rob Walker, "The Trivialities and Transcendence of Kickstarter," *New York Times* (August 5, 2011); Beth Teitell, "Kickstarter Boosts Funding and Angst," *Boston Globe* (April 9, 2013); and Chen's talks at TEDxTripoli and Do Lectures, on YouTube. The Anindya Ghose quote appears in Robert Strohmeyer, "The Crowdfunding Caveat," *PC World* (September 26, 2013).

For information on the Do Good Bus, I turned to StartSome

Good.com. For GE's partnership with Quirky, I spoke with GE's chief marketing officer, Beth Comstock, and consulted Joshua Brustein, "Why GE Sees Big Things in Quirky's Little Inventions," *Bloomberg Businessweek* (November 2013). Other discussions of crowdsourcing inside companies included Victor Luckerson, "This New Kind of Kickstarter Could Change Everything," *Time* (January 2014), "Crowdsourcing Happiness," www.cocacola.com, and Daniel Neville, "Crowdsourcing Beer—the Samuel Adams Crowd Craft Project," IdeaBounty.com.

The Lost Art of Stalking

The material about Sam Walton's stalking the competition comes from Sam Walton with John Huey, *Made in America*. The advice about stalking competitors on LinkedIn comes from Meghan Casserly, "Stalking Competitors (and Nine More Things Entrepreneurs Screw Up on LinkedIn)," *Forbes* (January 22, 2013). The Post-it story draws on the book *3M, A Century of Innovation* (2002) and Nick Glass and Tim Hume, "The 'Hallelujah Moment' Behind the Invention of the Post-it Note," CNN.com (April 4, 2013).

Estée Lauder's story is told in her memoir, *Estée* (1985); Evans's *They Made America*; and Nancy Koehn, "Building a Powerful Prestige Brand," *HBS Working Knowledge* (October 30, 2000).

— CHAPTER 3: CHAOS IS YOUR FRIEND —

For Walt Disney's story, my chief source was Neal Gabler, *Walt Disney* (2006). Also helpful were Timothy S. Susanin, *Walt Before Mickey* (2011) and Daniel Gross, *Forbes Greatest Business Stories of All Time* (1997).

Champagne for Your Enemies

Cari Lightner's story is told on the MADD Web site. For Michael J. Fox, I consulted his two memoirs, *Lucky Man* (2011) and *Always Looking Up* (2011). Petra Nemcova's story was told most fully in Leslie Bennetts, "Petra's Story," *Vanity Fair* (May 2005).

The figures on Cairo traffic come from the documentary *Cairo Drive*. The CNN correspondent who tweeted was Ben Wedeman. In addition to Endeavor's own materials on Bey2ollak, I consulted Chris Schroeder's excellent *Startup Rising* (2013).

Marian Croak's story appears in Sarah Kessler, "The Surprising Link Between 'American Idol' and Text-to-Donate Fundraising," *Fast Company* (October 2013) and "Helping Disaster Victims with One Simple Text," an interview with Croak, TheDailyBeast.com (October 28, 2013).

For the Veuve Clicquot story, I consulted Tilar Mazzeo's wonderful biography *The Widow Clicquot* (2008). As background for how uncertainty and adversity promote entrepreneurship, I recommend Dan Senor and Saul Singer, *Startup Nation* (2009).

Hug the Bear

The Warren Buffett quote about capitalizing on downturns appears in his op-ed "Buy American. I Am," *New York Times* (October 16, 2008). The Kauffman Foundation study is Dane Stangler, "The Economic Future Just Happened," (June 9, 2009). Their data on new-business formation come from the Kauffman Index of Entrepreneurial Activity, available at www.kauffman.org/what-we-do/research/kauffman-index-of-entrepreneurial-activity.

I have benefited tremendously from Jim Collins's books, *Built to Last* (1994), written with Jerry Porras; *Good to Great* (2001); and *Great by Choice* (2011), coauthored with Morten Hansen. His quotation in this chapter appears in Allan Cohen, "Forget the Recession. The Right Time to Start a Business Is Anytime You Have a Great Idea," CNN.com (February 4, 2002).

For background on the situation in Greece, I relied on the excellent report published by Endeavor Greece with Haris Makryniotis, *Entrepreneurship and Investment Opportunities in Greece Today* (October 2013). I also consulted Niki Kitsantonis, "With Start-ups, Greeks Make Recovery Their Own Business," *New York Times* (March 24, 2014).

The Johns Hopkins report is Lester Salamon, S. Wojciech Sokolowski, and Stephanie Geller, "Holding the Fort" (January 2012). Diana Aviv is the president and CEO of Independent Sector. Her quote comes from Catherine Rampell, "More College Graduates Take Public Service Jobs," *New York Times* (March 1, 2011). This article is also the source for statistics on AmeriCorps and Teach For America applications.

J. K. Rowling's story has been told by many outlets, but most revealingly by the writer herself in her 2008 commencement address at Harvard, available at HarvardMagazine.com. Other sources include Ian Parker, "Mugglemarch," *New Yorker* (October 1, 2012) and Rowling's own Web site, which includes several posts on the origins of the Harry Potter series.

Admit You Screwed Up

L. L. Bean's story is told by Pat Taub, *100 People Who Changed 20th Century America*, ed. Mary Cross (2013); M. R. Montgomery, "The Marketing Magic of L. L. Bean," *Boston Globe Magazine* (December 27, 1981); and "Leon L. Bean," *Entrepreneur* (October 10, 2008).

The story of Bonobos's Cyber Monday crisis comes from: Andy Dunn, "Bonobos Founder," *Inc.* (June 28, 2012); Alystair Barr, "Bonobos Caught with Pants Down on Top Shopping Day," Reuters (December 21, 2011); and Jon Schlossberg's entry on Quora headlined "Why Did Bonobos Have Such an Epic Fail on Cyber Monday 2011?" (November 29, 2011). The adulating Facebook comment was posted on the company's profile page on November 30, 2011.

To tell the story of Reed Hastings and Netflix, I relied mostly on primary sources on the company's blog, including "Netflix Introduces New Plans and Announces Price Changes" (July 12, 2011), "An Explanation and Some Reflections" (September 18, 2011), "DVDs Will Be Staying at Netflix.com" (October 10, 2011). The quotes given to James Stewart appear in two *New York Times* columns: "In 2013: Rebounds, Traders and Rights" (December 27, 2013) and "Netflix Looks Back on Its Near-Death Spiral" (April 26, 2013).

I learned about the "apology watch" from Dov Seidman in early 2014. The effort was announced in two *New York Times* pieces on February 3, 2014: Andrew Ross Sorkin, "Too Many Sorry Excuses for Apology" and Dov Seidman, "Calling for an Apology Cease-Fire." I also consulted Dov Seidman, *How* (2007).

Once upon a Time

Alfred Chandler's quote appears in John Seaman, Jr., and George David Smith, "Your Company's History as a Leadership Tool," *Harvard Business Review* (December 2012). For the story of Howard Schultz's return to Starbucks, I consulted Schultz, *Pour Your Heart Into It* (1997) and *Onward* (2011), as well as Adi Ignatius, "Howard Schultz on Starbucks' Turnaround," HBR.org (June 2010). Schultz's famous Valentine's Day memo is available through the *Wall Street Journal*: www.online.wsj.com/news/articles/SB117234084129218452. And I personally heard Adi Ignatius interview both Howard Schultz and Angela Ahrendts at the ninetieth anniversary celebration of the *Harvard Business Review* in November 2012.

Other sources for Angela Ahrendts's story include Ahrendts, "Burberry's CEO on Turning an Aging British Icon into a Global Luxury Brand," *Harvard Business Review* (January–February 2013); Rupert Neate, "How an American Woman Rescued Burberry, a Classic British Label," *Guardian* (June 15, 2013); Jeff Chu, "Can Apple's Angela Ahrendts Spark a Retail Revolution?" *Fast Company* (February 2014); and Jill Krasny, "Why Apple Poached Burberry's CEO," *Inc.* (October 16, 2013).

Shift Happens

The study of businesses in emerging markets was conducted by Mauro Guillén and Esteban García-Canal and is discussed in "Execution as Strategy," *Harvard Business Review* (October 2012) and *The New Multinationals* (2011).

— CHAPTER 4: YOUR ENTREPRENEUR PERSONALITY —

The material in this chapter is the result of a decade-long effort at Endeavor to define these profile types. I'm deeply indebted to our partners at Bain & Company, especially Chris Bierly, Vikki Tam, Eric Almquist, and Paul Markowitz, who have worked tirelessly over several years to test and refine our exclusive diagnostic process. While hundreds of Endeavor entrepreneurs have taken our self-assessment test to identify their types, the famous figures I use as examples throughout this chapter have not. Their types are based on my own evaluation of their careers and reputations.

For the story of the Myers-Briggs Type Indicator, I consulted Lillian Cunningham, "Does It Pay to Know Your Type?" *Washington Post* (December 14, 2012); the Web sites of the Myers & Briggs Foundation (www.myersbriggs.org) and CPP, the company that now administers the MBTI (www.cpp.com), as well as Mary McCaulley, "The Story of Isabel Briggs Myers," (July 1980) at www.capt.org/mbti-assessment/isabel-myers.htm. I also enjoyed Gary Chapman's bestseller *The Five Love Languages* (2008) and Anthony Tjan, *Hearts, Smarts, Guts and Luck* (2012).

Diamonds

The story of Tesla Motors is adapted from Tad Friend, "Plugged In," *New Yorker* (August 2009) and Ashlee Vance, "Elon Musk, the 21st Century Industrialist," Businessweek.com (September 13, 2012). His feud with the *New York Times* was ignited by John Broder, "Stalled Out on Tesla's Electric Highway," (February 8, 2013). I also recommend Chris Anderson, "The shared genius of Elon Musk and Steve Jobs," *Fortune* (December 2013). The story of Jobs's reality distortion field is told by former Apple engineer Andy Hertzfeld at www.folklore.org/StoryView.py?story=Reality_Distortion_Field.txt. Jony Ive's quote appears in Isaacson's *Steve Jobs*.

Stars

The primary source for Wolfgang Puck's story was Emily Ross and Angus Holland, *100 Great Businesses and the Minds Behind Them* (2004). Other sources included Dinah Eng, "Wolfgang Puck's Dining Revolution," *Fortune* (November 20, 2013); Puck's story as told to Liz Welch, *Inc.* (October 2009); "Meet the Chef," *JustLuxe* (February 2012); and Randall Frost, "Wolfgang Puck: Recipe for Success," BrandChannel.com (February 3, 2003).

Lance Armstrong's story was widely covered in the media, and a number of sources are available. The drop in donations and the quote from Livestrong's external affairs officer come from Eriq Gardner, "Livestrong Struggles After Lance Armstrong's Fall," *Hollywood Reporter* (July 25, 2013).

Transformers

I consulted a number of sources for Herb Kelleher's story, notably, Kevin Freiberg and Jacquelyn Freiberg, *Nuts!* (1996). Others include Jennifer Reingold, "Southwest's Herb Kelleher," *Fortune* (January 14, 2013); Joe Brancatelli, "Southwest Airlines' Seven Secrets for Success," *Wired* (July 2008); " 'Never Say Never' on Bag Fees," CNBC.com (January 24, 2013); and "Is Southwest Airlines Always the Least Expensive?" a study by Topaz International.

The story of Burt's Bees comes from Louise Story, "Can Burt's Bees Turn Clorox Green," *New York Times* (January 6, 2008); Jonathan Evans, "Burt of Burt's Bees Is Living in a Turkey Coop," *Esquire* (September 13, 2013); Roxanne Quimby with Susan Donovan, "How I Did It," *Inc.* (January 1, 2004); and a Brigham Young University case study, www.emp.byui.edu/nygrenm/B283/Roxanne%20Quimby%20Case.pdf. The Change.org petition decrying Clorox's takeover of Burt's Bees was created by Danise Lepard and is titled "Clorox, Make Burt's Bees Products Like They Were! Keep It HONEST!"

Ben & Jerry's admission that it is "beginning to look like the rest of corporate America" came in its 2004 "Social and Environmental Assessment," which is available at www.lickglobalwarming.org/company/ sear/2004/sea_2004.pdf.

Rocketships

For a complete listing of Bezos sources, please see the works listed under Chapter 1. The quote about Bill Gates comes from Evans, *They Made America*. The Bill and Melinda Gates Foundation's annual reports and grant-making policies are posted at www.gatesfoundation.org/How-We -Work/General-Information/Our-Approach-to-Measurement-and -Evaluation/Evaluation-Policy.

— *CHAPTER 5: THE WHITEBOARD* —

The lessons in this chapter have been culled from years of selections panels and services provided to entrepreneurs. In recent years studies by Endeavor's research arm have found quantitative and qualitative evidence to support many of the conclusions drawn here.

For Henry Ford's story, I consulted Douglas Brinkley, *Wheels for the World* (2004); Michael Blowfield and Leo Johnson, *Turnaround Challenge* (2013); Thomas P. Hughes, *American Genesis* (2004); and Lindsay Brook, "Top 10 Ford Model T Tech Innovations that Matter 100 Years Later," *Popular Mechanics* (September 25, 2008).

Close Doors

For the Liquid Paper story, I relied on Catherine Thimmesh, *Girls Think of Everything* (2000) and Ross and Holland's *100 Great Businesses and the Minds Behind Them.* For more on Phil Knight and Nike, see J. B. Strasser, *Swoosh* (1993); Chuck Salter, "Innovation: Phil Knight's 'Not Exactly Textbook' Moves," *Fast Company* (July 18, 2007); and Geraldine Willigan, "High-Performance Marketing: An Interview with Nike's Phil Knight," *Harvard Business Review* (July 1992). His quote about the swoosh design comes from Brian Clarke Howard, "'I Never Get Tired of Looking at It,'" *Daily Mail* (June 16, 2011).

Fire Your Mother-in-law

In this section, I relied heavily on Endeavor's research, as well as statistics on family-owned businesses from the University of Vermont (www.uvm.edu/business/vfbi/?Page=facts.html) and the Family Firm Institute (available at www.ffi.org/?page=globaldatapoints).

Usher's interview with Oprah is available on YouTube. The chief source for Lucille Ball and Desi Arnaz is Thaddeus Wawro, *Radicals and Visionaries* (2000). In addition, I consulted Kathleen Brady, *Lucille* (2001); Karin Adir, *The Great Clowns of American Television* (2002), and Susan Schindehette, "The Real Story of Desi and Lucy," *People* (February 18, 1991).

Minnovate

The term "minnovate" was coined by Dan Isenberg, and it appears in his book *Worthless, Impossible, and Stupid* (2013).

For more information on Gore, I suggest Lucien Rhodes, "The Unmanager," *Inc.* (August 1, 1982); Richard Daft, *Organization Theory and Design* (2007); Robert Safian, "Terri Kelly, the 'Un-CEO' of W. L. Gore, on How to Deal with Chaos," *Fast Company* (October 29, 2012); Alan Deutschman, "The Fabric of Creativity," *Fast Company* (December 2004); and "Gore: Success with Simplicity," *HR Insights* (July–August 2012). Gore's own Web site has a wonderful history of the company at www.gore.com/en_xx/aboutus/timeline/index.html.

Kleenex's story comes from Robert Spector and William Wicks, *Shared Values* (1997) and Burton Folsom, "From Kleenex to Zippers," *Freeman* (December 1, 2005).

For Barbie's story, I consulted Mary Cross, ed., *100 People Who Changed 20th-Century America* (2013) and M. G. Lord, *Forever Barbie* (2004).

Drop the Pens

The California accelerator mentioned here is Blackbox. It issued two reports in 2011: Max Marmer, Bjoern Herrmann, Ertan Dogrultan, and Ron Berman, "Startup Genome Report" and "Startup Genome Report Extra on Premature Scaling." I also consulted Austin Carr, "Blackbox's Startup Genome Compass Uses Science to Crack the 'Innovation Code,'" *Fast Company* (August 29, 2011).

Sources for Jobs's story are Isaacson, *Steve Jobs* and Isaacson, "The Real Leadership Lessons of Steve Jobs," *Harvard Business Review* (April 2012). The Sony quote comes from Hiroko Tabuchi, "How the Tech Parade Passed Sony By," *New York Times* (April 14, 2012).

The LEGO story is told in Jay Greene, "How LEGO Revived Its Brand," *Bloomberg Businessweek* (July 23, 2010); Gregory Schmidt, "Lego Builds an Empire, Brick by Brick," *New York Times* (February 14, 2014); and Wharton School, "Innovation Almost Bankrupted LEGO," www.knowledge.wharton.upenn.edu.

Dream Big but Execute Small

American Giant's story comes from Farhad Manjoo, "This Is the Greatest Hoodie Ever Made," Slate.com (December 4, 2012) and "The Only Problem with the Greatest Hoodie Ever Made," Slate.com (March 21, 2013); Kai Ryssdal, "Could Being Named the 'Best Ever' Be Bad?" NPR's *Marketplace* (March 26, 2013); and Kate Dailey, "American Giant," BBC.co.uk (March 10, 2013).

For the details on Blackbox's Startup Genome project see the sources mentioned under "Drop the Pens." The water buffalo quote by Mark Chang came from an interview in *Digital News Asia* in May 2013. Miguel Dávila's story is based on my interactions with him, as well as Isenberg, *Worthless, Impossible, and Stupid.*

Eat the Elephant One Bite at a Time

For anyone interested in tales and tips about survival, I heartily recommend Ben Sherwood, *The Survivors Club* (2009).

– CHAPTER 6: LEADERSHIP 3.0 –

Agile

The history of agile comes from research conducted by my husband, Bruce Feiler, for *The Secrets of Happy Families* (2013), which has abundant examples of how we've used these techniques in our home, for better and worse. You can see Bruce's TED talk on these themes (with me in the audience) at www.ted.com/talks/bruce_feiler_agile_programming _for_your_family.html.

The story of Heier's potato-peeling washing machine comes from Navi Radjou, Jaideep Prabhu, and Simone Ahuja, *Jugaad Innovation* (2012). George Lois's insights on the power of small teams come from Justin Rocket Silverman, "Quit Your 'Group Grope' Now," *Fast Company* (August 12, 2013). For more on Bezos, see the works listed under Chapter 1. Bezos also shared his insights on agile leadership in a personal conversation with my husband in late 2013.

The 2013 survey on workers' fear of failure was conducted by the American Management Association, www.amanet.org/news/9206 .aspx.

I consulted a number sources for the WD-40 story, including Nicole Skibola, "Leadership Lessons from WD-40's CEO, Garry Ridge," *Forbes* (June 27, 2011); Ken and Scott Blanchard, "To Encourage Innovation, Eradicate Blame," *Fast Company* (August 20, 2012); and Helen Walters, "Three Innovation Lessons from WD-40," ThoughtYouShouldSeeThis .com (September 22, 2011).

Scott Cook discusses the birth of SnapTax in his talk "Leadership in the Agile Age," www.network.intuit.com/2011/04/20/leadership-in -the-agile-age. Also helpful was an April 2004 *Inc.* profile by Michael Hopkins on Scott Cook as part of the series "America's 25 Most Fascinating Entrepreneurs."

For Ratan Tata's prize for best failure, I relied on Rita McGrath, "Failure Is a Gold Mine for India's Tata," HBR.org blog (April 11, 2011).

Accessible

The 2012 Dreamforce panel with Jeff Immelt and Colin Powell is available at blogs.salesforce.com/company/2012/09/gen-colin-powell-and-ges-jeff-immelt-talk-about-leadership-and-the-economy.html. The Weber Shandwick report on executive sociability is in "The Social CEO: Executives Tell All" (January 15, 2013).

For the story about Barack Obama, I consulted Bobbie Johnson, "Barack Obama to Use BlackBerry as President, According to Reports," *Guardian* (January 21, 2009); Joshua DuBois, "The Prayers Inside the President's BlackBerry," CNN.com (October 22, 2013); Michael Hastings, "How Obama Won the Internet," BuzzFeed.com (January 8, 2013); Laura June, "President Obama's Reddit AMA Reaches over 5 Million Pageviews," TheVerge.com (August 31, 2012); and Obama's AMA itself, available at www.reddit.com.

Aware

The best resources on the power of powerless communication are Adam Grant, *Give and Take* (2013) and Susan Cain, *Quiet* (2012). I encountered the term "flawsome" at the 2012 Fortune Most Powerful Women conference, in a talk by Wendy Clark of Coca-Cola. Trend watching.com also has good material on the term at www.trendwatch ing.com/trends/flawsome/.

While the video that started the Domino's controversy has been taken down, the pizza relaunch Web site is still accessible at Pizza-Turnaround.com. The developments also received plenty of media coverage: Stephanie Clifford, "Video Prank at Domino's Taints Brand," *New York Times* (April 15, 2009); Bruce Watson, "Domino's Pizza Reborn?," DailyFinance.com (March 5, 2010); and Bruce Horovitz, "Domino's Pizza Delivers Change in Its Core Pizza Recipe," *USA Today* (December 16, 2009).

The Spoleto videos can be seen at www.youtube.com/watch?v =Un4r52t-cuk and www.youtube.com/watch?v=ebe-3s4TLfQ. My relationships with Danny Meyer and knowledge of his philosophy of hospitality began when my husband worked as a maitre d' in the Union Square Café. You can read Bruce's James Beard Award–winning article at www.gourmet.com/magazine/2000s/2002/10/therapistat thetable. The quotes in my book appear in Danny's bestselling book *Setting the Table* (2006).

Authentic

Tony Dungy's moving personal story comes from his memoir, *Quiet Strength* (2008). Other accounts include Matthew Kaminski, "A Coach's Faith," *Wall Street Journal* (September 12, 2009); Pat Yasinskas, "A Dungy Story You May Not Have Heard," ESPN.com (January 12, 2009); and Gene Wojciechowski, "Dungy Delivers Profound Message in Son's Eulogy," ESPN.com (December 28, 2005).

Brené Brown, the author of *Daring Greatly* (2012), is today's leading voice on vulnerability. A report on her talk at *Inc.*'s 2013 Leadership Forum is available at www.inc.com/kimberly-weisul/leadership-why-the-best-leaders-are-vulnerable.html.

Finally, my husband has written widely, and beautifully, about how cancer affected him, me, and our entire family. I recommend his inspiring 2010 memoir, *The Council of Dads*, as well as "'You Look Great' and Other Lies," *New York Times* (June 10, 2011) and "Cancer Survivors Celebrate Their Cancerversary," *New York Times* (December 6, 2013), which marks the moment he was declared cancer-free after five years.

— *CHAPTER 7: A CIRCLE OF MENTORS* —

Mentorship is a crucial part of the Endeavor model, and we've spent years trying to make sure we do it as effectively as possible. Tom Friedman dubbed us "mentor capitalists" in a section on me and Endeavor in *The World Is Flat 2.0* (2006). I will always be grateful for his support.

The term "360° Mentoring" was the title of an article by Elizabeth Collins, in the March 2008 issue of *Management Update*, a newsletter from Harvard Business School Publishing. This article is also the source of the Kathy Kram quote about networked mentoring. I also consulted Kathy Kram's seminal *Mentoring at Work* (1985).

For Bill Campbell's story, I consulted Jennifer Reingold, "The Secret Coach," *Fortune* (July 21, 2008); a two-part article by Ozy.com's Carlos Watson titled "Guru of the Valley" (December 18 and 19, 2013); Miguel Helft, "Bill Campbell on Coaching RockMelt and Google vs. Apple" and "Coaching Silicon Valley," *New York Times* (November 8 and 15, 2010).

Get Yourself a Simon Cowell

Nick Bilton's *Hatching Twitter* (2013) includes a gripping account of the early years of Twitter. The quotes on *American Idol* and *The Voice* come from Lara Martin, "'X Factor' USA's Simon Cowell on Judges' Role," DigitalSpy.com (September 14, 2011); Cortney Wills, "'X Factor' Finalists Alex & Sierra Notch iTunes No. 1, Show Sales Potential," *Hollywood Reporter* (December 12, 2013); and Carla Hay, "Christina Aguilera, Adam Levine Take Aim at Simon Cowell and 'The X Factor,'" Examiner.com (October 27, 2012).

Cut the Cord

Beyond my many personal conversations with Ala' Alsallal of Jamalon, Fadi Ghandour, and Diego Piacentini of Amazon, I also relied on Christopher Schroeder's excellent telling of Ala's story in *Startup Rising*.

Gerry and Melissa Owen's story comes from Carol Shih, "Fourteen Eighteen Coffeehouse in Downtown Plano Has Already Become a Neighborhood Favorite," *D Magazine* (September 30, 2013); Peter Cohen, "3 Start-Up Tips from 'Yale's Professor of Coffee Shops," *Inc.* (September 17, 2013); Mark Oppenheimer "Taste-Testing a Second Career, with a Mentor," *New York Times* (September 15, 2013); and Duncan Goodall's profile on PivotPlanet.com, www.pivotplanet.com/advisors/486.

Phone a Frenemy

The Kram and Isabella study mentioned in this section is titled "Mentoring Alternatives," *Academy of Management Journal* (March 1985). The British Telecom anecdote comes from Jeanne Meister and Karie Willyerd, "Mentoring Millennials," *Harvard Business Review* (May 2010). Larry Page's account of his last visit to Steve Jobs comes from Brad Stone, "Google's Page: Apple's Android Pique 'For Show,'" *Bloomberg Businessweek* (April 4, 2012). Walter Isaacson's account of the encounter comes from his biography of Jobs as well as his *Harvard Business Review* article "The Real Leadership Lessons of Steve Jobs."

Not All Mentors Have Gray Hair

John Donahoe shared the story of his relationship with Brian Chesky to me over a dinner in 2012. He later recounted the tale at *Fortune*'s Brainstorm Conference in July 2013, www.tech.fortune.cnn.com/2013/07/23/brian-chesky-john-donahoe. I also drew from Mike Isaac, "eBay CEO John Donahoe on the Importance of Design," AllThingsD.com (July 29, 2013).

A good overview of this subject is Leslie Kwo, "Reverse Mentoring Cracks Workplace," *Wall Street Journal* (November 28, 2011). Chaudhuri and Ghosh's article on reverse mentoring is titled "Reverse Mentoring," *Human Resource Development Review*, vol. 11, no. 1 (February 2015). For the Mentor Up program at P&G, I consulted Tara Parker-Pope, "P&G Makes Pitch to Keep Women, and So Far the Strategy Is Working," *Toledo Blade* (September 10, 1998). In addition to Sheryl Sandberg, *Lean In* (2013) this new conception of career paths can be found in Patricia Sellers, "Power Point: Get Used to the Jungle Gym," *Fortune* (August 6, 2009).

— CHAPTER 8: THE PURPOSE-DRIVEN WORKPLACE —

The story of Globant's headquarters comes from my many private conversations with two of the cofounders, Martin Migoya and

Guibert Englebienne. Also valuable were Ken Stier, "IT Outsourcer Globant Sells Innovation, Wows Google, LinkedIn," *Bloomberg Businessweek* (April 8, 2011) and a Harvard Business School case by Mukti Khaire, Gustavo Herrero, and Cintra Scott (2011).

Psychic Equity

Beyond Endeavor's research on workplace culture, I relied on many sources. For those on W. L. Gore, please see the works listed under Chapter 5. I also have reviewed data available at the Gallup Web site; Rob Goffee and Gareth Jones, "Creating the Best Workplace on Earth," *Harvard Business Review* (May 2013), which cites the Hay Group data; and Shawn Achor, "Positive Intelligence," *Harvard Business Review* (January–February 2012).

For Dan Ariely's research, I consulted *Predictably Irrational* (2010), and Ariely's "What's the Value of a Big Bonus?" *New York Times* (November 19, 2008). Nancy Lublin discusses job titles in her book *Zilch* (2010). Also valuable were Ashley Ross, "Job Titles Retailored to Fit," *New York Times* (August 30, 2013); and ABC News, "Sugar High," *Nightline* (September 30, 2013).

Assorted strategies to foster psychic equity are discussed in Paul Kretkowski, "The 15 Percent Solution," *Wired* (January 23, 1998); Ryan Tate, "Google Couldn't Kill 20 Percent Time Even If It Wanted To," *Wired* (August 21, 2013), "Facebook's Wi-Fi Spreads in the Wild," *Wired* (June 18, 2013), and "LinkedIn Gone Wild: '20 Percent Time' to Tinker Spreads Beyond Google," *Wired* (June 12, 2012); Amanda Lewan, "Quicken Loans Innovates with a 'Small Business' Culture," Michipreneur.com (March 5, 2013); Jessica Lessin, "Apple Gives In to Employee Perks," *Wall Street Journal* (November 12, 2012); and Bo Burlingham, *Small Giants*, (2006), which profiles Jay Goltz.

Daniel Pink, *Drive* (2011) contains great insights on the science of motivation.

Culture Club

Many of the strategies Jenn Lim discussed with our entrepreneurs also appear in Tony Hsieh, *Delivering Happiness* (2010). The story of Debbi Fields is told in Edward Horrell, *The Kindness Revolution* (2006) and Ross and Holland, *100 Great Businesses and the Minds Behind Them*. Jim Collins's *Good to Great* is a valuable resource for information on the value of assembling a strong team. I also recommend Reid Hoffman, Ben Casnocha, and Chris Yeh, "Tours of Duty," *Harvard Business Review* (June 2013), which contains interesting insights on hiring and firing in the entrepreneurial age.

Kevin Ryan has been a good friend for many years and shared insights on hiring and firing with me on multiple occasions. He expressed these eloquently in "Gilt Groupe's CEO on Building a Team of A Players," *Harvard Business Review* (January–February 2012).

If You Can't Beat 'Em, You Know, Like, Join 'Em #FOMO

I have learned a tremendous amount about millennials from the many talented members of that generation who've worked at Endeavor and from the hundreds of young entrepreneurs we've supported around the world.

For much of the latest research, I am indebted to Lynne Lancaster and David Stillman, *The M-Factor* (2010), as well as Jeanne Meister, *The 2020 Workplace* (2010), both of which informed many of my ideas. *The M-Factor* is also the source for the stories about the FAA and Thomson Reuters. For the FAA, I also consulted Chuck Bennett, "FAA Kids Are in 'Control,'" *New York Post* (July 14, 2008).

The following sources provided information on Warby Parker's story: Jessica Pressler, "20/30 Vision," *New York* (August 11, 2013); Neil Blumenthal's interview for Adam Bryant, "Corner Office," *New York Times* (October 24, 2013); Neil Blumenthal, "Give Me More Millennials," *Inc.* (July 15, 2013); and Leigh Buchanan, "Warby Parker CEO," *Inc.* (June 2013).

For data on millennials in the workforce, I consulted the 2012

Jessica Brack report, "Maximizing Millennials in the Workplace," which is available at www.kenan-flagler.unc.edu, and a 2013 PricewaterhouseCoopers report, "PwC's NextGen," which is available at www.pwc.com. The Net Impact study is Cliff Zukin and Mark Szeltner, "Talent Report," available at https://netimpact.org/docs/publications-docs/talent-report-what-workers-want-in-2012-full-report. For data on Generation X, I consulted Marcie Pitt-Catsouphes, Christina Matz-Costa, and Elyssa Bensen, "Workplace Flexibility," a 2009 report by the Boston College Sloan Center on Aging and Work, which is found at www.bc.edu.

For information on hackathons, I consulted Drew Olanoff, "Facebook Shares the History of Its 'Hackathon,'" TheNextWeb.com (May 23, 2012); Alyson Krueger, "Hackathons Aren't Just for Hacking," Wired (June 6, 2012); and Pedram Keyani, "Stay Focused and Keep Hacking," Facebook.com/Engineering (May 23, 2012). For the British Airways hackathon, I consulted Zoe Fox, "The Hottest Spot for Hackathons? 30,000 Feet in the Air," Mashable.com (June 13, 2013). For information on the pediatrics hackathon hosted by the Boston Children's Hospital, I relied on the event's Web site, www.hackingpediatrics.com.

For DreamWorks's story, I turned to Jessica Grose, "The Animated Workplace," Fast Company (March 15, 2013); Joel Stein, "Millennials: The Me Me Me Generation," Time (May 20, 2013); Todd Henneman, "DreamWorks Animation Cultivates a Culture of Creativity," WorkForce.com (August 4, 2012); and Nancy Davis, "DreamWorks Fosters Creativity, Collaboration and Engagement," SHRM.org (July 5, 2012).

Put Out Your Family Photos

I have known and admired Sheryl Sandberg for over twenty-five years. Her breakthrough book, *Lean In* (2013), ignited breakthrough conversations in my office and offices around the world. The *Inc.* magazine piece by Darrell Cavens of Zulily, "The Way I Work," appeared on April 30, 2013. The results of the BabyCenter.com study are available at www.babycenter.com/100_press-release-dad-survey_10383601.bc.

– CHAPTER 9: GO BIG AND GO HOME –

The Tom Friedman quote appears in "Need a Job? Invent It," *New York Times* (March 30, 2013).

Get Going

The Rainbow Loom story draws on a number of sources, including Catherine Clifford, "Inventor of the Wildly Popular 'Rainbow Loom' Weaves the American Dream with Rubber Bands in a Detroit Basement," *Entrepreneur* (August 26, 2013); Camille Sweeney and Josh Gosfield, "How a DIY Dad Took the Toy World by Storm with Rainbow Loom," *Fast Company* (August 21, 2013); Catherine Kavanaugh, "Rainbow Loom's Creator Weaves Success from Playtime Inspiration," *Crain's Detroit Business* (December 15, 2013); and Claire Martin, "Rainbow Loom's Success, from 2,000 Pounds of Rubber Bands," *New York Times* (August 31, 2013).

Beyoncé's stealth album release received considerable media attention, including Matthew Yglesias, "How Beyoncé Got Us to Pay for Music," Slate.com (December 13, 2013); Jon Pareles, "A December Surprise, Without Whispers (or Leaks)," *New York Times* (December 13, 2013); Ben Sisario, "Beyoncé Rejects Tradition for Social Media's Power," *New York Times* (December 15, 2013); and Matthew Perpetua, "Beyoncé Sold Nearly a Million Copies of Her New Album in Three Days," Buzzfeed.com (December 16, 2013).

Costica Bradatan's quote comes from his "In Praise of Failure," *New York Times* (December 15, 2013).

Katrina Markoff's story is informed by the following sources: David Burstein, "Vosges Unwraps Chocolate's Wild Side," *Fast Company* (February 9, 2012); Emily Bryson York, "Chicago Chocolate Artisan Known for Vosges Preps Wild Ophelia for Mass Market," *Chicago Tribune* (March 14, 2013); *Fortune*'s profile on Markoff in the 2011 edition of its "40 Under 40" series; and Becky Anderson, "Sweet Success," CNN.com (July 10, 2012).

Go Big

I am grateful to Robert Pasin for sharing the Radio Flyer story with me and for sending us those wagons! I also consulted Reshma Memon Yaqub, "Backstory: Radio Flyer," *Inc.* (October 30, 2012); Kristin Samuelson, "Office Space: Robert Pasin, Radio Flyer," *Chicago Tribune* (July 23, 2012), "How Robert Pasin Dug Deep to Help Radio Flyer Evolve Its Brand and Its Products," *Smart Business* (January 2013), and "Radio Flyer Toys Bring Smiles, Create Memories," *Business Ledger* (June 10, 2010).

The story of the Doritos Locos Taco comes primarily from two articles in *Fast Company*: Austin Carr, "Deep Inside Taco Bell's Doritos Locos Tacos," (May 1, 2013) and Anya Kamenetz, "Taco Bell, the Late Todd Mills, and the Actual Invention of the Doritos Locos Taco," (December 5, 2013). Courtney Subramanian, "Taco Bell Sells $1B in Doritos Locos Tacos Because 'I Worked Late, I Deserve a Treat,'" *Time* (October 16, 2013) was also valuable.

Go Home

The phrase "the genius of the AND" is discussed in detail in Collins and Porras, *Built to Last*. My thinking about the value of going home was shaped by Clay Christensen's beautiful and moving *How Will You Measure Your Life?* (2012).

The origin story of the phrase "go big or go home" is told anonymously by the packaging designer on the Web site Answers.com, available at www.wiki.answers.com/Q/Who_coined_the_phrase_'go_big _or_go_home'.

Tina Fey's story comes from the hilarious and thoughtful *Bossypants* (2013). Kenneth Cole shares the story of his incident with his daughter in Alison Beard, "Life's Work: Kenneth Cole," *Harvard Business Review* (December 2011).

— *JOIN #TEAMCRAZY* —

Finally, if anything in this book has intrigued you about our work at Endeavor, I invite you to visit our Web site, www.endeavor.org. You can find abundant examples of our research, videos, ongoing studies of our impact, links to our country affiliates, and portraits of all the entrepreneurs we've worked with since 1997. For more information about me, this book, and my speaking schedule, as well as to contact me directly, please visit www.lindarottenberg.com or www.crazyisacompliment .com. You can also keep the conversation alive at www.facebook.com/ LindaRottenbergAuthor or www.twitter.com/lindarottenberg. I look forward to hearing about your crazy dream and how you managed to get going, go big, and go home.

INDEX